African Lives

"In *African Lives*, journalist Denis Boyles explores the white experience in Africa through a series of portraits, colonial and contemporary, skillfully juxtaposed. . . . His story is skillfully written, neither melodramatic nor despondent."

Christian Science Monitor

"Part history, part travelogue, *African Lives* records Boyles' journeys in search of the haunts of Henry Stanley . . . and the East African literary-expatriate colony recently restored to fame by the movie *Out of Africa*."

Chicago Tribune

"This breezy collection of observations and anecdotes about some of darkest Africa's most preposterous white tribes ought to pop a few corks on that continent's cocktail circuit. . . . Boyles delivers a book full of barbs that—surprisingly—carry only a few lingering stings. His is the kind of 'good humor' that's thought to be out of fashion today, but in fact has timeless appeal."

St. Petersburg Times

"Supplementing his experiences in Africa with tales from other books and adding gossip, freelance writer Boyles here wisecracks his way through the Dark Continent, singling out exploits of adventurers he has met or heard about. . . . Fun to read."

Publishers Weekly

AFRICAN

LIVES

White Lies,
Tropical Truth,
Darkest Gossip,
and Rumblings of Rumor—
from Chinese Gordon
to Beryl Markham,
and Beyond

DENIS BOYLES

BALLANTINE BOOKS • NEW YORK

Library of Congress Catalog Card Number: 88-92228

ISBN: 0-345-35666-7

This edition published by arrangement with Weidenfeld & Nicolson, a division of
Wheatland Corporation.

Cover design by Richard Aquan

Cover photo courtesy of The Bettmann Archive

Manufactured in the United States of America

First Ballantine Books Edition: September 1989

10 9 8 7 6 5 4 3 2 1

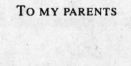

To my parents

Contents

Author's Note

THERE ARE A LOT OF PLACES where the bloody head of mankind pokes through the windshield of creation. But in Africa—where, despite a generation of urgency and famine, we in the West have pinned all our badges of best intentions—men have made governmental malpractice the centerpiece of a brilliant display of corruption, murder, hatred and impoverishment. The United Nations estimates that nearly $130 billion is required for a five-year period ending in 1990 just to address "priority" items in a proposed program for economic recovery.

There are probably a lot of reasons for this sort of thing, but I don't know any of them. I'm no expert on African politics. Happily for me, no one else has ever demonstrated any measurable expertise on that flammable subject either. Instead, there exists a wide variety of observations on Africa, of which this book is another.

My interest in Africa is confined to the white experience on that continent. In this book, that interest manifests itself as a mild blend of casual history, anecdotal anthropology and personal journalism. Like many other journalists, I am concerned about truth, or at least my own version of it. However, I commend to the reader's attention the fact that truth in Africa is clearly much more fashionable than anywhere else, insofar as it changes day to day or every few miles or from tribe to tribe.

"Europeans," as many black Africans are wont to call all white Africans regardless of ancestry, are the most widely dispersed and despised tribe in Africa, rivaled only by Asians in the antagonism they engender within the continent and unrivaled in the animosity they stimulate among those outside it. (Among many moot points: History is a shopping list of things that everybody wishes hadn't happened but did anyway, and the European invasion of Africa is probably one.) During their brief period of ascendancy, Europeans wrought a few significant changes and many superficial ones. In their decline, they exert a peculiar influence.

Sub-Saharan Africa has a long and probably quite varied history. Nobody knows for sure what it is, but there are plenty of theories. Maybe there were ancient warrior empires, ancient spiritual centers, ancient merchant princes who built ancient Venices everyplace. Maybe poets and astronomers wandered the forest primeval, and maybe men lived in peace and harmony with one another and with their friend Nature. Maybe not. What we know for certain about that part of Africa are the events that have transpired in the past century or so, since Europeans first arrived in bulk and either brutally quashed the peaceful product of a protracted renaissance or began a thankless struggle against disease, slavery, famine and tribal warfare.

Either way, that cycle of European involvement—which began slowly and reluctantly, sometimes even involuntarily, reached an apex of sorts during the half-dozen decades or so of colonial rule and ended in quick disengagement and a tangle of loose ends—has defined African history and, along the way, provided some pretty good stories.

Some of them are in this book. Most of them aren't. Africa's a big place, the Dark Continent and all that, and lots of things can happen in the dark.

In addition to sources cited in the text and in the notes, I used several books to provide an overall survey. Especially useful was David Lamb's *The Africans* and Sanford J. Ungar's brilliant and comprehensive *Africa: The People and Politics of an Emerging Continent.* Both books are wonderful examples of solid reporting and research. Among newspapers and periodicals, the *New York Times*'s correspondents covered the continent better than anyone else—especially Sheila Rule, James Brooke and Clifford D. May, whose dispatches are consistently well informed, and, earlier, Joseph Lelyveld, who has a good eye for the absurd. Their work made mine easier.

Furthermore, this is not a nature book. Nature is Africa's endangered cash crop, so to speak, and readers who wish to know more about the continent's vanishing wildlife would be well advised to see specific, appropriate titles. I can especially recommend Peter Beard's *The End of the Game,* a sensitive and quite beautiful treatment of that side of the African story.

For this book I owe particular thanks to Bob Datilla, my agent; John

Herman, my editor; and Spence Waugh, for her invaluable research assistance. There are others, of course, like my friends Georg and Christine Kajanus, who more than once had me show up penniless on their London doorstep. I also must thank Peter Bloch at *Penthouse* magazine, Elizabeth Chapman, Joe DeNicola, Sarah Dickerson, Monica Gesue, Craig Heiserman, Maggie Kassner, Gini Kopecky, Karen Kribemey, Arval Morris, Tom O'Day, P. J. O'Rourke, Alan Rose, Gregg Stebben, Bob Waldman and Alan Wellikoff, all friends and colleagues, for their support and encouragement. I also owe gratitude to Pete Knight and Don Eazell at Wellington Press, who, although perhaps inadvertently, gave me the stimulus I needed to embark on this project. I was given a great deal of practical support by various air-cargo crews and aircraft owners, and a good measure of friendship by a large number of people in Europe—notably Claude Hamilius, Lyliane Hubert, Kurt Kister of *Süddeutsche Zeitung*, Norbert and Christiane Missault-de Soete and their family, and Alain Soubry—and, of course, many, many others in Africa, who would, because of the contentious nature of this book, I'm certain, prefer to remain nameless. Finally, I must thank George Leinwall, the noted Baltimore bibliophile, who, many years ago, first introduced me to Burton, Emin Pasha and other early adventurers.

None of my friends and acquaintances, by the way, will agree with everything in this book, and all of them will be appalled at any errors in these pages, all of which are mine.—D.B.

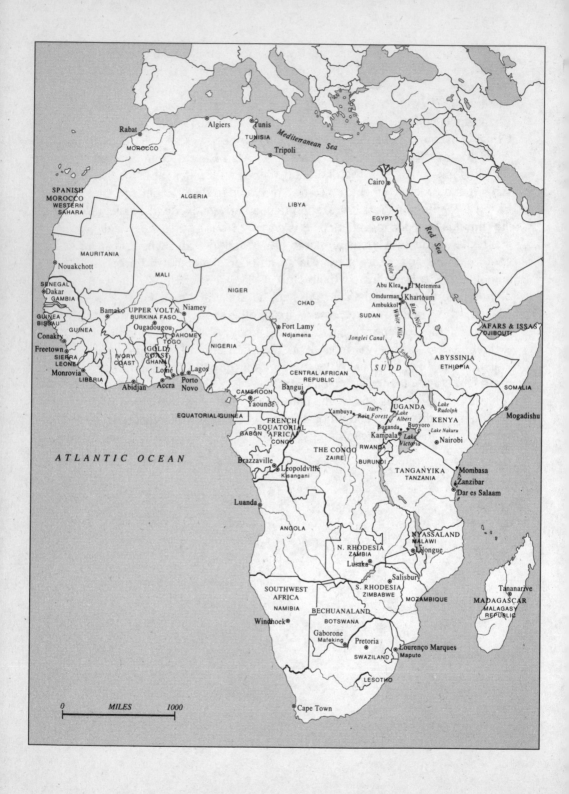

SPANISH
MOROCCO
WESTERN
SAHARA

Rabat
MOROCCO

Algiers

Tunis
TUNISIA

Mediterranean Sea

Tripoli

Cairo

ALGERIA

LIBYA

EGYPT

Red Sea

MAURITANIA

Nouakchott

MALI

NIGER

CHAD

SUDAN

Nile

Abu Klea
Omdurman
Ambukkol
El Metemma
Khartoum

Blue Nile

White Nile

AFARS & ISSAS
DJIBOUTI

SENEGAL
Dakar
GAMBIA

Bamako
UPPER VOLTA
BURKINA FASO

Niamey

Fort Lamy
Ndjamena

Jonglei Canal

GUINEA
BISSAU

Conakry

GUINEA

Ougadougou

Sobat

SUDD

ABYSSINIA
ETHIOPIA

Freetown
SIERRA
LEONE

IVORY
COAST

DAHOMEY
TOGO
GOLD
COAST
GHANA
Lomé
Lagos

NIGERIA

SOMALIA

Monrovia
LIBERIA

Abidjan

Accra

Porto
Novo

CENTRAL AFRICAN
REPUBLIC

Bangui

Yambuya
Ituri
Rain Forest
Lake
Albert

Lake
Rudolph

Mogadishu

CAMEROON

Yaounde

UGANDA

Buganda
Bunyoro
Kampala

Lake
Nakuru

KENYA

Nairobi

EQUATORIAL GUINEA

FRENCH
EQUATORIAL
AFRICA

GABON

CONGO

THE CONGO
ZAIRE

RWANDA

BURUNDI

Lake
Victoria

ATLANTIC OCEAN

Brazzaville

Leopoldville
Kisangani

TANGANYIKA
TANZANIA

Mombasa
Zanzibar
Dar es Salaam

Luanda

ANGOLA

NYASSALAND
MALAWI
L. Nongue

SOUTHWEST
AFRICA

NAMIBIA

N. RHODESIA
ZAMBIA

Lusaka

Salisbury
S. RHODESIA
ZIMBABWE

MOZAMBIQUE

MADAGASCAR
MALAGASY
REPUBLIC

Tananarive

BECHUANALAND

BOTSWANA

Windhoek

Gaborone
Mafeking

Pretoria

Lourenço Marques
Maputo

SWAZILAND

LESOTHO

0   *MILES*   1000

Cape Town

PART ONE

THE INVENTION OF NAKURU

I.

And you really must complain,
About Muthaiga Club champagne.
The most expensive kind of wine
In England is a matter
Of pride and habit, when we dine.
Presumably the latter,
Beneath an equatorial sky
You must consume it or just die;
And stern indomitable men
Have told me time and time again,
The nuisance of the tropics is,
The sheer necessity of fizz.

—*Doggerel ascribed to Denys Finch Hatton,
quoted by his biographer, Errol Trzebinski*

A WHITE MAN in Africa stands out a bit from the crowd and attracts a certain kind of attention—darkest gossip, a white lie or maybe even the whole tropical truth, take your pick.

Here's a digressive example: I had a choice—I could have dined in Wamba, charming place, where I dropped off the adventuresome nurse and her girlfriend, and passed the night trying to chat with the locals about native culture and regional agricultural recovery. Or I could travel two hours over the second-worst road in the world through a hot and dusty, scrub-filled slice of Kenya's Northern Frontier District to a game lodge where they serve a really good stuffed roast loin of pork.

So maybe I was driving the rental jeep a little fast for the lunar surface, but a simple slalom for a pedestrian shouldn't have punctured a tire the way it did. The fellow I'd almost run down didn't seem offended. In fact, when he approached and said something that seemed vaguely destinational, I just waved him inside. Really, it was his appearance that won me over: red cloak, skin dyed red to match and several pounds of green rocks piled ceremonially on his head. Besides, he was damned polite—and I

3

liked him a lot more than the three chaps to whom I'd given a lift earlier, all of whom certainly sang very well, but one of whose goats had pissed in the back.

We didn't have a lot to talk about, but, despite a tremendous language gap, we gave it a try. Every time he'd say something, I'd answer in international cultural cognates: Levi's. Nothing there. Lionel Richie. Nope. Pelé? We Are the World? Ingrate. Rambo, hey, Disneyland? Nah. Coca-Cola? Got one. "Coca-Cola." It sounded wistful, almost sad, the way he said it, like it meant something. He said it again, but this time with an awkward embellishment. "Coca blah blah Cola blah." Not really a real thing. So I tried one more.

"Patrick Shaw."

"Patrick Shaw." Bingo. "Patrick Shaw."

"Patrick Shaw?" I was surprised.

"Patrick Shaw," he said, and away he went, imaginary guns blazing, imaginary bad guys keeling over, falling on my gearshift.

Riding in a police car a few days later at the Murang'a Road roundabout in the middle of Nairobi, I could see kids pointing; one waved. Everybody stared. It was as if Kim Basinger were tied up on the roof rack.

It wasn't the car—a standard-issue Volvo with a bar of big, blue lights on top. It was the driver, a white man named Patrick David Shaw. Mr. Shaw is a school administrator in Nairobi. He's also a senior police official, and he had a big problem.

"Look," he said to me at the end of a long interview. "I want you to be careful what you write about me. . . . I like to keep a low profile."

Stands to reason. A white cop in a big, black neighborhood, worried, as he told me, about "becoming a target." Unfortunately Mr. Shaw is not only one of the most famous men in East Africa, he is also—at something over six feet tall and well in excess of 300 pounds—one of the largest. He could get nailed in a cross fire between Stevie Wonder and Ray Charles. And if he wants a low profile, he has cause to worry—although not because of anything I write. For Mr. Shaw, along with a handful of others—magnificent monuments to British eccentricity and high moral purpose—is all that remains of a once-glittering imperial society.

One of the nice things about imperialism, British-style, is the residue it leaves behind, the faint ring that marks the high water of righteous ambition or idle preoccupation. Kenya was once a peach of a colony, home to the thousands of settlers, missionaries and merchants, misfits, eccentrics, romantics and truth seekers who followed the improbable railroad from Mombasa to Uganda and, making quick and dirty deals with warring natives and their slave-trading Arab cohorts, created the place. Especially between the wars, it was the posting of choice for a generation of well-meaning, purposeful Britons, keepers of the only empire in all history that was an almost completely haphazard and accidental construction built on a solid foundation of ethical conviction and the best of intentions. The empire's gone. But the souvenirs are terrific. For Kenya, one of the most fortunate and enlightened of African countries (despite recent flirtations with a local variation of Africanization, a politically convenient concept of racial discrimination with a long history of demonstrated failure—sort of the ultimate in affirmative-action programs—but always the refuge of choice for governmental incompetence), has an interesting and ongoing tradition not only of making room for white tribesmen, but of relishing their exploits, embroidering them, spinning transient myths out of wild speculation.

Of course, gossip is the currency of information in most parts of Africa, a continent of unparalleled possibilities, where a man can go to bed a policeman or staff sergeant and wake up a field marshal or president, where nations resemble cults, where a half-dozen decades of colonialism have excused another quarter-century or so of lethal corruption and famine-inducing social mismanagement, and where most hard news comes in explosive canisters.

But there's a marked difference between Kenya, one of the very few relatively stable and coup-less countries left on the continent, and many of the other nations of sub-Saharan Africa. A casual visitor can spend just a few days in places like Kinshasa, Lagos or Luanda and see that they are, indeed, the work of an angry and vengeful God. Kenya, on the other hand, was built by John Bull and Walt Disney as a joint venture for well-dressed people who want to see Africa in a few days without a lot of fuss. Tourism is the country's second-largest industry (after coffee), so the tourists must like what they see: colorful coastal towns with palm-studded, Club Med–grade beaches; cool, quiet highland lakes and deep, wet forests; rolling, grassy hills and trout-filled streams and rivers; prosperous farms carved out of rich, red earth; game parks with abundant exotic wildlife; and Nairobi, the African convention capital.

Nairobi is a new town in a new country—the city was founded in 1899, four years after the colony* itself, with the arrival of the railroad from the

* Actually, the British protectorate, which included Kenya, was established in 1895. Full colonial status wasn't granted until 1920.

coast. Before that it was a virtually deserted, treeless plain backing up to a large papyrus swamp. Nairobi, if not terribly picturesque, is at least full of comforting Western amenities. Elspeth Huxley, in one of her books,* says that when she first arrived in Nairobi, it had the appearance of an Indian town, an atmosphere she suggests has been much diminished. But Huxley knows the city too well. To a less familiar visitor, Nairobi still has an Asian patina, a characteristic evident not only in the older architecture, which looks very much like standard-issue British colonial architecture, as found in lesser cities throughout India, but also in the merchant class, which seems to be overwhelmingly Asian. In the center of the city there's an abundance of new, Western-style high-rise buildings, but they've been adapted for local use: Windows are flung open because the air conditioning is on the fritz; huge throngs clutter the pavement in front of government skyscrapers; men's-room mosaics, those little tiles in various shades of blue, decorate the lower registers of some buildings. The shopping districts include much older, temporary structures that somehow became permanent; huge arcades cover the sidewalks, filled with vendors selling everything from shoeshines to four-year-old copies of *Redbook* magazine; inside the ramshackle shops, clerks sell cotton safari jackets and I ♥ KENYA T shirts to tourists, who, during the long season—from May until January—block the pavement and jam the city streets with chartered minibuses just back from fruitless excursions through the local game parks. Phenomenally persistent con-artists ply the crowds selling fake elephant-hair bracelets, and in front of the New Stanley Hotel, black marketeers offer terrific exchange rates to dollar-laden visitors who sit sipping Cokes. At night, muggers walk their beats through the city center, waiting to waylay visiting Europeans with a lame story about starving relatives in Uganda, just before the bludgeons fall.

Once, not too long ago, you could sit on the terrace at the Norfolk Hotel and think about where you were, in Africa, breathing the dust of deadly deserts and trackless savannas; now you stare at the morbidly modern buildings of the local university. There's an inoffensive market in Nairobi, enough good restaurants to warrant the successful publication of a dining-out guide, a so-so casino and a half-dozen first-class hotels. News organizations that feel they have to have somebody someplace in the sub-Saharan part of the continent stick their bureaus in Nairobi, because while the city may have little in common with the other capitals of Africa, at least a fellow can make a phone call from there. (It certainly isn't for

* *Out in the Midday Sun.*

convenience, since usually the quickest way to get from one flash point in Africa to another is to fly via Europe.)

But if Nairobi seems oddly out of sync with its geography, you can get back in touch with Africa by simply motoring out of the city for a few miles, where the common places of the city change to shantytowns harboring the victims of the continent. Traffic moves at a furious pace along these well-pitted macadam strips, their shoulders eroded into five-foot-deep ditches. There is not enough room for two lanes of opposing trucks and buses; there's a near-miss every split second, and at night it can terrify the most jaded driver. I once drove a minibus-load of journalists into town along one especially terrifying road; it was well after dark, and by the time we arrived everyone was huddled on the rear two seats, their eyes closed tighter than mine. After all, one of the few characteristics Kenya does share with the rest of black Africa is that everybody drives like a maniac there, too. On an almost daily basis, a madman piloting a careering, jam-packed *matatu*—small Japanese pickups sporting camper shells (but not, perhaps, brakes or steering) that serve as sort of ad hoc intercity buses—pays a bloody visit to oncoming traffic, wiping out commuters a dozen at a time.

If grim speculation has a vital role elsewhere in Africa, in Kenya, where things actually work—including the light switches, the postal service, the economy and a reasonably high proportion of the adult population—rumor has a more sublime role. Newspaper editors in Kenya have learned from their British and American colleagues that with a relatively unfettered and independent press, gossip doesn't necessarily have to inform, it only has to entertain. (A front-page headline in one national daily reads: SEDITION: SEVEN ARRESTED IN TOILET. The villains, it was revealed, had been caught in the can reading a pamphlet published by the illegal, apparently leftist and somewhat mysterious Mwakenya organization.*) At diplomatic receptions in Nairobi, in bars and restaurants, good gossip provides the pocket change for a sort of social barter economy. At one dinner party, for example, in return for some meaningless chatter about a local pilot, I got twenty minutes on the elderly and impoverished European aristocrats who, nattily attired in the same frayed evening clothes, each night crashed a different party or reception to rustle up some dinner.

* The name, I was told by Kenyans, means nothing. The organization is apparently a loosely constructed fraternity of middle-class, urbanized Kikuyu and Luo who complain a lot but accomplish little. Most accidents—train wrecks, bridge collapses, that sort of thing—are blamed on the Mwakenya by Daniel arap Moi's government, lending them an appearance of power they don't really possess.

A French diplomat told me the one about the rich Englishman, a pilot and scholar, who had moved to town and taken control of the local classical society, and who, on being asked to fly the Archbishop of Canterbury to a distant game park, took his airplane to cruising altitude, switched on the autopilot and said, "I hope Your Grace won't mind," as he reached down into his flight bag and pulled out his needlepoint. "Thank God," said the Archbishop, reaching into his own bag for his embroidery.

So, in a country where there's almost never anything good on TV, rumor and gossip are the national pastimes, played at a variety of venues—in the exclusive Muthaiga Club, or in embassies, or in the Kenya Regiment, or at the East Africa Flying Club.* Although gossip is enjoyed by everyone, for most First World visitors it has a certain attraction when the participants and the subjects are white residents. For them, Kenya is a very small world indeed. There are only 50,000 resident whites in the whole country, but most of them are two-year contract employees of governmental organizations or multinational corporations and don't count. White Kenya is a tiny town and has many of the same incomprehensible peccadilloes found in small towns elsewhere.

Unlike most small towns, however, the white community in Kenya has more colorful characters than Mayberry R.F.D., and every year or so, the focus of gossip shifts slightly—but only slightly, since the principal

---

* The British, among all the world's races, possess the greatest genius for forming clubs. In Kenya, you can see a perfect manifestation of this remarkable talent at the Muthaiga Club—if you can get a member to stick his neck out far enough to extend an invite. It's a large, rambling, pink building that looks the sort of establishment that would normally contain the living remains of ancient silent screen stars. Inside, there's a large dining room and a bar, where gentlemen of English origin stand, posture-perfect, exchanging polite xenophobic observations, until they topple over, drunk. (As far as I know, there are no black members there, but there is a Belgian, an aristocrat, no less, whom I overheard complaining that he couldn't seem to get the chap who tends the rolls to acknowledge his baronial title. "But I am *not* an esquire, you see," he said. "Don't they have barons in England?") To Beryl Markham, a famous East African flyer and a long-time resident, the club consisted of "rooms in which the people who made the Africa I knew danced and talked and laughed, hour after hour." The club has a terrific stuffed lion on display, but I forget the story behind it.

The Muthaiga Club is downright chummy compared to the East Africa Flying Club, where you can sit for hours staring at poor, dead Maia Carbery's picture over the fireplace mantel, and nobody will speak to you, except the waiters, for fear that you may be a non-flying non-member, or worse, not English. When I was last there, they were holding a contest in which the person who guessed the identity of a club member in a baby picture stuck on the wall won an hour aloft or something. I only knew one member—Punch Bearcroft—but I got it right. Bearcroft said so.

Americans also form clubs—there's something called the Mount Kenya Safari Club, for example, which is now owned by an American movie star, I think. It's a hotel. Anyone can join, but it's not worth it.

players are well-established personalities. For example, Shaw is a perennial: They call him "Gunner." So was the late Dr. Hugh A. W. Pilkington, M.A., D.Phil., if you please, who was killed in Canada in 1986 when struck by a car, and Michael "Punch" Bearcroft, founder of the famed Kenya Flying Police and perhaps the only one-armed helicopter pilot in the world. Other players are yanked out of the country's short history and are feverishly discussed by the locals like missing BMOCs at a class reunion. Not long ago Lady Delamere was the favorite topic, following the publication of James Fox's *White Mischief,* a book that surveyed the scandal surrounding the murder of Lord Erroll in 1937. These days, of course, an important central character is Karen Blixen (sometimes better known as Isak Dinesen).

One of the easiest places for a casual visitor to catch up on the latest is at the Norfolk Hotel. There the children and grandchildren of the empire chug White Caps and lounge around in T shirts like Californians on a school break, ignoring the tourists, who, clad carefully in Banana Republic khakis, sip Tusker Export, grimace tightly and avoid salads while telling each other lies designed to convince themselves that life in the bush is a bitch.

In fact, I was sitting in the terrace bar at the Norfolk one night, swapping lies with a couple of other journalists, when one of them, Kurt Kister of *Süddeutsche Zeitung,* looked over my shoulder, froze, then whispered, "Kurtz."

I turned to see a huge white man in his early fifties, maybe, his head nearly shaved, his safari shirt bulging over a gun of some sort, stroll casually through the bar. People made way—they had to, the guy really was big—and the usually indifferent waiters stood nearly at attention, waiting to see which of them would draw the man's table.

"He looks like death," Kister said almost eagerly. "He looks very, very dangerous."

I must confess, at first I wasn't so interested as I should have been. Sure, he was big, and sure, he looked like the thing in the closet at night. Whatever variety of sidearm he carried must have been at least eighteen inches long, the noisy bar had quieted considerably and the crowd allowed a wide circle for the man at the table. But we'd been discussing topics appropriate to traveling bachelors, and the newcomer clearly didn't qualify.

Alas, Kister was really insistent. "I bet he kills men with his bare hands," he said. "I think he pulls people apart for fun." Personally, I never liked German movies, all that weltschmerz leavened with dashes of sturm und drang. I'm more a musical-comedy sort of chap, myself. But it was too late; Kister's screen was filled with blood: "He hunts men down at night."

It was all idle gossip, local sport, which we played for a vacant half-hour or so, unwittingly with one of the principal characters on the local stage, and it was, as it turned out, an example of the way that rumor and invention illuminate reality.

2.

He shoots first, all right. But he never, ever
asks questions later.

—*A Nairobi-based airline employee, of*
Patrick Shaw

IF SUCCESS can be measured in terms of gossip—and I suppose it can, or *People* magazine wouldn't exist—then Patrick Shaw is one of the men most likely to succeed in East Africa. A cover line on one Kenyan women's magazine read, "The Mysterious Patrick Shaw"; inside was a page of photos and a paragraph or two of laudatory copy without a single direct quote. I never heard anybody in Kenya gossiping about Madonna or Jesse Jackson or Bruce Willis or W. E. B. Du Bois. But I heard a lot of great stories about Patrick Shaw.

Here's a safe bet. Ask any boatman at Lake Naivasha, any bartender in Nyeri, any schoolkid in Meru, any shopkeeper on Muindi Mbingu Street in Nairobi what they think of Patrick Shaw, and if they express anything other than fearful admiration and respect, sometimes even reverence, it's because they're either a guilty white or a potential murderer. It's weird. Asking about Patrick Shaw in Kenya is like asking about the Red Sox in Boston: It's a guaranteed conversation starter. And everybody's got a kicker, a fantasy parable.

"They cannot kill Patrick Shaw," a university student out canvassing for charity told me with unmistakable pride. "They have tried to kill him— once, another policeman even shot at him four times from very close—but they cannot do it."

"He frightens the criminals into surrender," a Nairobi merchant said. "He knows everyone who breaks the law, and he warns them twice that he will stop them. Then he goes to their parents and tells them, 'I have warned your son twice that he must stop breaking the law. I will not warn him a third time,' and they [the criminals] give themselves up.

"Once, he caught a very dangerous man who was a member of a gang. Patrick Shaw said to him, 'You must tell me who the others are, and I will release you.' So the man named the others in the gang. Then Patrick Shaw took the man out to the countryside one night and said, 'Okay. Now you can go.' When the man started to run, Patrick Shaw shot him. A prisoner trying to escape." (I found no basis in truth to this allegation, by the way.)

The imaginative French diplomat at the dinner party had waxed cinematical about Shaw. He was with the police, the diplomat had said, and every night he found somebody to make his day. "He never sleeps. He cruises the streets all night in his police car, looking for troublemakers. When he finds them, he shoots them, no questions asked. If you've done something wrong here, he's the one man in Kenya who will find you. To the criminals, he's the most feared man in the country."

A woman had been eavesdropping. "A white man? How disgusting." The Frenchman only shrugged.

"The people think he is like a god," a local journalist told me at breakfast one day. "They think he cannot die, and that he is everywhere. Even I don't know how he does it. If there is a robbery in Gigiri [a distant, fashionable northern suburb of Nairobi] at 3:30, he is there. And if there is trouble in the town at 3:35, he is there, too. It doesn't matter if it's day or night. Patrick Shaw is there."

There was more: He has a direct line to President Daniel arap Moi, and uses it not infrequently. Once, in 1979, while acting on a radio report that a band of marauding Ugandans had been sighted, Shaw rushed to the scene, only to find one of the bad guys standing at his car window. The man shot and ran, and the bullet passed through Shaw's shoulder, through his chest, and out the other side. Shaw drove himself to the hospital, and two days later was out looking for his assailant. More recently he put down an unruly strike by simply showing his face and promising to have a word with the management. Similarly, the story goes, he ended a series of student demonstrations at the university by calmly ordering the kids back to class. He can break up a crime ring with a well-timed, firm request.

While there's undoubtedly more than a little truth to most of these stories, the journalist maintained that for Shaw, the truth served as well as fiction, kind of like the power of advertising.

"He likes going for the dangerous ones," the journalist claimed. "His greatest day," he said, must have been June 26, 1978, when he finally shot dead one of Nairobi's most notorious robbers, Nicolas Mwea Wakinyonga.

Wakinyonga, naturally an object of intense speculation himself, had a reputation as a sort of local Robin Hood ("He never robbed the poor people," a bartender told me later). In the spring of 1978, however, he had expanded his scope somewhat, committing a series of bank robberies in Nairobi, Kakamega and Thika, killing an oil-company executive along the way. Wakinyonga's favorite hangout was the Nyakiambi Lodge and Night Club, in the western suburbs on the highway to Nakuru, just before the road surface and the local demographics fall apart. On that particular Monday night, Wakinyonga was lounging around the bar, a little snookered maybe, and bragging that he hoped Shaw would show up with the police so he could "shoot them all." Some wishes are easier to grant than others, and when Shaw and the police arrived, Wakinyonga let loose with a Czech-made automatic pistol, wounding three people, including one of the cops, but of course not Shaw, who promptly shot the guy. Wakinyonga, by the way, had finished digging his own grave at his nearby homestead just hours before he dug another one at the Nyakiambi Lodge and Night Club.

I asked the journalist if people feared Patrick Shaw. He looked at me like I was nuts. "Of course," he said. "But the ones who fear him the most are the thugs. They hate him. They wish him dead, but unfortunately for them, he never dies." While some feel that, as a white man, his work with the police should be curtailed or even stopped altogether, most others, according to the journalist, recognize that the tremendous increase in population—Kenya's 4-percent population growth is the fastest in the world—and the resultant increase in crime make him "the man Kenya needs, as all criminals fear him."

Then why did everyone I spoke to about Patrick Shaw ask me not to print their names? "That's normal anywhere in Africa if you ask about the police or the government," he said. "And I am telling you things I wouldn't write for myself. Besides, people are afraid of him."

He paused, then smiled. "One other thing," he said. "He is not a very good friend of journalists."

"I certainly hope you're not pulling the wool over my eyes," Shaw said the morning of our interview. "I am generally suspicious of journalists."

"You should be."

"One particular one . . . [who] works for the BBC. He tried a lot of nasty business. If I ever get my hands on him, I'll break his bloody neck."

I looked at the ceiling of Shaw's office at the Starehe Boys' Centre and School, then switched to the walls, where dozens of certificates ("For

Excellence . . . ," "For Courage . . . ," "For Dedication . . .") hung next to clusters of photographs of royalty, the Kenyan elite and schoolchildren. I tried to think of something else, but could only come up with the story that Kister had related when I told him about my scheduled interview: Apparently Shaw was a favorite but elusive target for interviewers, and had several well-tested methods of avoiding the press. Once, when a Swiss correspondent approached Shaw for a brief interview, Shaw stood up, put his face next to the journalist's ear as if to whisper something, and said, "Move!" at the top of his lungs. You could quote him.

So Shaw had imposed some strict rules for our chat. When I had asked for an appointment, I had said I was interested in his job at the Boys' Centre, his position as head of the Boy Scouts and his involvement with the President's Award Scheme, a sort of outdoor survival program. He said he'd be happy to talk about his work with kids but not about his work with the police. "I am with the police, you know," he said confidentially.

So I didn't ask him, even as the police radio crackled on his school desk, and even after he'd shouted into the telephone that he wanted a photo of yet another renegade policeman, this one suspected of shooting some motorists with a Soviet AK-47 on the Naivasha road when they'd stopped to buy pineapples.

While Shaw showed me his school, I spent the morning thinking about my neck and the crazy world we live in. It was a little frustrating, listening to him talk about education when what I wanted was to hear about shoot-outs in nightclubs. Still, Shaw's history more or less mirrored the brief history of his nation: He explained how he'd come to the country—along with many other young men—from the United Kingdom in August 1955, during the Mau Mau Emergency,* ostensibly as a civil servant in the

---

* Although ultimately successful, the Mau Mau uprising owed its final victory to changing times rather than military superiority. The Mau Mau's secret Kikuyu societies were variations on the clandestine groups adopted by the forest-dwelling Kikuyu as the best means by which they might protect themselves against the warlike Masai. The Mau Mau took tribalism to an extreme, especially after its leadership was assumed by Jomo Kenyatta. The organization was always primarily intended to enhance Kikuyu tribal ambitions, but Kenyatta successfully persuaded British well-wishers to portray the movement as a tool for independence. Its strategies were marked by a reliance on terrorist acts and the gross mutilation of victims, almost all of whom were unsympathetic blacks of other tribes. By the time the Mau Mau uprising was suppressed by the British in 1956, some 14,000 blacks had died, along with fewer than 100 whites, most of whom were soldiers and police.

After independence, the Kikuyu consolidated their hold on the government of Kenya. Some degree of economic growth was achieved by what can only be described as an official policy of personal ambition and greed. As Nicholas Harman noted in an article in *The Economist* (June 20, 1987), "By substituting personal acquisitiveness for state control, the Kenyans gave Adam Smith's old diversified magic a chance." Kenyatta often

employ of the Ministry of Agriculture. And, in fact, he had had an early posting to Lake Baringo, where he worked briefly on an irrigation project, and a five-year stint in Eldoret, where he worked as farm manager at a government experimental station. But in both places he was on the police reserve, and by 1961 he was in Nairobi, working not only as the showground manager at the Royal Kenya Agricultural Society and as secretary of the Young Farmers Club of Kenya, but also as part of the mobile police emergency unit.

Shaw had a friend in Nairobi, Geoffrey Griffin, who, during the Emergency, had been in charge of detention camps for delinquent boys. Perhaps consequently, he became director of the National Youth Service, which ran community centers and other programs for children, including a very small educational facility—disguised as a "club" and consisting of a couple of small Quonset huts—for wayward boys in the Starehe district of Nairobi.

It's clear, even from casual research into the school's development, that Griffin was the one with the vision while Shaw was the one with the persistence to carry it out. With justification, he was proud of the school, with which he had been associated since 1962.

"We started with two tin huts, and today we have 1,350 boys here," Shaw told me during the tour of the school's rambling, '60s-modern campus, where all of the buildings have been donated by various charities (the Save the Children Fund, under Shaw's guidance, is especially active at Starehe). "And we are also the top school academically; last year about 200 boys got first-division O-levels.

"We are much more than a school. We have very high standards of discipline and education, and we are a home to most of these boys, since at least 75 percent of them are orphans or destitute. The school is open 365

---

upbraided government officials for not lining their pockets sufficiently (a charming and illustrative anecdote can be found in Paul Johnson's *Modern Times*). As Daniel arap Moi, Kenyatta's successor as Kenya's president, solidifies the one-party rule of the Kikuyu-dominated Kenyan African National Union, other tribes are apparently denied governmental power and consequent wealth; the Samburu are especially neglected, while the Luo are being pushed out of favor by the Kelenjins, members of Moi's own tiny tribe. The Kikuyu have adopted most of the traditions of the British, including a private ownership of agricultural land. (In black Africa, only Kenya and Zimbabwe encourage the freehold of farmland; as a result, the two nations are extremely successful food producers.) The resulting stability encourages investment in Kenya, much as political stability used to do in South Africa.

A similar stability exists in Tanzania, but because of wildly inappropriate, post-independence centralized economic schemes masterminded by the country's textbook-socialist leader, Julius Nyerere, there is no economy there in which anyone might wish to invest.

days a year because many of these are boys who have no home." There is one white student at the school and a "good number" of Asians, mostly the sons of Indians and Pakistanis; the vast majority, of course, are black Kenyans.

Shaw escorted me through metal- and woodshops, a huge dining hall, automotive workshops, a fire and civil-defense facility, band rooms, chemistry, computer and physics labs, a library and an infirmary, an auditorium and a chapel, a small mosque and athletic fields. He boasted about the school's international reputation: "We've had kings and queens, princes and princesses, and presidents visit here. Princess Anne [patron of the Save the Children Fund] has been here twice." We detoured through the job-training and placement center (Starehe graduates are routinely placed at the top of the list for job openings by personnel directors) and ran into a boy who was bound for West Germany as part of a foreign-study program. I found a copy of the mimeographed student newspaper, the *Scan*, which ran a story about a kid who had eaten "2,780 baked beans one by one, with a cocktail stick" in thirty minutes. Not bad.

Starehe Boys' Centre is a good school by anyone's standards, and is certainly remarkable for a school where only 5 percent of the students pay full fees (less than $1,000 per term) and where most pay nothing at all, supported entirely by contributions from individuals* and local and international charities, as well as by substantial grants from the Kenyan government. It provides the only free secondary education in the country, although Shaw and the other Starehe directors have been urging the government to establish a similar school for girls. According to Shaw, however, the authorities have not been able to come up with a woman administrator willing to work eighteen-hour days, seven days a week, as the staff does at Starehe.

Although it has been officially designated a model school, Shaw said, it exists outside the government's Education Ministry. "We remain independent," he explained, noting that "Starehe does its own management, and the government has never tried to lay down a law."

Shaw's role on campus is a bit mystifying. He doesn't teach ("You'll *never* get me to do that," he said flatly), and he admits that education, per se, is not particularly interesting to him; he prefers instead "the development side." He is unmarried and has an apartment on campus, but he never sleeps in the bed Starehe provides for him, opting instead for a straight-backed chair, perhaps because of his size. "I have trained myself to sleep

* Donations can be made by check to the Starehe Boys' Centre and School, P.O. Box 30178, Nairobi, Kenya.

for ten minutes at a time," he told me, "then wake up feeling completely
refreshed." Quite naturally, his police work has an enormous impact on
the students, for whom he is the hero-in-residence, as well as on his ability
to put together support for the school. "I couldn't have done most of the
things I do for the students at Starehe if I weren't a senior police officer,"
Shaw said. "Most of my notoriety comes from my work with the police."

Ah, yes, the police, you said? "I won't tell you exactly how I got into it.
But in fact, I work for them more than I do for the school—except I'm not
paid for it."

People do often get carried away with peculiar hobbies. I knew a man
once who collected pocket combs, and another who invested a lot of time
and money acquiring 3-D glasses. But Shaw is the first person I ever met
who spends, quite literally, all his free time driving around looking for
armed and dangerous people who do terrible things.

He was, I suggested gently, the object of occasional conversation here
and there.

"Yes, I know. People do talk . . . after all, a lot of people would have
lost their lives if it weren't for the work I've done."

"Yes, but . . ." I thought better of it. Besides, I realized, Shaw was not
only acutely aware of his image, he had in fact nourished it to some
degree. For example:

"People ask, 'How do you get to the scene of an accident before it even
happens?'

"The answer is very simple. A lot of those mobile police units are very
slow if they think they might get into any danger." Their tactic, he said,
was to wait for Shaw and the other CID officers to arrive first, which
suited him fine. "I have a very firm policy: The sooner a senior officer gets
to an incident the better. Generally the situation gets under control before
it deteriorates into a situation that you can't control."

During our drive through Nairobi, Shaw elaborated on strategies and
tactics, talking about close calls and good cases, like the time he helped
corral a half-dozen P.L.O. and Baader-Meinhof terrorists who were
attempting to blow up an El Al airliner. There was also the time hotel
bombers had managed to slip away before their bomb went off (it was
actually a double-bombing attempt, but Shaw had spotted the second one
just before detonation), but would, Shaw thought, eventually be nabbed:
"We know who did it. We've got the photographs, but we don't know
where the terrorists are. The Israelis will get them one day. MOSSAD
[Israeli intelligence] are very good."

Shaw went on to recount a number of other exploits, asking me at the
end not to "put in any details," which was fine, since it would only

decorate the already baroque rumors that surround his activities. "Plus," he added, "being a European, quite frankly I don't want too much publicity as a police officer. I mean, the police are very pleased to have me, but at the same time they don't like anybody getting too much publicity.

"I want to be honest," he was saying. "I do a job because I like it, not because I want to get credit or money out of it. No doubt, I could spend my time gaining a lot of money, but as long as I have enough to live on, I'm not interested."

I was sort of paying attention. But I have to admit that when you find yourself riding around in a car with a guy like that, what you really want to hear is something like, "Hold on, pal, this isn't going to be pretty," or, "Look, when the shooting starts, you hit the floor." You start hoping for TV, the big payoff, the punch line. Instead, you get Fiji.

"Working in commerce five days a week, that would drive me nuts. I couldn't stand working in [the] U.K. I would never go back to U.K., even if I were thrown out of here. It would drive me nuts, that place: the people and the traffic and the weather, in that order."

So where, I asked, would you go?

He fell silent for a while. "I don't expect to go away from here, but you never know. I wouldn't go further south," he said, referring to South Africa. "I don't know. Fiji, maybe, or Australia. There is going to be the most awful blowup in South Africa."

We pulled up in front of the Norfolk Hotel and I felt home free. But as I started to open the door, Shaw stopped me.

"Remember," he said. "I want you to be careful what you say about me." I nodded and shuffled and rolled my eyes.

The next night I loafed around the Norfolk listening to a group of white locals discussing politics. They gossiped about the way Moi, like Jomo Kenyatta before him, had carefully balanced the roles of the police and the army to ensure stability, and speculated on whether that balance was going out of kilter and whether there would be a coup this year or next or never, until two of the party, young women born and raised in Kenya, suggested I move with them to a less crowded table for dinner.

We made small talk, stared at steaks and discussed the future for whites in Kenya (they thought there wasn't much of one: "They're pushing us out," one said), until I decided to see what I could do to add to my collection of Shaw stories.

"You should be careful of him," one girl said. "My father worked with him for years and always liked him. But he hates you lot—journalists."

"He was friendly to me," I ventured.

They both looked at me with disbelief. "Not bloody likely," one said. She paused. "You mean you spoke to him?"

"That's impossible," said her friend. "I heard he gives notice to journalists who even ask to interview him. He's worried what they might say."

The first girl agreed. "I think he can detain you just on suspicion," she said. "[A reporter] from the BBC was here once, and spoke with Patrick Shaw. And now Shaw's looking for him. I mean, that's what I heard."

Just a rumor.*

* Shaw, fifty-two, died of a heart attack early in 1988, as this book was going to press. I arrived in Nairobi shortly after the funeral and before the end of breakfast. I collected seven different stories, all inspired by the fact that his casket had been closed during the service. One local publication cited Shakespeare in their obituary for Shaw: "Know that the grave doth yawn for thee thrice wider than for other men." But no irony was intended.

3.

I HAD A LUNCH in Africa, in a train station overlooking Nakuru, where
they build tractors.

Of course, there are a few other restaurants in the vicinity of Lake
Nakuru. But if you ask me, the best restaurant in town is upstairs at the
railway station, where everything—waiters, trains, time—stands still. For
one thing, the view—inside and out—is terrific.

Inside the ticket hall in Nakuru station, which is of recent colonial
construction and not especially notable, there's dead optimism—a line of
dusty, shuttered ticket windows—and nobody's home. Neglect swirls
across the floor, and a small chalkboard announces the late-night departures of the Tuesday and Thursday trains. At the top of the stairs, just
before you reach the massive mid-'50s murals depicting elegant passengers boarding railway carriages for Nairobi and the coast, there's a
quartet of toilets: two for gents, two for ladies, an "oriental" and a
"Western" style for each. You can choose, but there's no difference; it's
a lesson. Beyond the toilets is an empty cocktail lounge, just remodeled by
somebody after a long stay at a TraveLodge in Tucson. And straight ahead
is the restaurant.

It's easy to catch people off guard, barging into a train station restaurant
just like that. Three women and a man, the only other customers, stop
talking, but only briefly. The waiters, after exchanging confused glances,
straighten their white jackets and make for the kitchen, probably huddle,

20

then re-emerge. Towels flutter over arms, a starched tablecloth is produced, a small tent-card advertising the chicken special disappears and is replaced by an index card bearing a hastily written suggestion for a four-course Sunday dinner.

No dicey renovation here. A few Kenya Railways picture-posters are lost on three wash-green walls, while huge windows dominate the other. Lots of light, the dust floats, it's very still. But outside, below the station plaza, a busy and confusing open market stretches downhill along the road that leads away from town. THE HOME OF MASSEY-FERGUSON reads the sign over the highway, which leads on to the gray concrete low-rent housing project, where the communal water supply's been cut off by the local government after a squabble with the landlords, and where crowds of children, each nattily attired in one school uniform or another, compete for space with cars and trucks on the crumbling tarmac.

It's the wet season, and beyond Nakuru—a Kenya highlands farming community more or less like any farming community anywhere, like, say, Mankato, Kansas, with a twist and an entrepreneurial sense of poetry ("Moonlight Service Station")—you can see fields green as Devon warp into the surrounding hills. At the station restaurant you can eat a reasonable roast beef with Yorkshire pudding on china decorated with the Victorian logo of the Uganda Railway, pour tea from old East Africa Railway silver into a cup bearing the modern "KR" of Kenya Railways, stare out the window and watch the whole, hopeful invention of Nakuru.

With a little hindsight, maybe, you could watch a nervous baroness, Karen von Blixen-Finecke, the lean, dark-haired woman with the big hat, wander the streets looking for her dog. She and her husband, Baron Bror, had left three identical hounds—Askari, Pania and Dusk—in the care of a motorcycle-riding bookkeeper named Erik Wilhelm Tancredo von Huth after their car had broken down. But what with one thing and another, the one named Dusk had wandered off, and now the baroness was busy stalking Nakuru, shouting, "Dusk! Dusk!" like a frenzied town crier, and offering a reward of 300 rupees for the safe return of her pet.

Everyone was enlisted in the effort to find Dusk. The baroness, who, under the name Isak Dinesen, would later write sensitive memoirs of her life in Kenya, was an overly concerned woman anyway and by now she was in a state of agitated intensity, damning von Huth and Nakuru ("cursed place") alike, and organizing rescue parties. By car and by horseback, the Blixens bothered town and valley and probed deep into the hillside settlements, asking everyone they met if they had seen the missing Dusk. This went on for three days until everyone grew tired of it and decided to go home. "It was all so distressing," she later wrote her mother. A few days later, the dog was finally found, involved in some sort of suicide-murder arrangement with a zebra.

Karen Blixen was a woman who loved her dogs, and while Pania was her favorite, Dusk, she thought, was a fine dog too. In a letter home, Dusk was characterized as "in every way . . . so much better than most human beings . . . faithful . . . beautiful and intelligent," and Blixen later told an interviewer that as a teenager she had dog "fantasies," in which she was surrounded by ten pups at a time. Indeed, only the day before the tragic disappearance, Blixen had jumped in front of a train at Kikuyu station to push one of her clever pooches out of the way of an oncoming local, and got herself bounced off the engine in the process. "The pluckiest thing I have ever seen in my life," remarked Lord Delamere, who at the time was seated safely in one of the railway carriages, but who was damned plucky himself.

Once the squire of Vale Royal in Cheshire, Delamere had become king of Nakuru. His nearby sprawling cattle operation—along with the workshops built by the railroad—had made Nakuru into a town of convenience for the growing community of local settlers and traders who had believed the earnest recruitment promises of Delamere's agent in England. ("The most beautiful country imaginable," Delamere had written to him, "with enormous timber trees, evergreen grasses and clovers, perennial streams everywhere and a temperate climate. It will grow anything, and to my mind it is a chance in a thousand for a man with a little money. Settlers at present in this country say that it compares with the best of New Zealand.") Delamere opened a tavern on the main road, where, standing on the bar, he organized indoor rugby matches, sometimes diving headfirst into the scrum, and later he built a small hotel around the corner, where his favorite pastime was to roust the occupants, arm them with oranges and spend the night breaking all the windows in the place. His neighbors grew to know him, for he was a frequent visitor. But they never quite understood him. Wrote one neighbor to a friend in May 1917:

He's the sort of person you would hesitate to express a thought to that seemed perhaps a little far-fetched. . . . Not that he wouldn't understand it, he would, no one better; but he would dismiss it probably with ridicule. His perceptions, his keen wit and an amazing faculty he has for, so to speak, detaching himself and *never* giving himself away make him very strong in dealing with most people and all sorts of material things. You never really get to know him. I doubt if anybody ever has. He won't be known, but he likes to know others. It's rather "take all and give nothing" with him.

Bad news: A white woman in the restaurant has declined the roast beef and ordered a ham sandwich instead. The waiter is incensed; he knows the protocol and is miffed at the woman's inability to follow rules; a ham sandwich is nobody's idea of Sunday dinner but hers, and a mild flap ensues when he refuses to serve her a beer.

Now the dog was gone, and so was the train, along with Lord Delamere and the bookkeeper. The baroness had long ago returned to the first act of her melodrama, about which she wrote at length in books that would subsequently become an immensely popular film, *Out of Africa,* about a couple of quite handsome and elegantly attired expatriates who had a deeply meaningful relationship at a financially troubled coffee plantation in what is now the Nairobi suburb of Karen.

In fact, the Blixens' home, Mbongani (which, as Karen Blixen's thorough and sympathetic biographer, Judith Thurman, notes, translates as "house in the woods"), was too small to use for the production. The serious, bespectacled Danish caretaker tells sightseers at the rather pleasant but unprepossessing stone bungalow—situated next to Karen College, around the corner from Karen Country Club and just up the street from Karen Hairdressers—that shooting the film at Mbongani "would have destroyed the house," so they used the house of Mama Ngina, First President Jomo Kenyatta's widow, instead. The tourists listen, then ask for directions to the movie locale. (I asked one Frenchwoman why she was so eager to see where the movie had been shot. She told me she wanted "to see how it really was.") They certainly don't wait to hear the caretaker explain why Blixen's sweetheart, Denys Finch Hatton, always wore a hat ("He was quite bald, you see"). Some visitors linger, however, for now that Meryl Streep is Karen Blixen, a certain exaltation of the author quite naturally has taken place. When pilgrims—as opposed to tourists—are told that she sat in this clubby window seat looking at those rain-green hills while she wrote, they dutifully sit at the window, gaze out at the chap doing yardwork and strike a contemplative pose. Companions snap the picture.

Meanwhile in Nairobi, long after the film has completed an unsuccessful run following a premiere attended almost exclusively by local whites who, months later, would still delight in discussing Robert Redford's skin condition with visitors, letters from irate Kenyans are still appearing in the daily press, wondering why the film wasn't about two black Africans instead.

I was sitting in a coffee bar in Nairobi one morning gossiping with a local writer, a lifelong Kenyan with an acute sensitivity to local history, when the current feature topic came up. "Blixen was quite intense, quite passionate," she said. "And I think she actually believed the things she said, even though we all often knew better. That affair with Finch Hatton, for example." She paused for effect, then ever so slightly lowered her voice. "We all knew he had other *tendencies,* wandering off all the time with those boys," she said, referring to Finch Hatton's frequent and lengthy excursions into the bush accompanied only by native youngsters. "But she was quite imaginative, and nobody wanted to say anything."

Like hell. The settler community did a brisk trade in back-fence news, and Blixen was the subject of perhaps thousands of conversations during her relatively brief sojourn in Kenya, from early 1914 until 1931, when the coffee plantation was finally sold. "First it was Bror," said a retired farmer, "and his affairs, and there were quite a few of those." (Enough, anyway, to provision a case of clap, which he promptly donated to his wife.)

"But eventually Karen and Denys and Berkeley Cole became a set, although nobody could quite understand what interest she could have in men like that, I mean intimately, of course. . . . Oh, we all liked them, especially Denys, but it was rather strange. There were rumors. . . . She could be very peculiar at times. A bit much." (Her biographer says, "Her clothes were ideas," but, alas, not all ideas are good ones. "She dressed rather odd," the farmer told me. Always too much makeup, too many frilly dresses, strange hats—an appearance Thurman's sources verify. "But of course I understand she was a really first-rate author.")

And finally there was her attitude toward Africans, which was conditional, convenient, vividly patronizing and no doubt deeply offensive to both the white and native communities. Complaining that during hard times, most settlers took "very little interest in their natives," Blixen wrote to her mother that "the future of this country depends on *native labour,* and it is in one's own interest to take care of their children just as much as calves and foals."

In the early days of its colonial existence, Kenya was crowded with troublesome, rich white kids, sent off to a distant corner of the empire where their embarrassing behavior wouldn't be quite so readily noticed. Karen Blixen, for example, was the eccentric child of a wealthy bourgeois family; her husband, Bror, was poor but seriously aristocratic and, at first, not much good at practical things: Once, when he was thirsty, he drank a bottle of Lysol, mistaking it for soda water, and almost died. It was a good match in many respects, and in fact the Blixens were a happy couple as they made their way toward the equator with money in their pockets and coffee on their minds. Urged on by the baroness, who very much believed in life-as-art, they added a charming bohemian touch to local society. One gets the impression that later in the century they'd turn up at a performance-art festival in Oregon or organize a group of their friends and put up the money for an off-off-Broadway production of *Mother Courage*.

I met only two people who had known Karen Blixen in Kenya, but both of them agreed that she was pretentious and affected, and they liked her better in the movie. To those whites she considered beneath her she appeared aloof, even downright rude, although in her letters home she spoke of her "black brothers," usually being careful to either underline the phrase or set it off in quotes to make sure her egalitarianism was well understood.

Her democratic ideals were somewhat situational, however. All her life she insisted on being addressed by her title, and she once wrote that, sure, Bror had been a pain but "it was worth having syphilis in order to become a 'Baroness' " (although she added a healthy number of disclaimers— "the world being as it is," and all that). Thurman quotes a friend of Blixen's: Karen "had an idiotic reverence for the aristocracy." In fact, she had an obsession with the aristocracy; as she once wrote, it defined her existence. More, it provided a suitable context for her self-conscious revolt against her own middle-class background. And Kenya provided an ideal setting.

Blixen's East Africa, for all its rigors, was a fairly settled country by the time she arrived on the eve of World War I. The Kenya colony especially was already yielding a good crop of bad-boy aristocrats, including a wide range of reckless cadet sons and other relatively improvident peers, the most prominent among whom was the third Baron Delamere.

Delamere had gambled his entire fortune on his East African future. His Kenyan estates were huge, and at first they lost a lot of money. So he borrowed more and invested it in applied science, trying to develop livestock and grains that would survive the local environment and provide the basis for the country's growth. He started a small chain of butcher shops to exploit the local market, along with a grain-milling operation (using Kiswahili names, he called the latter "Grain, Ltd.," and the former "Meat, Ltd."), neither of which he profited from, but both of which had a signal effect on local agricultural enterprises. An ardent admirer of Cecil Rhodes, the quintessential British empire builder, Delamere became a spokesman for the settlers in their endless squabbles with colonial bureaucrats (official policy was to defer to native rights in all areas of conflict) and was one of the principal opponents to Colonial Secretary Joseph

Chamberlain's peculiar proposal to turn over some 5,000 square miles of the Mau Plateau to a Zionist group led by Dr. Theodor Herzl, who hoped to establish in Kenya "an antechamber to the holy land" for Russian Jews.* Delamere also championed the cause of the Masai, who, while they robbed him blind, showed up at his shanty† every night and told him some good stories about livestock. On Delamere's rare days off, his idea of a good time was to race passing trains for ten miles or so with his American trotter or ride into Nakuru and cause his customary, good-natured—but usually expensive—trouble. It wouldn't be an exaggeration to say that Delamere was more responsible for the success of Kenya Colony than was anyone else. "There was hardly an industry in which he had not experimented, a society to which he had not belonged, a political issue in which he had not joined," his biographer, Elspeth Huxley, wrote. "The thread of his existence had become inextricably woven into the web of Kenya's development."

* Chamberlain's 1902 offer came in response to a particularly severe pogrom then under way in the Bessarabian region of Russia. The eccentric proposal was greeted warmly at first by many humanitarians, but finally was met by severe dissent within the Zionist movement itself. At the Zionist Congress at Basel in August 1903, delegates from Bessarabia raised the loudest objections to the scheme, saying they preferred the chance of massacres to settling in a pre–holy land someplace in Africa. The proposal finally carried, with a vote of 595 to 177, but most of the Russian delegates, who had led the opposition, left the meeting in a huff. Zionists around the world were concerned that the establishment of Herzl's antechamber would diminish the ongoing effort to establish a homeland in Palestine. Finally, according to Elspeth Huxley, a three-man Jewish deputation was sent to Kenya in 1904 and traveled to the proposed settlement area, where they were met by threatening Masai and roaring lions. They stayed three days, left, and reported, in Huxley's words, "the district to be, on the whole, unsuitable for the settlement of fugitives from Russia." Most Zionists were relieved by the report; in 1905, the Zionist Congress at Basel formally declined the British offer, although interest was revived somewhat later, when the proposal was championed by Winston Churchill. Popular historian Charles Miller sees the episode—which took place when Arthur James Balfour was Prime Minister—as a preliminary to Balfour's subsequent commitment, in 1917, to the establishment of a Jewish state.

Kenya did, however, attract some Jewish pioneers. One of the earliest was Abraham Block, the patriarch of a family of remarkably talented hostelers. Until quite recently, Block Hotels ran most of the country's game-park resorts; the family still retains the venerable Norfolk Hotel, in Nairobi.

† I mean it, it was a dive. Mud floor, slat walls, no windows. According to Elspeth Huxley, the place was filled with livestock, oak antiques, Masai warriors and fine china. "That's a rather dreary place over there," a neighbor wrote home. "There's something about it that always depresses me and somehow there's a sort of bareness about Delamere's surroundings that I can't explain." His first wife put up with it for a while, but finally, when Delamere was away in Cheshire, she bought a prefab. She later went insane, and died in England.

Because of Delamere's pervasive involvement in the development of the country, I regard Huxley's biography of Delamere, *White Man's Country* (1935), as a decent political history of Kenya Colony.

injury. It had been a good trip for Delamere—the only one he made to Africa without hurting himself—and he decided to return to Africa as soon as he could find a suitable wife. In 1899 he married Lady Florence Cole and took her off to Kenya. Unfortunately, once there he caught a severe case of malaria and in 1900 returned to Vale Royal.

They tried again, in December 1902, setting sail from England to Mombasa, this time to stay. For Delamere, home wasn't where the heart was, it was wherever they could carry him on a stretcher so he could mend a spinal concussion acquired when he landed on his head after his horse tripped over a pig hole. He was carried to a plain near Njoro on the slopes of the Mau escarpment, where, after recovering, he built the Equator Ranch. He soon discovered the area was unhealthy for both livestock and wheat, and so he used it as a laboratory to provide heartier stock for his new ranch—Soysambu, situated around the flamingo-clogged, soda-bitter water of Lake Elmenteita on the floor of the Rift Valley—which he supported by putting Vale Royal more and more in hock. In 1909 the family estate was put into receivership, and Delamere's African adventure was left to float on its own merits.

Delamere's tribulations became the stuff of legend. If anything wrong could happen, it would happen to Delamere. After enormously expensive experiments with different strains of livestock and grain, Delamere was ready by 1917 to upgrade his stock, and, after a great deal of difficulty, managed to obtain a half-dozen fine Shorthorns. Huxley quotes a letter-writing neighbor who, in July 1917, describes their fate:

> I told you, I think, what difficulty there always is in getting bulls. The last effort was the most disastrous yet. Delamere got six bulls from Australia, and we had arranged that I should take over three of them on their arrival. After much trouble and expense they were safely landed about a month ago. Bearing in mind what happened to the last lot of six which I landed, all of which died within a year of their arrival, we thought we would send those to the government laboratory near Nairobi to be inoculated with various diseases. We were told there was not much risk, but we might perhaps lose one out of the lot.
>
> They have however killed the whole six and this within a month of their arrival, so that's settled that lot pretty effectively. They cost us about £70 each landed. I don't so much mind the actual loss in money, but what I do mind is being left without any bulls. That is where the real loss lies.

Delamere's livestock and crops managed to find nearly every stock and grain disease common to East Africa, and his effort at large-scale farming very nearly failed. He must have turned a profit eventually, though, because Soysambu became, and is still, an impressive place—great, green fields neatly divided by white fences, barns bigger than Macy's, and a large stone house set far from the mud track that I drove along behind the property. Lady Delamere—Hugh's daughter-in-law—is in residence, but not for the likes of me. Or anyone else, for that matter. "Lady D," as the locals call her, is the Queen Mum of Kenya, the leader of the pack of "vanilla gorillas," as middle-class blacks and short-term whites call lifelong white Africans,* and you can't just pop in for a cup of tea. Kenyan society starts in Soysambu. Besides, there's a certain problem with bandits, you see, and nobody takes any chances.

In Nairobi, the vast shantytown that ebbs and flows according to the schedule of the bulldozers sent to periodically raze odd parcels of temporary neighborhoods is but one symptom of Kenya's (and Africa's) biggest problem—a population boom. The strain has caused a near paralysis of public services, bloated the unemployment figures and given rise to a new spirit of criminal exuberance.

"They are truly audacious," a UN staffer in Nairobi told me. "I've heard of gangs of thieves walking right into houses while people were having dinner parties."

The police are stretched a bit thin. If you come home to find the place lousy with thugs, you can call the police, all right, but you have to pick the cops up at the station since most police cars are broken down. As a result, nearly all white residents hire guards to watch the house—a practice followed in many other parts of Africa. "Even then, you aren't so safe," said a local flying instructor, Denise Morchand-Holz. Morchand-Holz is a dark-haired American who came to Kenya twenty-three years ago as a tourist and now operates her own air-charter company, headquartered among the bougainvillea-clad hangars, shacks and offices at Nairobi's rambling, old Wilson Airport.† She is, perhaps, the only woman to operate an independent flying service anyplace in Africa—the Boys' Club of continents—and as such she is accorded a certain tomboyish respect by

* Simian references do not have universal appeal. Recently, a white Kenyan was sentenced to six weeks in the pokey for calling a black Kenyan a "baboon."

† Wilson Airport is the operations center for most small charter carriers—especially those contracted by touring companies to ferry tourists to game parks. Wilson Airways, whence the airport received its name, was one of the first commercial aviation ventures in East Africa, and one of the more successful. It has long since been absorbed by the endless parade of pre- and postindependence air carriers operating under the flag of one or more East African states.

other pilots—but not by the ubiquitous thieves of Nairobi. After recounting her own misadventures at the hands of a gang of thugs, she began cataloging the ills that had befallen other residents. For example, Beryl Markham, a pioneer aviatrix who died in 1986 at age eighty-three, was the victim of a gang masterminded by her own house guard. "They made her a prisoner," Morchand-Holz told me. After they beat her severely, they tied her to her bed with barbed wire. As it turned out, for Markham it was the last in a long line of exciting episodes, and one she barely survived.

Markham was one of the great adventurers, a *Boys' Own* heroine who seemed to relish every passing challenge, and whose life reflected the incestuous nature of Kenyan society, where everyone seems to know everyone else—one way or another. The daughter of a horse trainer named Charles Clutterbuck, Markham was born in England in 1902. At the age of four she was taken to Kenya, where she was raised in the bush—on a farm down the road from Delamere's Equator Ranch—and given only a rough education, mostly by her father. The first Lady Delamere became her surrogate mother, and Lord Delamere loomed large in her childhood as a man of "legendary" generosity but also possessed of a "wholly unjustified" temper. "Delamere looked and sometimes acted like Puck," Markham later wrote, "but those who had the temerity to scratch him found a nature more Draconian than whimsical underneath."

At sixteen she married a local farmer; divorce followed, and by the time she was eighteen, her father had gone bankrupt. When Clutterbuck left for Peru, she stayed behind and began training horses on her own. In 1927, when she was twenty-four years old, she married Mansfield "Monte" Markham, a rich member of local society, and quickly moved up the ladder until her 1928 triumph, a liaison with the visiting Duke of Gloucester ("Any fair lady was fair game to him," she told a documentary film crew, "and he certainly hunted me"). One important result of the liaison may have been the son she named Gervais Markham, who was born in '29 (Monte Markham threatened to name Gloucester as a party to his divorce suit; after the threat was dropped, however, Beryl Markham was given a small annuity by Buckingham Palace).

A prodigious smoker and drinker, the tall, thin and graceful Markham vied with Karen Blixen for Denys Finch Hatton's affection—and won. In fact, Markham was to have flown with Finch Hatton in his Gypsy Moth on his fateful flight to scout elephants near Voi, and was only dissuaded from going by Tom Black, her revered flying instructor. Finch Hatton's death affected her deeply at the time, and in her memoirs she notes that Finch

Hatton "has been written about before, and he will be written about again. If someone has not already said it, someone will say that he was a great man who never achieved greatness, and this will not only be trite, but wrong; he was a great man who never achieved arrogance. . . . He would have greeted doomsday with a wink—and I think he did."

By 1931 she was as thoroughly engaged in aviation as she had formerly been in horses, flying passengers and mail throughout East Africa in her two-seater Avro Avian, often finding work as a game scout with Bror Blixen, who had finally picked up a few practical skills and whom Markham clearly liked. To her, "Blix" or "Blickie" was "six feet of amiable Swede and, to my knowledge, the toughest, most durable White Hunter ever to snicker at the fanfare of safari or to shoot a charging buffalo between the eyes while debating whether his sundown drink will be gin or whisky." To Markham, Blixen's most obvious charm was in his smile— "caught, like a strip of sunlight, on a familiar patch of leather—well-kept leather, free of wrinkles, but brown and saddle-tough. Beyond this concession to the fictional idea of what a White Hunter ought to look like, Blix's face yields not a whit. He has gay, light blue eyes rather than somber, steel-grey ones; his cheeks are well-rounded rather than flat as an axe; his lips are full and generous and not pinched tight in grim realization of what the Wilderness Can Do. He talks. He is never significantly silent."* Against the advice of Black ("Sheer madness and damnably, bloodily dangerous," he thought), Markham spent several years flying for Blixen and visiting hunters, like Winston Guest, and for local airline operators.

In 1936 she made her celebrated flight from England to North America, and in 1939 she was at work at Paramount Studios in Hollywood, where she met Raoul Schumacher, whom she subsequently wed. Schumacher was a writer, and despite the persuasive claims of Mary S. Lovell, Markham's biographer, it is still widely assumed in Kenya that he was the ghostwriter of Markham's memoir, *West with the Night,* a finely crafted book unlikely to have been written by someone who never professed an eagerness or even an ability to write. (A prefatory author's note in the memoir expresses Markham's "gratitude to Raoul Schumacher for his constant encouragement and his assistance in the preparations for this book.") Certainly, if it's his, the book is his best work. If it's hers, it's her only work, aside from a few magazine stories also written during her marriage to Schumacher.

During an abortive coup in 1982, while still recovering from the beating

* Markham herself maintains a rather significant silence on the subject of Karen Blixen.

administered to her by her domestic thieves, Markham was wounded by a gunshot while running roadblocks to make her regular luncheon appearance at the Muthaiga Club, a dedication to social ritual still much admired by club members.

West with the Night, which appeared in 1942, was greeted with wide critical acclaim ("Bloody wonderful," said Ernest Hemingway): It was reissued in 1983, when Markham was quite destitute. A year after her death, in 1986, the book was on the *New York Times* paperback bestseller list. While the book omits some cumbersome details, it adequately describes the social circle that defined Kenyan society. Beryl Markham's life, compared with Karen Blixen's, was truly memorable. How come Streep and Redford didn't make a movie about *her?*

PART TWO

SALVATION ARMIES

4.

And I remember saying to one of the officials, "I wish I could see something old"
. . . And the official said, "Oh, but you're
going to." I said, "How delightful! What
are we going to see?" And he said, "You
are going to see a very ancient fort." And I
said, "Yes, and who built it?" And he said,
"Lord Lugard."

—*Violet Bourdillon, the wife of the new*
Governor of Uganda, 1932

RUMOR DIVIDED by lies plus witnesses equals history (even if all the equational expressions are out of whack). Remember? In school they used to tell you, History is fun! about an hour after they told you, Numbers are your friends! H&R Block disabused me of the latter notion, but history—well, it's not fun, exactly, but I like the ordered accretion of gossip, the catalogs of compromised truths.

Besides, history makes interesting conversation. In Europe, people argued for a long time about what happened in history until they changed the subject and the story went cold. It was settled: Romans, barbarians, monks, gravity, Germans, tourists. But in Africa, history's still subject to negotiation; all the cats are not yet out of all the bags. When your great-grandfather was born, the European population of Africa was seven or so; overnight, the Eurotribe invaded and colonies popped up on mystery maps. In the middle of nowhere, salvation armies marched to no place and accomplished nothing. Year after year, it's the old tired tune: Everyone writes a memoir—*Letters from Camp Africa*—then everyone goes home. The most precious product of imperialism was a harvest of good stories: On the table in front of me are stacks of two-reelers (*The Story of Emin's Rescue as Told in Stanley's Letters; In Darkest Africa; The Lunatic*

Express; White Man's Country; Fire and Sword in the Sudan), episodes grim and chilling, Saturday matinees for grownups.

The British, with their charming sense of the absurd, are best at these cautionary tales with their unchanging themes: If light is shed in darkness, peace and prosperity follow. And the plots are all the same, too: Boy meets challenge, boy loses challenge; an army, an expedition or a civil service is sent in to fix the mess. So the weight of the narrative always falls on character and setting. I don't know what happy circumstance led England to the gross overproduction of colorful characters. But fortunately, there was abundance of colorful imperial settings—like Africa—in which to place them.

Of course, there were mistakes. Even the settlement of Kenya, for instance, was an accident typical of Great Britain's African colonial history. Less than a century ago, Kenya was just a large, mostly inconvenient chunk of real estate that stood between Uganda and the sea. (That "sterile region," the Foreign Office called it.)

But England had an interest in the sea because she had an interest in India, and if some enterprising Frenchman or zealous Egyptian were to fill the Suez Canal—Britain's costly link with Bombay—with junk, communication with India would become dependent on well-policed sea-lanes in the western reaches of the Indian Ocean. England also had an interest— although a somewhat less urgent one—in Uganda, partly because the Germans, French and Belgians also were interested in Uganda, partly because the area surrounding Lake Victoria had become a major theater in the war against slavery and an outpost of British missionary and commercial activity, but mostly because Uganda was at the headwaters of the Nile, the fortune of Egypt—which brings us back to the Suez and to India. So Kenya, as it was not then known, was happily surrounded by the four pillars of British imperial wisdom: open routes to India, which required the British to stabilize coastal areas and other strategic regions; the suppression of the slave trade, an imperative of religion and the Victorian sensibility; mercantile adventurism, which was, on the one hand, the instrument of British foreign policy to help further the first two causes, and on the other, the basis on which it was thought the benefits of civilization might be made known to the "Great Unclad" (to use a popular contemporary term); and alarm at the inroads made by other European powers, since such expansion threatened stability, Victorian values and potential commercial growth.*

---

* The impulse behind British imperialism is given a comprehensive analysis in *Africa and the Victorians* (1961), by Ronald Robinson, John Gallagher and Alice Denny.

My favorite source for much of this section is the first volume of Margery Perham's outstanding biography, *Lugard: The Years of Adventure, 1858-1898* (1956).

*   *   *

For millennia, the only part of East Africa that mattered was the part you could see from a boat offshore; the busy coastal strip extending north and south from Lamu and Mombasa had been frequented for thousands of years by traders from India, the Levant and the Persian Gulf, whose business consisted mostly of carting away dhowloads of ivory, spices, minerals, boys and girls, in exchange for grain, tools and fabric.

But by the eighth century, some of the traders had become settlers— colonists, if you like. Sunni Muslims from Persia and Arabia tossed out whatever tribes were living in the area at the time and established a flourishing network of what historian Basil Davidson calls "city-empires." Sweet places still, Lamu, Mombasa, Malindi, if you look past the beached and floundering Danes, Brits and Dutch. Not African, really, more Afro-Arabic, a good combination. Out of the hotel, down to the sea, and you can stand there with your back to the uncertainties of Africa and squint across the water into the rising sun of the Orient, with all the oil of Araby and all the tea in China, while around you are the remains of the carved coral, carpet-and-alabaster wealth of ancient Zinj, as they called these coastal settlements. In Mombasa stands giant Fort Jesus, built by the Portuguese at the end of the sixteenth century, a hundred years after they had come looking for India (if Renaissance sailors hadn't always got lost looking for India, we'd have a mighty tidy map today). The Portuguese wrecked the place, but the signs of Zinj are everywhere: in broken buildings, in medina streets and on the lips of the locals; Kiswahili the ancient confusion of Arabic and tribal tongues is still the koine of East Africa.

Then began one of those slo-mo juggling acts that pass as regional history: The Zinjians didn't like the Portuguese because the Portuguese were ruthless, just as you'd expect, and when a Turkish freebooter named Ali Bey showed up in Mombasa in the late 1580s and promised to liberate the place, the populace rose up and tossed out the Europeans. In 1589, however, the Portuguese came back; at the time, they were busy trying to subdue India and hence were possessed of the predictable anxiety about securing the route to their colony. They sent a fleet from Bombay to blockade Mombasa harbor and a siege developed. After a while, a large contingent of Zimba warriors showed up and volunteered to help the Mombasans fight the white devils. When the city gates were opened to them, the Zimba, a tribe of vicious but wily cannibals, promptly ate most of the residents, and then left. So the Portuguese took back Mombasa,*

---

*What goes around, comes around, as we used to say in the '60s. A couple of years ago, a Portuguese air crew, stranded on the northern frontier of Zaïre, was eaten by local residents.

and, to show they would stay, built Fort Jesus. Some forty-odd years later, another revolt, this one led by a newly anointed local sultan most wonderfully named Don Geronimo, succeeded to the extent that all the Portuguese in Mombasa were killed. But two things about the Portuguese: They're very stubborn, and apparently there are a lot of them. So a few years later, the Portuguese returned, fought a battle or two and set up shop in Fort Jesus again.

Farther north, the Arabs in the Persian Gulf territory of Oman, another Portuguese possession, were also causing trouble, and by the mid-seventeenth century, they had seized Muscat and forever driven out the Portuguese. The people of Zinj asked the sultan of Muscat to help them do the same, and by 1730 the Portuguese were pushed south into Mozambique, where they stayed for almost two and a half centuries. The Omanis occupied Mombasa, where they established a foothold, and swiftly moved to annex Zanzibar and most of the coast to their own empire. For well over a century, the locals chafed under their latest conqueror and reminisced, no doubt, about the good old days when the colony was theirs, while the new Omani sultanate of Zanzibar grew in strength and influence until eventually the famous sultan, stammeringly named Seyyid Said, who ruled for much of the first half of the nineteenth century, decided in 1832 to make his home there.* Other than the neighborhood characters, nobody cared; even the Portuguese lost interest as soon as their Indian hegemony passed to the British. Zanzibar grew rich trading in slaves and ivory.

Meanwhile, back in Europe, another continental civil war was brewing. Napoleon, eager to probe English weaknesses in India, had invaded Egypt in 1798, defeating the Mameluke vassals of the Turkish sultan, and in 1799, he had written to the Omanis to inform them that France was going to occupy Egypt (along with Mysore, India) and that the sultan of Muscat was about to receive the blessings of French protection. Unfortunately for Napoleon, the British intercepted and read the letter first, and, ever fearful of threats to India, induced the sultan to sign a rancorously Francophobic treaty, the first step in what historian Charles Miller describes as "a long political chain reaction, which, in the end, virtually forced East Africa

---

* At a crucial period in her history, Zanzibar was lucky to have been governed by a series of relatively stable sultanates. Seyyid Said came to power in Oman in 1806, spent much time in Zanzibar, and ruled until 1856. His son, Majid, was a loafer but nonetheless managed to hold things together in Zanzibar despite the vain attempts by his brother, Seyyid Bargash, to usurp power. Bargash, for his trouble, was housed comfortably in India until Majid's death in 1870. As sultan, Bargash proved to be a faithful ally of the British. He died in 1888.

down England's throat," since it compelled England's attention to a part of the continent that wasn't Egypt.

For England to have neglected the sultan of Zanzibar's coastal possessions—which, after all, stretched along the coast from Somaliland to Mozambique and inland along the slave and trade routes—for so long was quite unusual. The British method of imperial expansion, until now almost completely directed toward India, had always been to establish safe and unfettered means of communication to any new, far-flung outpost before making claims to any intermediate territories. Once the sultan's provinces were finally seen by the British as important to the security of India, London determined that Zanzibar and vicinity must remain in the hands of a friendly government and that the political stability of those possessions must be ensured to prevent their falling under French or German domination. As we've seen, so sensitive was the affection Great Britain felt toward India's tranquility that by the end of the century, English armies would be tramping up and down the Nile, worrying about the intentions of tribal leaders on the shores of Lake Victoria, in case somebody should steal all the water in northeastern Africa, drive Egypt into chaos and thereby threaten the trade between Liverpool and Lahore. Amazingly, those fears were quite well founded.

In many respects, England was ill advised to pursue any imperial ambitions whatsoever—a fact often driven home in parliamentary debates, where the acquisition, however incidental, of foreign protectorates, colonies and the rest was bitterly condemned. Until very late in the game, an empire was something the English really couldn't afford, definitely didn't want and ultimately would lack the will to keep. How much happier that island would have been had the citizens resolved to simply make themselves a more interesting version of Iceland. So why were so many Britons so eager to risk their lives in unknown, unpronounceable corners of the uncharted world?

We know that if life were logical, all hypotheses would be much less interesting than all proofs (Blackpool, 1986—A Labour Party poster: "FREE NAMIBIA! FREE SOUTH AFRICA! SANCTIONS NOW!"). But it's a crazy world, and these days, the more ponderously enlightened elements of the British left annoy reasonable people because of their noisy and aggressively proprietary approach to moral indignation. A hundred years ago, the British monopoly of ethics was much easier to justify because it was different in two important respects: First, it was predicated on the notion that right and wrong were objective values, not subject to whimsical alteration; and, second, it was spread across the political and social spectrum. It simply wasn't possible to send a virtuous nineteenth-century English lad to a part of the planet like Zanzibar without finding that he had immediately become involved in trying to "civilise" the damn place.

Not that there wasn't a market in Zanzibar for civilization. The island was a foul-smelling, unhealthy pit. Dead bodies floated in the harbor, and live ones were sold by the thousands in the marketplace. Zanzibar—like the rest of Africa—was utterly without Protestant charm, a void that God invented British outrage to fill.

Britons had seen the benefits that industrial innovation and hard work had wrought at home. Believe it or not, England in the eighteenth century was a money-making proposition, and by the nineteenth century some of that wealth was being used to educate children, combat disease, democratize justice and defend the realm—all within the theoretical context of fair play and rectitude. Especially rectitude: Every schoolboy knew that God spoke only English because He spoke only to them ("Wogs start here," a British peer once told me on arriving at Calais from Dover), often in the measured tones of Jeremy Bentham.

It was not difficult for Victorians to perceive that there was a proper, British way to do things, which if diligently pursued would inevitably ensure the greatest good for the greatest number of people. This was the imperial message, and there were many ways of carrying it to the world: It was tailor-made for folding carefully inside the Bible of a Church Missionary Society evangelist; you could fly it high from the jack staff of a gunboat, lock it safely in a diplomat's dispatch box, or wedge it tightly next to a bedroll on a Tommy's back.

But the ideal vehicle for deliverance was prosperity. Most Victorians believed firmly that economic growth brought in its wake moral improvement and intellectual vigor. The best weapon against the forces of darkness and evil, as Prime Minister Henry J. T. Palmerston suggested to Parliament, was Commerce "leading civilization with one hand, and peace with the other, to render mankind happier, wiser, better." And who better qualified to escort Commerce and her cronies than the British? At least at the outset, they were willing to do the job at considerable cost to themselves; whatever profit would come as a result was considered secondary, but certainly well deserved. As more than one British colonial administrator noted, it didn't pay to scrutinize the balance sheet too closely. Any pretensions to profit from African involvement existed as a consequence of the civilizing mission the British saw for themselves. Whereas bringing Western notions of civilization to the benighted was the rhetorical, often self-serving rallying cry of even the most cynical European colonial powers, the British actually meant it.

In East Africa they had their work cut out for them. The period of initial involvement by the Europeans coincided with a fairly lengthy period in African history that featured widespread violence, social chaos and the ancient dragon of slavery.* Local wars and mass executions coexisted with bloody migrations of nomadic tribesmen; early missionaries and explorers described fields full of sun-bleached skeletons and foul ponds of mud and blood; famine and flood did their fast two-step across the continent, while vast territories were depopulated by disease. Through this fantastic landscape coursed the Arab slavers, briskly trading hardware for human livestock and ivory. Perhaps, as some historians suggest, it is wrong to subject all this to European analysis and pronounce it bad.† In any case, it was about to change.

By the time the English finally arrived in East Africa, the population was overwhelmingly an immigrant one. According to Davidson, the migration of "small but strong groups"—branches of tribes desiring increased territorial possession—that had for centuries wandered Africa worked into a familiar pattern: Once they found a new homeland, "they conquered or otherwise settled down with its indigenous people, acquiring governing power through their superior techniques and organization, and thereby conserved their own traditions at the expense of the traditions of the people among whom they had settled." Sometimes these conquering invaders would assimilate as thoroughly as possible (as did a few Hamitic tribes and the Arabs and, to a considerably lesser extent, the French, Portuguese and Spanish). Others, like the fratricidal Kikuyu and the Masai, a particularly vicious Nilotic tribe, both of whom arrived in eastern Africa sometime well after the Portuguese did, simply took whatever land they could win, and kept it by force.

Each of the European powers brought a unique brand of colonial administration and policy to Africa. The French, until the end of World War II, relied shamelessly on one form of forced labor or another, even though only the African colonies sided with Charles de Gaulle's Free French during the war. The Portuguese were worse; for three centuries,

---

* According to Basil Davidson, who wrote *Africa in History* (1968), however, slavery was a relatively new phenomenon, although that observation is certainly open to question; strictly speaking, the largest part of sub-Saharan Africa has anthropology, not history. But really, it doesn't matter; the social patterns that obtained at the beginning of the nineteenth century were unpleasant ones in almost anyone's book.

† On the other hand, if Davidson is right, maybe in an African context it was worse.

they traded labor with the South Africans as if it were a commodity (a policy still pursued by most of the states bordering South Africa—including Mozambique, and, to a lesser extent, Angola, two former Portuguese colonies). The Belgians ran the Congo like a primary school; while the native population had excellent medical care and social services and the literacy rate was the highest in Africa, the Belgians never bothered training a native civil service, and when independence was declared (with just six months' notice) in 1960, there wasn't a native officer in the colony's security force. The British were different; all of their policies had one goal: They sought to control events in the region by influence rather than by fiat.

For example, through their brilliant consul general in Zanzibar, John Kirk,* the British cajoled, wheedled, threatened and whined to get their way. They wanted slavery abolished, and, much to the consternation of slaving coastal tribes such as the Mazrui, the Arabs and, of course, Seyyid Bargash, by now sultan of Zanzibar, eventually it was. They wanted French, German and other foreign involvement in East Africa curtailed, and, though through blind good luck, it ultimately was. They wanted the area made safe for commerce, and for whatever good it did (trade possibilities were extremely limited), it was. And, most of all, they wanted Uganda and the equatorial lakes secure for the sake of Egypt and India. That wasn't so easy.

The region that now constitutes Uganda was at the time a battlefield between several important tribal kingdoms. If there was a "classical" civilization of some note in central Africa during the eighteenth and early nineteenth centuries, the kingdom of Buganda, along the northern edge of Lake Victoria, was it.† Relatively speaking, it was an island of order in a

---

* Sir John Kirk, a naturalist, was appointed vice-consul in Zanzibar in 1866 and consul general in 1873 after serving as David Livingstone's medical officer on the missionary's Zambezi expedition of 1858–60 and the Lake Nyasa exploration of 1861. At Zanzibar, Kirk's skill as a botanist was rivaled only by his extraordinary talent as a diplomat. He was Seyyid Bargash bin Said's friend and confidant, a role that frequently caused him discomfort in executing the government's often contradictory policies. He left Zanzibar in 1886; less than two years later, Bargash, who had acceded to the sultanate in 1870, was dead at the age of fifty-one. By 1890, Zanzibar was a British protectorate and Kirk was a director of the Imperial British East Africa Company.

† A number of sub-Saharan African kingdoms and empires are thought to have existed as long ago as A.D. 500, a date later Arab scholars gave as the founding of the Ghanaian kingdom. The Muslim kingdom of Mali dates back to the fourteenth century, and a number of political entities, such as the Hausa States and Benin, flourished during the fifteenth century. It would, of course, be inappropriate to assess these societies in a European context. Essentially, they were tribal groupings.

sea of anarchy. Society was organized in a reasonably efficient manner, with the kabaka, or king, at the top; beneath him was a prime minister who sat in a parliament composed of tribal chiefs, courtiers and other nobles. The parliament, called the Lukiko, exercised genuine power (among other things, it nominated the kabaka), providing a check on the king's prerogatives. The provincial areas were under the control of civil servants, and below them, nearly a million workers and slaves, who were bound in allegiance to their local chief. Among the upper classes, at least, literacy was prized and civility was highly regarded; music and the arts were patronized; the army and navy were almost models of modernity. Equally advanced were the techniques of torture and execution, for the Buganda practiced lavish mass executions—thousands were killed at a time—as part of conventional social rituals (at the anointing of a new kabaka, for instance), and even slight misdemeanors were punishable by mutilation. The Buganda were, of course, usurpers; they migrated from the Abyssinian highlands in the mid-1500s (Rwanda and Burundi are other migratory Hamitic sites).*

The Bunyoro, to the northwest, were yet another Hamitic tribe, more aggressive but less successful than the Bugandans, who were their arch rivals. There were constant slave wars between the two kingdoms, and equally frequent incursions into the neighboring kingdoms of their cousins, the Tojos and the Nkoles.

The paramount chiefs, wholesale murderers all, fought with one another, then formed alliances and instantly broke them. Meanwhile, Arab traders played one tribe against the other in an effort to make the area as unstable as possible, thereby securing a free hand for themselves.

For hundreds of years, the Buganda had asserted their superiority over their neighbors, and the conflicts between them had assumed a predictable, if malignant, routine. But by the middle of the nineteenth century, the erosion of traditional, moderating tribal customs by Arab influences, combined with a consolidation of power by the kabaka, had created a

* Margery Perham sorts out the name game: Ganda is the Bantu root; Baganda refers to the tribe; the language is Luganda; an individual Baganda is a Muganda; and Uganda is a Swahili corruption of the name of the kingdom, Buganda.

In addition to Perham, Lord Lugard's *The Rise of Our East African Empire* (two volumes; 1893) gives an accurate and detailed view.

For an overview, see Charles Miller's *The Lunatic Express* (1971)—undoubtedly some publisher's idea of a good title for a book that provides a useful popular history of East Africa while detailing the construction of the Uganda Railway.

For more specific analyses, *The Uganda Journal* is an irresistible source of scholarship on the history of the region.

dissolute and bloodthirsty monarchy. John Hanning Speke and James Grant had briefly visited the kingdom in 1863, without effect. But in 1875, Henry Stanley, that most indelicate explorer, passed through and told Mutesa, the modestly depraved but extremely cunning kabaka, about "Europe and heaven," and promised to send him missionaries, which he summoned by sending off a letter to the *Daily Telegraph*. The letter appeared in November 1875, and by July 1877, Anglican missionaries were at work. In November 1878, Alexander Mackay, a Church Missionary Society devotee of Stanley's, had arrived to organize the Ugandan mission; and before the next year was out, the French Catholic order of White Fathers was working the same territory. By this time, Mutesa was becoming as anxious about the invasion of his territory by white intruders as he was about the constant threat of his longtime foes, the Bunyoro, who were led by the fearless Kaberenga* and armed by the ubiquitous Arabs.

The arrival of the Christian missionaries provided Mutesa with an opportunity to set each faction against the other, while he enjoyed the fruits of Christian commerce—notably, better firearms than those he had been obtaining from the Arabs. Predictably, the Protestants and the Catholics were soon conspiring with Irish zeal to make martyrs of each other, urging their rapidly growing ranks of followers to join militias and fight for Jesus.

In October 1884, Mutesa died and was succeeded by a seventeen-year-old maniac named Mwanga, who had a great deal in common with a couple of subsequent Ugandan leaders. The pernicious Arabs pointed out to Mwanga that Christianity as practiced by the white evangelists fell somewhat short of its promises and that the Europeans had designs on his country. Mwanga believed them, and after a slow start, he began devising keenly imaginative ways of terrorizing the missionaries and murdering their followers, a persecution that boosted the numbers of Christians faster than Mwanga could kill them off.† Finally, in October 1885, he sent an

---

* Kaberenga fought fiercely against Sir Samuel Baker when Baker, as governor of Equatoria, tried to establish provincial installations in Bunyoro territory. Sometimes in league with the kabaka of Buganda, sometimes against him, Kaberenga was, as Alan Moorehead notes, the prototypical African-nationalist guerrilla leader. He was finally imprisoned on the Seychelles in the company of Mwanga, an ousted kabaka (see subsequent footnote), and died at age eighty on his return to Uganda.

† According to Perham, Mwanga enjoyed an equal addiction to marijuana and sodomy. In May 1886, he became concerned that some of the young boys at court were objecting to his sexual appetites. So he lined them up and asked the Christians among them to step forward. Thirty did so. Mwanga then gave them the choice of submission or slow roasting. All thirty chose the fire and died.

assassin to the border of Masailand to murderously greet the newly appointed Anglican bishop, James Hannington.

Encouraged by the failure of Salisbury's government to react to the killing of Hannington, Mwanga unleashed all the rage his insanity could muster. At last the kabaka's excesses had grown intolerable even to his own chiefs, and in late 1888, he was sent into exile on the south shore of Lake Victoria, at which time the Arabs mounted an attack on the Christians, and drove them out, too. A few months later Mwanga was back again, and a month after that, he was on the run once more. The Arabs were busily manipulating the monarchy, installing and replacing kabakas on an almost mensual basis.* The Catholics were vociferous in their dislike of the English, and were praying for intervention from any quarter, so long as it wasn't from England. The Protestants were angling for British protection, and getting nowhere.† A missionary-turned-gunrunner named Charles Stokes was selling everyone weapons with alarming results, and when the Christians finally retook the capital, the streets were filled with corpses.

The Foreign Office, wanting to avoid direct involvement in Uganda, turned to Sir William Mackinnon's philanthropic, deeply debt-ridden but grandly named Imperial British East Africa Company (IBEA), which had laid claim to not only the souls but also the commerce of the sultan of Zanzibar's possessions, to implement British policy while keeping its own hands clean.

Chartered companies like the IBEA, by no means new weapons in the imperial arsenal, were granted government-approved monopolies over whole nations. In fact, most of the empire had been built by simply annexing territory in the wake of these quasi-official enterprises. The British East India Company, of course, was the model; often called "John Company," the firm had run India for two centuries before colonial rule was initiated. (The Great Mutiny in India in 1857 might be seen to have been as much a revolt against big business as against the British government.) Like the British East India Company, other chartered companies— the Hudson's Bay Company, the British South Africa Company, the Royal Niger Company and the rest— operated a complete range of governmental

---

* The Arab activity in Uganda coincided with a widespread uprising by the slavers against Europeans in East Africa. The German sphere was especially troubled.

† The situation of the missionaries was very grave. The British government of Lord Salisbury—who at the time was also Foreign Secretary—resolutely refused to send them aid. Other European powers seized on this neglect to show that Britain had relinquished its claims to the territory.

services, including post, treasury and, of course, an army. Normally the flag followed trade; in East Africa, however, there was almost no trade to follow. It confused the situation enormously.

Salisbury finally had assumed a new and more concentrated interest in Uganda. Cooked Christians were one thing, but the government had come up with an even more forceful reason to restore order in the region: The Germans were on their way to Lake Victoria. Led by a bookish-looking, sado-egotist named Karl Peters, the column, representing the Society for German Colonization, was burning and shooting its way into the interior, coercing local chieftains to sign unintelligible treaties along the way.*

Peters, in a way, represented the most efficient model of all African explorer-exploiters. He was driven, ambitious and possessed of some intellectual software—he had been awarded his doctorate for his paper, "To What Extent Is Metaphysics Possible as a Science?," while still in his early twenties. In photos, Peters looks like the sort of grad student who gets a job in a bookstore—he's a tiny, thin man, with a pince-nez at the end of a long nose. In one photograph, Peters is shown seated at a table, wearing a white uniform jacket with golden epaulets as wide as his teeny head. He's shuffling through a big bundle of paperwork, and looks for all the world like a history major with a Napoleonic complex doing his homework.

Apparently deciding that metaphysics wasn't a growth field, Peters, like other, less malignant personalities, became attracted to the reckless potential Africa could offer a small man with a big gun. In 1884 he established the Society for German Colonization as part of his plan to grab as much of the sultan of Zanzibar's mainland empire as possible, then coerce the German crown into annexing it into a German-African empire. Unfortunately for Peters, the Germans had little interest in an East African land-grab, and when he—along with two confederates, all carrying fake

---

* Treaties, a balm to what Frederick Lugard called "the sensitive official conscience," were a passion among early European representatives. "Treaties were produced by the cartload," Lugard wrote in *The Dual Mandate in British Tropical Africa* (1922), "in all the approved forms of legal verbiage—impossible of translation by ill-educated interpreters. It mattered not that tribal chiefs had no power to dispose of communal rights. . . . The treaties were duly attested by a cross, purporting to convey the assent of the African chief, and this was sufficient. In some cases, it is said, the assent had been obtained by the gift of a pair of boots, or a few bottles of gin—the Kaiser had sent a parcel of opera-hats working with a spring. . . . Ignorance of African conditions, and perhaps a latent feeling that the end justified the means, induced the rulers of the nations of Europe to accept these treaties without too close a scrutiny, and to persuade themselves that the omelette had been made without breaking any eggs. . . . In some cases the native ruler was himself an alien conqueror, holding in subjection tribes with which he had no affinity; in others he was a despot . . . exercising a bloody tyranny; in others again, pagan tribes carried on an internecine warfare, and were powerless to defend themselves against organised slave-raiders."

names and wearing hokey disguises—finally arrived in Zanzibar in November 1884, the German consul delivered his government's warning that Peters could set up all the colonies he wanted, but it would all be on his neck: The German government would offer him neither "imperial protection nor any guarantee for his own life and safety." Peters figured that it would probably be easier to persuade the Chancellor to become an East African colonizer if the colonies were already in place. So ten days after his arrival in Zanzibar, Peters and his associates boated over to the mainland and disappeared.

By February 1885, Peters was back in Berlin with treaties of "eternal friendship" bearing a dozen or so nervous and sloppy X's from uncomprehending chiefs who had been bullied into serving up to the Society for German Colonization some 2,500 square miles of what is now Tanzania. The German press and public were delighted; Bismarck was happy to see him, but not so eager to ratify his treaties as Peters would have liked.

Bismarck, of course, had a plan. He was wrapping up the final stages of the Berlin Conference, which his government had convened to help establish binding agreements for the incipient African sweepstakes, in which the European powers gave a priori recognition of one another's claims on the continent—provided only that when territories were annexed, they be efficiently administered (the official term was "effective occupation").* Bismarck withheld making public his claims until the conference adjourned on March 2, then rushed the treaties off to the Kaiser, who placed all the affected territory under German imperial protection. At the end of April, the Germans notified Sultan Bargash that the Zanzibar territories were no longer his to govern, and at once Consul General John Kirk cabled the Foreign Office that if Bargash wasn't given protection for his mainland territories, a powerful German sphere of influence in East Africa was inevitable. When the sultan sought to reestablish his authority in the disputed area in June 1885, two German cruisers showed up and anchored off the East African coast, near Lamu; in August, five more German warships steamed into the harbor at Zanzibar. While a frustrated Kirk waited in vain for helpful instructions from London,† Bargash gave in and recognized all of Germany's claims.

* The Berlin Conference, convened by Germany in November 1884, sought to formalize various European claims to African territories by granting recognition of "spheres of influence" to those claimants who demonstrated their ability to occupy and develop coastal areas and their "hinterlands." The rules of colonization were thus quite conveniently vague, but the conference did serve to institutionalize the "great scramble."

† England was reluctant to anger Bismarck, since, at the time, its interests were being threatened by Russia in Afghanistan and in Asia Minor, and by French opposition to the British seizure of the Suez Canal and the occupation of Egypt.

In the wake of England's submission in East Africa, the balance of power in that part of the world shifted radically. In short order, Kirk was recalled, appeasement became the de facto policy of the Foreign Office, and Germany expanded its initial territorial claim to embrace all of present-day Tanzania.

England was left with the northern portion of Bargash's empire—the area that now comprises Kenya. The problem, of course, was that since England was in possession of the territory, it now had to demonstrate "effective occupation." To do this, England leaned more and more on the IBEA.

The events that had occurred since his arrival in Zanzibar in November 1884 gave Peters heart, and he headed inland to claim troubled Uganda for Germany. Like Stanley, Peters was almost completely unconcerned with either the inhabitants or the landscape of the strange continent through which he was traveling. His sole interest was his own reputation, and the sensitivities of a tribal chieftain or a vacillating missionary were meaningless to him. As a result, his progress through eastern Africa had been fast and efficient. Not to put too fine a point on it, but Peters was a thug, even worse than Stanley. An embarrassment to the German government of the time, he was eventually canonized by the Nazis.

Meanwhile, the IBEA's task in sorting out Uganda had become nearly impossible. Salisbury had followed the Gladstonian non-policies of vacillation and procrastination; as a result, a concerted antislavery program was delayed by a decade, costing perhaps a million Africans their lives. At the same time, the whole of East Africa, once England's for the taking,* had been left in a state of diplomatic limbo. The Germans, playing on London's fear of European collusion, had simply stepped in and within twelve months assembled an entire African empire. Nevertheless, a small IBEA force led by Frederick Jackson was dispatched from Mombasa in August 1890—several months behind Peters—to forestall German annexation.

The race to Uganda was a beauty, with Peters employing some very slick en route maneuvers—including a surprise visit to Jackson's camp while the Englishman was away and reading his mail (including a crucially revealing message from Mwanga begging for the IBEA's protection)

---

* Bargash had encouraged Great Britain to open up and occupy all his mainland possessions as early as 1876, well in advance of any basis for European protest or competition. Salisbury, who became Foreign Minister as negotiations were in progress, killed the idea.

and intelligence reports—even circulating news of his own death to generate more confusion. Needless to say, Jackson arrived in Uganda too late; Peters had already made an agreement with Mwanga and was headed back to the coast.

But as he victoriously emerged from the bush, Peters was met by a courier bearing some awkward news. The Germans and the English had just concluded a treaty giving Germany the small island of Helgoland—site of a coaling station and nothing else—in return for recognition of a British sphere of influence* in Zanzibar and the territories inland to Uganda. Peters was miffed, as you can imagine. He begged his companions to "say nothing more on the whole subject" but later complained about trading two African kingdoms "for a bathtub in the North Sea." The Kaiser, as it turned out, had developed a new affection for boating and decided Germany's future was naval, not native.

Now all that was left was for the British to consolidate their new possessions, and once again they turned to the IBEA, by now nearly bankrupt. Dutifully, in August 1890, the company sent out another column, led this time by Frederick Lugard, to Lake Victoria.

Lugard, a child of the middle class, looked more like a jockey than a general, with a mustache clearly designed to be worn by a man with a much bigger head. Nevertheless, the thirty-two-year-old had been awarded the Distinguished Service Order in Burma, and was a veteran of campaigns on the Afghan border and in Suakin. He was suffering at the time from a cardiac ailment—a girl-betrayal after an unexpected return to London. Lugard had subsequently sought comfort in the warming environment of the London Fire Brigade, a career move that surprised his family. "Fred turned up last evening looking better than when he first came home, but I thought rather wild!" his well-connected uncle, Sir Edward Lugard, wrote to Lugard's younger brother. "At last it came out that he had joined the Fire Brigade and went out every night (when they

---

* Germany and Great Britain had already signed an agreement in 1886 that recognized the sultan's possessions over the coastal islands—including Pemba and Zanzibar—and a ten-mile-wide strip along the coast. The agreement was a major concession to German ambitions in Africa and served to confirm the German protectorate of East Africa (now Tanzania), which had been declared in April 1885.

England seized the one-and-a-half-square-mile rocky island of Helgoland (or Heligoland) after World War II and, in 1947, after evacuating the 2,500 residents, blew it to smithereens in order to destroy German fortifications, along with a substantial stock of ammunition and heavy shells. According to a report in the *New York Times*, the blast registered as far south as Sicily. After using the place as a target for RAF bombing exercises, it was returned to Germany in 1952. In 1986, a half-million tourists visited the island.

were called out) to fires etc. on the engine!!" By December 1887, he'd cooled on that vocation and decided to "put an end to his life" by taking up the white man's burden and fighting against slavery in Africa. With £48 in his pocket, he shipped out, sleeping on the deck of an Italian packet boat and dreaming of suicide. Arriving in Abyssinia, he volunteered to help the invading Italians and was turned down cold ("My *heart* was never in that venture," he wrote later). So he drifted farther south, becoming more and more desperate for work and more and more broke. "If only I had some money," he wrote in his journal. "One can be such a hero with money in one's pocket."

Finally, arriving in Mozambique, he fell in with the British consul, Henry O'Neill, a former naval officer who had been posted to the coast to keep tabs on slaver activity in the Portuguese colony. O'Neill was one of Britain's angry soldier-diplomats, full of wrath at the Arabs and their collaborators, and in Lugard he thought he had found just the man to help execute one of his favorite projects.

So, in April 1888, Lugard was riding a canoe up a river in Nyasa-land, looking for an outpost of the African Lakes Company—another exploration-and-evangelism enterprise—where, commanding a makeshift company "army" of twenty-five game hunters, missionaries and doctors, he would spend much of 1888 and part of the following year trying unsuccessfully to dislodge a slave-raiding chieftain from a hideout near Lake Nyasa. When that effort, along with the company itself, went nowhere, he accepted a position with the IBEA in December 1889, where he found his ill-prepared commission to Uganda.

Even at a quickstep, the trek to Uganda took months, and on his arrival in December 1890, Lugard found himself in big trouble. Unbelievably, the situation had deteriorated even further, to the extent that he faced not only internal religious strife of a Lebanese magnitude but also the threat of invasion by an Arab army that had allied itself with one of the tribal chieftains. After bluffing the combatants into a stalemate of sorts, it became clear to Lugard that the eruption of a full-scale civil war in Uganda would result not only in the loss of the territory to British interests, but also in a horrible letting of blood, including his own. Lugard was sufficiently over his girlfriend's infidelity to consider carefully his position: He urgently requested reinforcements from the coast. Unfortunately the company was penniless, although quite ready to offer instructions: "Endeavour to be perfectly impartial . . . point out . . . the scandal which their differences present to the cause of Christianity . . . [and convey] a sense of the power of the Company." He would have to work it out himself.

The local true believers made his job as difficult as possible. To the

French Catholics and their supporters—called the Wa-Fransa—and the Anglicans and their adherents—the Wa-Inglcza—Lugard was just the enemy they needed. Each side complained of his partiality to the other, and both sides threatened violence against him, as well as against each other. Lugard had arrived with only 270 porters, about one-third of whom he guessed might make passable soldiers; he also had a beat-up Maxim gun and almost no ammunition.

Installing himself in a fort on Kampala hill, in the middle of what he called "this hornet's nest," Lugard worked hard to negotiate a peace and drill his porters into something vaguely military, and spent his leisure time writing reports to the Company: "The value of Uganda to the Company . . . per se, has been much overrated." He was unable, however, to gain the support of the kabaka, who had gone over to the French side, while the Ingleza proved to be worthless allies. The French missionaries conspired bitterly against Lugard, and, like their competitors, sent nasty letters about Lugard back to Europe. Finally the Arabs in the north grew restive, and Lugard used the Christians' common enemy as a means to create a little temporary domestic peace.

Leaving a small garrison at Kampala, Lugard set out through Bunyoro, fought some Muslims, then turned west, wondering as he went if anybody would be home when he returned to Buganda. Lugard desperately needed men but, stranded in the interior, he couldn't figure out where to get them. Fortunately, there happened to be an off-duty army loitering in nearby precincts.

You think of Victorian regiments, and you think of men in band suits with mustaches and good posture. But the Sudanese askaris that Lugard finally enlisted from the southwestern shores of Lake Albert looked like extras from a *Mad Max* movie. They wore animal skins and rags for uniforms, swore fealty to a government that had collapsed and disowned them, and plundered native villages for a living because they hadn't been paid in ten years.

If, when Lugard found them, they were buried in darkest Africa, not long before they'd been in the limelight, for they had served under two of the most eccentric European administrators in African history.*

* After suffering through a sequence of equatorial headaches, the subject of a later portion of this part of this book, Lugard went on to Nigeria to complete his career as an African empire builder. His notion of the "dual-mandate"—in which the colonial power ruled through native officials and institutions—became the accepted method of British rule until the very end. Perhaps no other colonial administrator outside India had so great an impact on the formulation of imperial policy. For more, see Margery Perham's biography.

5.

NORTH OF KHARTOUM and near El Metemma, I turned to the west, bent
over like a wayward Mussulman, and almost buried my face in the sand
looking for any sign of the British army, a souvenir of a late arrival.

What a no place. Life inside a light bulb, the hot vacuum of the
Bayuda—a dry patch in a big desert. There's nothing there but the story. It
could be four o'clock on the moon; all the scenery is in the shadows. And
so is all the history: It's hard to believe that a hundred years ago—on
January 19, 1885—an inexperienced officer of a British relief force
entrusted with a crucial rescue mission and operating against the clock
took one look and said, Looks good to me, let's stay for a while.

But El Metemma is a river town, and after a bloody march through the
desert, it might have looked better to the Englishman than it did to me.
The Nile's the rich neighbor here, donating a few hundred yards of shrubs
among which the citizens have built some dull, square buildings, and you
can stand right next to the water and wonder about the mystery of its
source and the great currents of history. Or you can wonder about how to
get back to Khartoum, where there's a hot shower and a cool drink.

After too much Sudan, Khartoum comes as a bit of a surprise, like one
of those giant, fiberglass dinosaurs that once advertised Arizona reptile
farms on old Route 66. For much of the day, Khartoum bakes. There are
some apologetic trees around town, but most of Khartoum is covered with
gravel, immense stretches of big dust that separate government buildings.
Little garden circles of stone are everywhere; there's gravel outside the

54

circle, and more gravel inside the circle. The biggest garden in Khartoum is behind the presidential palace—you can see slices of it through the security gate, like a Beverly Hills backyard, but you can't go there; visitors are politely turned away. In front of the palace is Khartoum's most prepossessing boulevard, the Shari al Niel—Nile Street—lined with the giant trees* planted by General Herbert Kitchener when he redesigned the place after he captured it from the Mahdists in 1896. All along the Nile, huge British-built government ministries hide behind thick walls and long stretches of burned grass. In the late afternoon, a giant, dark wall appears on the horizon; called the haboob, it's a tidal wave of Saharan detritus sent to replenish Khartoum's beige landscape. It blows over.

In government offices, sleepy clerks man surplus desks and wait for God's will to manifest itself. Someplace far to the south, they're revving up for more civil war, and away to the north, pretty girls are renting Peugeots to tourists in Cairo. In Khartoum, they're trying to fix the air conditioning at the hotel, while some jerk from New York lectures a bartender on how to make an egg-cream soda—out of the question, of course—but you can hear him everywhere, it's so quiet.

Night life in Khartoum has taken a beating lately. After the introduction of former President Gaafar Nimeiri's version of shari'a—fundamental Islamic law—the police showed up and seized every bottle of booze in town. "I almost cried," a longtime bartender at the Hilton told me. Once, a middle-aged German in evening dress took a seat at the piano in a hotel bar and played "Smoke Gets in Your Eyes" for bored or weepy-drunk guests every night; I recall his cuffs were badly frayed and partially patched, and I learned later he had gone native and lived in a two-room house in the outskirts, his goats and a cow in one room, his tuxedos and his Sudanese wife in the other. Now he was gone, they said, and I couldn't imagine where he could go. In those days, the hottest spot in town was the open-air beer garden and cabaret bearing the name of poor, dead Chinese Gordon, where it seemed there was always a Dutch magician running through his hat tricks. No more. The bright lights are dim now, and it's grilled chickens and Pepsi in an outdoor cafeteria, unless you know somebody who knows somebody.

Like El Metemma, Khartoum is also a river town, same river. The Blue and White Niles meet quietly in Khartoum. Kitchener laid out the capital of the Sudan like a big Union Jack, a handsome design for a flag but a lousy one for a town; the edges have been tattered by the rapid accumula-

---

* Gaafar Nimeiri, scared of snipers, killed many of the trees during the bizarre twilight of his long rule. The destruction of the trees has done almost as much to ensure popular resentment against his military regime as anything else.

tion of loose architecture, and the upper right-hand part of the cross of St. George ultimately disappears across the Blue Nile into the wistful industrial zones of Khartoum North.

On the other side of the water, off to the northwest, is Omdurman, where there are far fewer trees but a lot more people. Taxis fishtail around road-hogging camels, people shout in the streets, the huge market is alive with thousands of burnoused travelers and young men in the Carnaby Street regalia—bell-bottomed trousers, psychedelic shirts, platform shoes—that is the permanent fashion statement of the Third World. The open plazas are drained by dozens of small alleyways that vanish around immediate corners, and in the middle is the local Notre Dame, the resting place of the Big Trouble, the Tomb of the Mahdi.

Between Khartoum, and Omdurman is an amusement park built to impress delegates to a long-forgotten Organization of African Unity (OAU) conference; not long ago, goats grazed beneath the iron skeleton of a roller coaster. Now things are better, and the roller coaster's back on the tracks again, but the theme-park scene is a novel one in the Sudan and the crowds are somewhere else. No lines, no wait for the ride. Along the riverbanks are networks of trenches and redoubts, the sole survivors of Khartoum's battles.

To amateurs like me, Khartoum is to cities what cricket is to sports: incomprehensible, slow, unchanging but still interesting. Every arrival in Khartoum is the same: the same crush of cabdrivers at the airport, the same colorless drive to the same colorless hotel, where the first thing you see is the knees of the same seven-foot-tall Dinka doorman, whose smiling face descends from heaven and peers into the tiny taxi. Details vary, however. On my second visit, for example, the evening after my arrival the government imposed a curfew so that if the threatened invasion of Khartoum by thousands of zealous members of the Islamic Brotherhood from Omdurman took place, the twenty or so people who constituted the tourist industry wouldn't be wiped out overnight. So I sat in the bar with two Irish relief officers and a diplomat who tried to terrify us with local legends of murder, mayhem and martyrdom. It was ridiculous, said the man from county Mayo, who would die for Khartoum?

So much for the everlasting memory of heroes.

Between the Crimean War and World War I, the British army honed its gentlemanly skills on some of the more obscure playing fields of the world. The United Kingdom was understandably reluctant to wage open war against its European rivals, and although England's diplomatic skill had risen only marginally above the prevailing level of contemporary mediocrity, it was enough to trounce them all. Along the way, the British put together the largest—and, for the most part, one of the shortest-lived—empires in history. The Germans and the French might well have at each other in the outskirts of Paris; the British fought their battles in cartographic abstruseness against enemies who often elicited considerable scientific rather than military curiosity.

In the years leading up to the great scramble for African territory—a land rush in which the British, who already had what they needed, played a surprisingly small role—successive governments shied away from unwarranted annexations. As a rule, colonies and protectorates were added only after they had demonstrated sufficient economic vitality to merit membership in the empire; imperialism was the province of religion and private enterprise.

This attitude reached its zenith with the Liberal government of William Gladstone—G.O.M., they called him the Grand Old Man of Victorian politics—which took office in 1880, unseating the more deliberately imperialist rule of Disraeli. Gladstone was seventy at the time, and had already retired once, some five years earlier; he had returned, he said, to provide unity to a badly fragmented Liberal party, in which Joseph Chamberlain and Sir Charles Dilke led the Radical faction, while Lord Granville and Lord Hartington, cousins, led the Whigs.*

It was a government preoccupied by a great number of issues, notably land reform and home rule for Ireland, and possessed of a belief that the recent expansion of the electorate was accompanied by an anti-imperialist public sentiment. Lord Granville, the leader of his peers in the pursuit of leisure, was given the Foreign Office, which he promptly cluttered with unanswered correspondence and half-finished reports; the War Office went to Lord Hartington, a reluctant politician, but whose influence made his cabinet post essential to the health of the government. While acknowledging that Britain must provide security to the empire, continue its campaign against slavery and ensure the free flow of the Christian truth

---

* Much of this background to the problem of Egypt is found in *Africa and the Victorians* (1961), by Ronald Robinson, John Gallagher and Alice Denny; my principal sources for what follows, however, are Lord Cromer's *Modern Egypt* (two volumes; 1908); *The Mahdiya* (1951), by A. B. Theobald; the campaign journal of General Garnet Wolseley, edited by Adrian Preston and published as *In Relief of Gordon* (1970); *England's Pride* (1965), by Julian Symons; and the journals and memoirs of the principals involved in the siege of Khartoum.

Alan Moorehead's *The White Nile* (1960)—along with its companion volume, *The Blue Nile* (1962)—is the very best introduction to this part of the world. Everyone who has had occasion to write about central and northeastern Africa has found his brilliant, lucid general histories indispensable, and I'm certainly not an exception.

to the inhabitants of Africa, the government was uncertain whether tropical expansion was something the voters wanted, so they energetically ignored the whole issue.

Unhappily, there was a lot of unfinished business in some of the more inconvenient outposts of British interests. Egypt, for example, with its peculiar khedivial excesses, was an ongoing problem to which no one ever had a solution.

The khediviate, though nominally under Turkish suzerainty, was an invention of the European powers—chiefly the British and French—who sought to protect their financial interests in Egypt and ensure the security of the Suez Canal. For the British, especially after the strategic value of Constantinople started to decline in the 1860s, Cairo and the canal held the key to India, the colony by which all other colonies were justified. The French, however, had determined as early as 1798—when Napoleon invaded the country—to gain ascendancy over the Nile Delta, and thereby obtain the means by which they could control the Mediterranean and threaten their old foe in India. Subsequently, the French decision to fund construction of the canal (England had balked at such a commitment) presented Whitehall with a greater threat, since the completion of the canal would make possible the rapid deployment of forces from the Mediterranean, while the French financing of the project—along with other large French loans to the profligate khediviate—might give Paris the upper hand on the Nile. To eliminate the Napoleonic threat, the admiralty had simply dispatched the fleet. The elimination of the threat posed by the canal project, however, was enormously complicated by events in Asia Minor, the Near East and in Europe.

By the 1870s, the balance of power in Europe had been affected by renewed Russian ambitions, since the Crimean War, to control the Bosporus. Both France (in Cairo) and England (in Constantinople) had determined that "moral influence" rather than military intervention was a better way to control the tangled events in Egypt and Turkey, and allowed for the most practical use of the Ottoman possessions as a buffer against the Russians. ("Moral influence," the ad hoc formulation that propelled England's informal expansion, was defined by Lord Salisbury, one of its chief proponents, as "a combination of nonsense, objurgation and worry.")

In the face of Russian antagonism the two powers found it necessary to collaborate in the Near East, and a tacit policy of dual control was developed for Egypt, by which France and England collaborated to exercise control of the sultan and his vassal, the khedive. The French insisted on bleeding the Egyptians to recover invested funds, and the British—unwilling to spoil entente, since control of Egypt was one of those fancies that could trigger a war—reluctantly acquiesced. European paramountcy thus stripped both the Porte (the handy name given by historians to the Ottoman Turkish government) and its khediviate in Egypt of any legitimacy. The effect of such pronounced European control had predictable results.

In 1881, an Abdel Nasser–like soldier named Arabi fomented a nationalist uprising in the Egyptian army and set about ridding the country of foreign influence. When, after the usual round of massacres, it became necessary to send in troops, the French government, which had been by far the most hard-nosed about refusing to delegate real responsibility to the khedivial government and thus giving it much-needed credibility, found it impossible to get the Chamber to approve. Gladstone's government, left in the lurch by the French, sent in General Sir Garnet Wolseley—Gilbert and Sullivan's "very model of a modern major general"—and affairs in Egypt passed under the control of Britain, who substituted for military subjugation a more belligerent force—bureaucrats, headed by an old India hand named Evelyn Baring, who had first arrived in Egypt in 1877. From 1882, Baring (later Lord Cromer) was the de facto Farouk in Egypt. Britain had stumbled onto a foreign policy that, as usual, was bound up in Indian affairs, and the northeastern corner of Africa became as important to her as East Africa and the Cape of Good Hope. (The French looked elsewhere for hegemony and found it in northern and West Africa.)

The financial and political collapse of the Ottoman Empire had put a strain on the Anglo-French partnership, since neither could influence events in the state of chaos and anarchy that accompanied the Turkish disintegration. More than anything else, the rush to fill the vacuum created by an absence of Turkish power in northern Africa and along the Nile set off the scramble for African territory, each European player wary of the other and each using African real estate as game markers.

Now Gladstone had Egypt, a bankrupt Turkish possession noted for its Pyramids and governmental corruption. The country was a bother to him, interfering as it did with his domestic preoccupations, and he frankly didn't know what to do with it, so he turned the matter over to Granville, who turned the matter over to Baring. The result was a permanently temporary occupation of the country, along with the burden of supervising its crippling debts, its army, its foreign policy and its big backyard, the Sudan.

Egypt's interest in the Sudan has always seemed the product of curiosity, sort of a follow-the-thread game that has been going on for three thousand years or so. The Sudan was never worth much to Egypt, except as a source of slaves, but it was handy, and since it was never really very well defined as a political entity, it was easy. Usually a prosperous regime in Egypt would exercise itself by reaching south, just to see how far up the Nile it could go. And when times turned tough, the Egyptians retreated down the Nile, leaving the country in splendid isolation.

Sudanese kingdoms came and went, sometimes killing one another off in what must have been profoundly nonsensical wars, since—aside from the brush that grows along the banks of the Nile—there is nothing at all to fight about in much of the Sudan. But always there was an invasion from the north to reshape the Sudanese landscape, and after the tenth century, most of these were Islamic incursions. By the beginning of the nineteenth century, Egypt had annexed most of the northern and central provinces of the Sudan, and by 1870, when Sir Samuel Baker explored the equatorial lakes on behalf of the khedive, Egypt's Sudan extended as far south as the Ugandan kingdoms.

As a rule, imperialism relies heavily on economic benefit as a justification for its existence. But in the Sudan the financial situation was clouded by the fact that nobody had any money. Taxes were paid in cattle, some of which were exported to Cairo, and some of which were sold back to the taxpayers in exchange for slaves, who were also exported to Cairo. It was difficult keeping good books, of course, and before long, the Sudan existed chiefly as a playground for the oppressive, cruel and larcenous pashas sent by the Porte and the khedive to administer the country.

In 1869, the khedive Ismail, a visionary without genius, eager to improve his reputation among his European creditors, as well as out of what seems to be a genuine concern, sought to suppress slavery in the country and establish a more pragmatic basis for the Sudan's finances. He sent expeditions to the southern provinces with the intention of opening the upper Nile to commerce. After five years, he had accomplished little. An expedition sent to Bahr al-Ghazal had ended after its leader was killed by slave traders, and another, under Baker, had resulted in the precarious annexation of Equatoria; while Baker claimed to the khedive that he had "conquered and pacified the country as far as the equator," in fact his accomplishments were minimal. A few military posts had been established, but the native tribes had been made more hostile, slaving had increased, and the Sudan had been extended south to an ungovernable extent. In 1873, Baker resigned and Ismail began searching for a replacement governor for Egypt's most ludicrous province.

One night after a visit to Khartoum, I was sitting in an Egyptian pokey with eighty-odd Libyans and a North Korean. One man, refusing to believe I was really interested in irrigation projects, turned my baggage inside out and went through my notes. Another told me my detention was "purely technical, okay?" and asked me to help him find work in America. I tried to read from a beat-up copy of G. Birkbeck Hill's *Gordon in Central Africa: 1874–1879.*

It was hard to pay attention, but I didn't believe what I was reading anyway. Listen to this: "It will be a long time before much can be done to civilize [the Nilotic tribes]. . . . Poor creatures! they would like to be left alone. The Arabs hate these parts [Equatoria], and all the [Arab] troops are sent up for punishment; all their constitutions, unlike ours, cannot stand the wet and damp, or the dulness [sic] of their life. I prefer it infinitely to going out to dinner in England, and have kept my health exceedingly well."

Life in the hot swamp better than dinner in England? Evolution flat out in reverse, really. The author, I thought, must be quite mad.

As it turned out, for more than a century many people have thought Gordon mad. Nuts or not, Major General Charles George "Chinese" Gordon was an extremely charismatic figure of profound piety, spartan simplicity, military genius and mystical courage. They made a movie about Gordon once, and he was played by Charlton Heston. That should tell you something

A hundred years or so ago, Gordon was England's greatest hero, the ideal of the empire made flesh. Born January 28, 1833, into a military family, he had done poorly in officer training but earned his nickname in the 1860s in Nanking, where, armed with only a wicker cane and a sweet-smelling cheroot, the thirty-year-old brevet major of the Royal Engineers led a mutinous and motley militia called the Ever Victorious Army against the Taiping rebels, a bloody cult that featured, as its leader, a man who claimed that he left his concubine-laden bed every night to go bother God, until he claimed God finally relented and made him the Brother of Christ. As a reward, the emperor made Gordon a mandarin and gave him a yellow riding jacket "to be worn on his person," and a big peacock feather to be stuck on his hat, plus four suits "proper to his rank of Ti-Tu," on which he probably pinned the French Legion of Honor decoration given him for gallantry in the Crimea, and put the whole bundle in a wardrobe chest. For by now Gordon was a very famous figure,* and he hated fame.

Anxious to avoid the popular acclaim that greeted his return to England in 1865, Gordon disappeared into the obscurity of a useless military construction project in Gravesend, where he embarrassed his fellow officers by dashing around the streets distributing religious leaflets he himself had written. He bestowed pensions on impoverished elderly neighbors, visited the sick and dying—who often sent for him instead of the local vicar—and scouted the district for distressed kids who, he thought, would benefit from the religious and secular education he privately underwrote. Nearly all his salary went to his philanthropic hobbies, and the enterprise left him flat broke. The army, uncomfortable with such an eccentric, found a way to dispose of Gordon neatly enough: In 1871, they hustled him off to a post on a pointless Central European boundary commission, where, alas, he chanced to meet Nubar Pasha, the prime minister of the khedive of Egypt. Nubar, it seemed, was looking for someone to assume the governorship of Equatoria. Gordon nominated himself.

In 1874, when Gordon arrived in Cairo to discuss his post with the khedive Ismail, Equatoria hadn't even been properly mapped. As noted, Baker, the previous governor, had been unable to stop the routine raids by slave traders; the countryside was beset by bandits, making it necessary for travelers to convoy with armed guards; and the province itself was a Devil's Island for the malcontents and troublemakers of the Egyptian army, who looted native settlements with the same frequency as that of the Arab slavers, and who were often paid in slave girls. The biggest industry in Equatoria was the manufacture of horrible, deadly diseases. A terrible place.

Offered a salary of £10,000, Gordon shocked the khedive by taking only £2,000—most of which went to his Gravesend pensioners—and set about making arrangements for his departure. He quickly assembled a staff—Italian adventurers; American officers fresh from the Civil War; his own nephew, Willy Anson; and a welter of other European specialists eager to accompany the famous Chinese Gordon, and even more eager to make their mark in Africa, the outer space of the Victorian age.

The province took its toll on the Europeans, and one by one they were overwhelmed by malaria and other maladies that lived happily in the

---

* "Never did a soldier of fortune deport himself with a nicer sense of military honour, with more gallantry against the resisting, and with more mercy towards the vanquished, with more disinterested neglect of opportunities of personal advantage, or with more entire devotion to the objects and desires of his own Government, than this officer, who, after all his victories, has just lain down his sword," wrote the London *Times* on August 5, 1864.

dreadful climate.* But to Gordon, Equatoria was a perfect tonic. Within two and a half years, he had reliably mapped the upper reaches of the Nile for the first time,† established a 600-mile-long chain of garrison settlements, driven out the slavers, befriended the local tribesmen, initiated trade, disciplined the troops and made it possible for an unarmed man to walk alone from one end of the province to the other without molestation, something you certainly haven't been able to do since. Happily for the khedive, Equatoria even began turning a profit as produce and ivory traveled down the Nile to Khartoum on Gordon's fleet of river steamers. But as long as the government in Khartoum abetted the slave trade, Gordon felt his work in Equatoria was wasted; he resigned, and by the end of December 1876, he was back in London.

The corruption of the khedive (for whom Gordon professed an ironic affection‡) had infested Khartoum. Alan Moorehead pointed out that the khedive's governor-general "had developed a system of bribery and extortion that was wonderfully complete, even by Egyptian standards." This entrepreneurial spirit was bankrupting the Sudan, and the khedive, eager to preserve every penny for his own purse, determined to right the situation. He must, he felt, persuade the incorruptible Gordon to return as

* In a letter to his sister (written September 11, 1874), Gordon called the roll of his European companions:
"Your brother. *Well,* but a shadow.
"Kemp engineer. Well.
"Gessi. Well; has a severe fever.
"His Greek servant. Ill more or less: result no work.
"Berndorff, German, my servant. Ill.
"Mengies, German servant. Sent back ill.
"Russell. Ill, cannot be moved; invalided.
"Anson. Dead.
"De Witt, amateur like Berndorff. Dead.
"Campbell. Ill.
"Linant. Very ill, cannot be moved.
"Long. With King Mtesa; have not heard of him for six months.
"My place is a complete hospital."

† Mapping was one thing; exploration was another. He was paid to be a governor, he wrote, not an explorer. "If you ever go out to Africa on exploration business, go alone. . . . I consider it is quite unjustifiable that Englishmen should take men into dangers of which they are utterly ignorant, and should then leave them to their fate. Residence in these oriental lands tends to blunt one's susceptibilities of right and justice. . . ." Romolo Gessi, Gordon's most trusted lieutenant, was usually the one sent out to record new rivers or chart new lakes. Henry Stanley would have done well to follow Gordon's advice, as we shall see.

‡ The feeling was mutual. "When that man comes into the room," Ismail said of Gordon, "I feel I am with my superior." Absolutely correct, especially in view of the khedive's well-satisfied appetite for luxury. Gordon, on learning of Ismail's huge ill-gotten fortune, altered his view, saying the exile of Ismail "appears . . . quite right."

governor-general of the entire Sudan. On January 17, 1877, he sent Gordon a telegram saying, "I refuse to believe that, when Gordon has once given his word as a gentleman, anything will ever induce him to go back on his word." So, by February Gordon was again in Cairo, and, after obtaining a free hand and another reduced salary from the khedive—who, in his dealings with Gordon only, was always honest and fair—he arrived in Khartoum in May 1877.

Over the course of the next year, Gordon set about stripping away much of the power of the unscrupulous local officials and relieving the burden of bad government that had fallen on the poor. Corrupt Egyptian officials were dismissed and replaced by Sudanese and Europeans. He abolished flogging and slavery, class privileges, and army corruption and brutality. He sat listening to endless petitions and dispensed justice. He traveled enormous distances on camel- and horseback, often for months at a time, crossing from one end of the largest country in Africa (the Sudan is the size of a small continent, nearly one million square miles) to the other—in all, as much as 9,000 miles in less than three years. He once covered eighty-five miles in thirty-six hours. He also visited his strange collection of provincial governors and officials: the inexperienced former sailor Frank Lupton, governor of the Bahr al-Ghazal; the Austrian Rudolph C. von Slatin, governor of Darfur; the Italian adventurer Romolo Gessi, who had labored with Gordon in Equatoria and who continued as Gordon's most trusted officer; Carl Giegler, the taciturn inspector general of telegraphs; and, as governor of grim Equatoria, a very odd, skinny, near-sighted German physician and naturalist named Eduard Schnitzer, who had fled Bavaria to the pleasures of a Turkish harem and now preferred to be called Dr. Emin.

Gordon was everywhere, mounting successful expeditions against rebels and bandits one day, and the next, forcing an army of slavers to surrender by riding alone into their camp and simply ordering them to submit. "I am striking deadly blows against the slave-trade, and am establishing a sort of Government of Terror about it," he wrote. Traveling with a light escort of fewer than 300 troopers—whom he usually outdistanced—he ricocheted around the Sudan settling boundary disputes, receiving complaints, relieving taxes, making administrative reforms, chasing slave caravans and supervising the construction of a telegraph line. This sort of behavior might have been dismaying to the men back at the office in London, but it thoroughly thrilled the Sudanese, who loved him. Trade from Khartoum began to flow, and the capital transformed itself as commercial development blossomed.

But by January 1880, Ismail had been deposed; the British had installed a new khedive, Tewfik; and Baring, the consummate bureaucrat, had come to look after Egypt's affairs. Gordon, feared and despised by men of the official temperament, and, after all, a non-believer in a Muslim country, was once again in London, while in the Sudan, Ra'uf Pasha, whom Gordon had twice dismissed for corruption, incompetence and cruelty, had been installed as Gordon's replacement. Inevitably, a Muslim revolt broke out, led by Muhammad Ahmad, a Shi'a fanatic who claimed to be the Mahdi,* the promised Prophet, and threatened to consume both British and Egyptian interests in the Sudan.

Muhammad Ahmad's successes were spectacular; his followers defeated every army Egypt sent against them—including columns led by British officers like Hicks Pasha and Valentine Baker, the brother of the explorer Samuel Baker—steadily gaining more fanatic adherents, and at the same time adding a considerable number of captured weapons to his arsenal. By 1883 Khartoum itself was in serious jeopardy. In England, the fate of the Sudan became a popular issue, and letters in the press were championing Gordon as the man to straighten things out.

Gordon, meanwhile, exhausted after his latest round in the Sudan, went for a brief rest in Switzerland, where, in what he called "a moment of weakness," he accepted an appointment as private secretary to the new Viceroy of India, Lord Ripon. Before he even arrived, he was regretting his decision. "I have been an idiot," he wrote from someplace off Aden. "I hate India, and how I could ever have taken the post is past my comprehension. The endless sorts of quarrels which seem to be going on there by all accounts is enough to sicken one. I shall get out of it as soon as I can." It took him three days. "My views," he explained, "were diametrically opposed to those of the official classes."

* The Shi'a Muslims hold that the leader of Islam is the Imam, who must be a direct descendant of the Prophet, through his daughter, Fatima, and her husband, Ali. According to A. B. Theobald, conventional Islam holds there were twelve such direct descendants, but the last one died without issue. The Shi'as will have none of this. They believe that the son of the twelfth descendant mysteriously disappeared, and has remained hidden ever since. They call him al-Mahdi al-Muntazar, and claim he will return someday to deliver righteousness to an evil world and bring a golden age of true Islamic ascendancy.

Muhammad Ahmad's strict interpretation of Islamic law gave his regime a familiar Iranian texture, although the abstinence he preached was not part of the Mahdi's own daily program, which seems to have involved fun with girls and an occasional roaring toot.

In the chaos that followed Gordon's resignation, Muhammad Ahmad was the most successful of several Mahdis who all arrived inconveniently at the same time. My own favorite has to be the Mahdi with adherents in the eastern part of the Sudan, who claimed to be able to fly around on his bed.

That same week, he received a telegram summoning him to Peking; the position of the Chinese government was critical, and war with Russia seemed imminent. The War Office refused to allow him to go, so he surrendered his commission, borrowed some money and went anyway. "My object in going to China," he told a journalist, "is to persuade the Chinese not to go to war with Russia. . . . Inclined as I am, with only a small degree of admiration for military exploits, I esteem it a far greater honour to promote peace than to gain any paltry honours in a wretched war." Arriving in Peking, he confronted the imperial high ministers with his assertion that war with Russia was unthinkable; the capital would be in Russian hands within weeks of a declaration of war. The war party, however, was in the ascendancy, and the argument quickly grew rancorous. "It would be sheer idiocy to fight Russia," he finally declared. His translator, however, refused to interpret the word idiocy, so Gordon grabbed a bilingual dictionary, found the word and showed it to the assembled notables. Surprisingly, the shocked ministers followed his advice. Gordon then retreated to write a long treatise on Chinese defensive warfare, gave it to the government and left for London, where he found his resignation had been refused.

During November 1880, he traveled through Ireland, where he sought to understand the land reform and home-rule issues that had so long dogged Parliament. In December he published a plan that would allow for the compulsory purchase of large estates by a land commission—which, after reallocation, he reckoned would cost the government £300,000 per annum—and the free sale of leases and rents. "The state of our fellow countrymen [in Ireland] is worse than that of any people in the world, let alone Europe. . . . I am not well off," he wrote, "but I would offer ——— or his agent £1,000 if either of them would live one week in one of these poor devil's places and feed as these people do." His offer—along with his plan—was ignored.

Early in 1881, he finally found an appointment in Mauritius, "this Patmos of idleness," where he spent months "looking after the barrack repairs and seeing that the drains were in good order." Gordon had been refused an appointment in Basutoland, and by now the War Office seemed ready to ask for his resignation from the army.

Instead, the Cape government had a change of heart and asked him to come and help settle a violent conflict that had arisen between the natives and the colonial government. Gordon arrived, examined the issues, and sided with the natives. Colonial interests were repelled by Gordon's findings, and while he was in negotiations with one of the leading chiefs in an effort to end the bloodshed, the colonists spread the rumor that hostilities against the natives had broken out. His life having been placed in great jeopardy, Gordon, of course, resigned, and by 1882 was again in England, where King Leopold of Belgium was asking for his services. "You can name your own terms," Leopold wrote. "You know the consideration I have for your great qualities." Gordon postponed a decision, and instead spent most of 1883 in Palestine, where he tried to divine the location of the Garden of Eden, Golgotha, the Temple of Jerusalem and other biblical sites, and wrote to friends about news of the day, and especially about the deteriorating situation in the Sudan.

The sequence of events that finally led to Gordon's reappointment to the Sudan is as remarkable for its cynical contradictions as for its well-paced theatricality. It was an interesting month: On January 1, 1884, Gordon arrived in Brussels and came to an agreement with Leopold*; on the same day, a letter from Sir Samuel Baker to the *Times* advocated that Gordon be sent to the Sudan; on the 5th, the *Times* ran an editorial lamenting England's loss of Gordon to the Belgians; on the 8th, he was asked by the editor of the influential *Pall Mall Gazette* what course England should follow in the Sudan. Gordon, characteristically, said that Muhammad Ahmad should be defeated, reasoning that if he was allowed to gain control of the Sudan, the British army would be needed to drive him out eventually, since the presence on Egypt's southern flank of a revolutionary Islamic fundamentalist state would be intolerable, and the longer they waited, the more difficult it would become to accomplish the task. The interview was published on January 9, 1884. On the 10th, the Foreign Secretary, Lord Granville, pressed Baring to accept Gordon's appointment as Khartoum's rescuer; on January 14, the *Times* printed a letter from Gordon to Baker advocating a policy of military intervention in the Sudan; on the morning of the 18th, Gordon was asked by Wolseley whether or not he was willing to go to Khartoum to report on conditions in the Sudan; and that same afternoon, Granville, Hartington, Dilke and Lord Northbrook, the first lord of the admiralty, met with Gordon and asked him to go to the Sudan to either report on the situation or evacuate the garrisons—nobody was quite sure which, although Gordon was left with the impression he was to evacuate the troops, a notion confirmed in Dilke's notes and alluded to by Northbrook and Granville. This confusion of the orders was to play a convenient part in the government's subsequent policies regarding Gordon's mission.

* He was to have served in the Congo with Stanley, a working relationship that wouldn't have lasted past lunch.

In fact, the mission was confused from the start: Gordon, asked if he had any clothes other than the old suit and frock coat he was wearing, said no, "I'll go as I am." He also had no money, and as he was to depart that evening, Wolseley had to run around the London clubs taking up a collection for him while Gordon ate dinner. At Charing Cross, Gordon was handed £300 and a watch by Wolseley, while Granville bought his ticket; the Duke of Clarence, the commander-in-chief of the army, held open the railway carriage door, and Gordon, accompanied by Colonel J. D. H. Stewart, set off for the Sudan on the eight o'clock train for Calais.*

On January 21, the four cabinet members who had given Gordon his instructions gathered to try to figure out what the instructions were, exactly, but couldn't really decide. Granville's official orders, as communicated to Baring in Cairo, called for Gordon to report "on the military situation and on the measures to be taken for the security of the Egyptian garrisons still holding positions . . . and perform such other duties as may be entrusted to him by the Egyptian Government through Sir Evelyn Baring." This message crossed with one Baring had sent asking for an officer "with full powers civil and military to conduct the retreat" of the garrisons from the Sudan, and Baring assumed that Granville's orders gave him the power to expand the nature of Gordon's mission.† Gordon, who had the habit of expressing his every passing thought on paper, many of which were contradictory, wrote dozens of letters and telegrams as he rode through France, and although he had planned to go directly to Suakin on the Sudan's Red Sea coast and avoid Egypt altogether, Baring bid him come to Cairo, where he arrived on January 24. At a meeting with Baring and other officials convened to clarify his instructions and intentions, Gordon was ordered to evacuate the garrisons of the Sudan, given a credit of £100,000 to accomplish this task, and appointed governor-general of the Sudan by the khedive. Gordon's plan for restoring the sovereignty of the various local sultans was also approved, and he was given a proclamation announcing the Egyptian government's policy of evacuating the coun-

---

* Gordon's name had slipped the public's mind by this time, and when it was reported in the press that Chinese Gordon would go to the Sudan, not many people knew who he was. One contemporary account tells of a Pembrokeshire magistrate remarking to an officer of the Pembroke Dock garrison, "I see the Government have just sent a Chinaman to the Sudan."

† Gladstone was ill at the time of Gordon's appointment, and was told by Hartington only about the reporting aspect of the mission. When Gordon began taking a more active role, Gladstone became convinced he was willfully disobeying his instructions, and no amount of subsequent evidence or argument would make him change his opinion.

try. Baring, the most careful of diplomats, was later severely rebuked by the government for compounding their error.

Gordon's procession through the Sudan in February 1884 was marked by political plotting and wild celebrations. Tribal leaders met and made contingency plans to allow for an unforeseen outcome. Villages were festooned with banners; in Berber, thousands of Sudanese came to welcome him, and his greeting in Khartoum on February 18 was ecstatic—as bands played and fireworks exploded, virtually the entire capital turned out to see the man they hoped would deliver them.

He at once opened the gates to any who wished to flee to Muhammad Ahmad, and few took the opportunity. He made arrangements for the evacuation of the first contingent of Egyptian soldiers, formed a local council, burned all the tax records, turned political prisoners and debtors out of prison, destroyed all of Ra'uf Pasha's instruments of torture, vainly sued for peace with Muhammad Ahmad and, through a series of successful cattle raids, managed to reduce the cost of food. He flooded Baring with telegrams, and the British agent worked overtime trying to distill the sense of Gordon's information for retransmission to London.

Then things began to go very wrong. On March 13, the telegraph line was cut. The riparian tribes north of Khartoum revolted, and by the middle of the month the capital was cut off. By June, Gordon's situation was desperate; Muhammad Ahmad's troops had encircled Khartoum, and Gordon was able to communicate infrequently with Cairo only by sending out runners. (For several weeks, Baring wasn't aware of the interruption of communications, and in London, Gladstone grew angry at what he saw as Gordon's refusal to answer their messages, most of which, of course, Gordon never received.) He applied himself to strengthening the city's defenses, laying mines made of explosives concealed in old biscuit tins around the perimeter, and launched his river steamers on a series of forays up and down the Nile. When the city's economy began to collapse, Gordon printed his own currency and managed to achieve a small recovery, but food supplies ran dangerously low and, after a serious military setback in which he lost his best battlefield officer, Gordon's vastly outnumbered garrison was unable to clear a path out of Khartoum. It was thought Gordon would be able to hold out for no longer than a few months.

In Cairo, Baring was growing increasingly insistent that some measures must be taken to aid Gordon, but Gladstone remained adamant. In nearly every cabinet meeting, and at most parliamentary sessions, the question came up again and again. Gladstone had become obsessive about refusing aid to Gordon. In Parliament, he couldn't decide *exactly* how difficult

Gordon's position really was: Certainly Khartoum was "hemmed in," if that meant that "there are bodies of hostile troops in the neighborhood forming more or less of a chain around it." However, Gladstone continued, "I draw a distinction between that and the town being surrounded, which would bear technically a very different meaning." And as far as the telegraph line being cut, he, along with Granville, thought that was probably a good thing, since it prevented the receipt of Gordon's disturbing messages.

A consummate politician, Gladstone used every trick in the book to avoid committing the government to a rescue. Indian affairs, Irish home rule, land questions and financial policies were used to obscure the need for a decision on the Sudan. The delay of the inevitable expedition stretched on through the summer of 1884.* Even the Queen—mirroring the growing public sentiment that action must be taken—wired Lord Hartington, one of the pivotal members of Gladstone's waffling cabinet, and one of those who had convinced Gordon to take on the mission, "General Gordon is in danger; you are bound to try and save him." In short order, Gordon's plight became a sort of daily drama, with most of Britain a captivated audience. At public meetings, in churches, in the press, a great clamor arose for the rescue of Gordon, and his picture appeared in shop and home windows not only in England but also on the Continent. Both Gladstone and Granville managed to ignore the outcry, until finally, after a lengthy delay, a wire was sent to Baring, which was relayed by messenger to Khartoum—one of the few to get through—asking Gordon to state the reasons he "continues at Khartoum." It took months to get a reply: "You ask me to state cause and intention in staying in Khartoum knowing government means to abandon Sudan, and in answer I say, I stay at Khartoum because Arabs have shut us up and will not let us out." In his *Journals* Gordon makes it clear that even if he could have escaped, he would not do so if it meant abandoning the civilians and the soldiers who followed him so blindly. By summer 1884, Khartoum was held entirely by the transcendent will of Gordon.

Finally, on September 9, 1884, he dispatched Stewart and all the other

* Gladstone, a modern politician, was a master of form but miserly in substance. As with most political professionals, it was difficult to tell whether he was prompted by incompetence, stupidity or plain meanness; it must be remembered that he was now well into his seventies and had been suffering from repeated illnesses. At one point, he seemed to harbor the idea that the whole episode was a conspiratorial fabrication on Wolseley's part to gain power for his faction in the army. Or perhaps he just didn't believe Gordon and thought it was all a trick to get the government entangled in a Sudanese quagmire; perhaps he didn't want to spend the money; maybe he just forgot.

remaining Europeans, including the *Times* correspondent, Frank Power, in one of his river steamers to Cairo, and settled in to wait for the inevitable arrival of the Mahdi. "I have always felt we were doomed to come face to face ere the matter was ended," he wrote in his journal, with what would later be seen as a notable lack of precision. (Stewart, carrying dispatches and cyphers, never made it; the steamer ran aground and everyone aboard was killed.)

By early August, Hartington, whose influence was essential to the life of Gladstone's government, finally yielded to the pro-Gordon pressure. With Hartington's resignation on his desk, Gladstone at last allowed the passage of a bill setting aside £300,000 as a contingency fund in the event Gordon needed assistance; a fervent friend and admirer of Gordon's, General Garnet Wolseley was asked to prepare the necessary plans.

By September, Wolseley was in Cairo assembling his 11,000 troops for the 1,500-mile assault up the Nile. Lord Wolseley's decision to use the Nile route was roundly condemned at the time, and today seems just as ill advised. It should be noted, though, that Wolseley had come to fame by employing a similar strategy during the much less complicated Red River campaign in Canada, and to him, apparently, a river was a river.* He ordered the construction of hundreds of small whalers, suitable for rowing or sailing, and even imported to Egypt a batch of Canadian voyageurs to take care of the boats, but they turned out to be mostly unemployed insurance clerks and merchants and the like, and knew little about the whole business. Thomas Cook and Son had been contracted to deliver a portion of the column up the Nile, but a contractual disagreement over the supply of coal resulted in a long delay halfway into the campaign. Moreover, the column itself was extremely unwieldy, stretching for many miles from one end to the other. Camels for the special mounted units were often difficult to come by, and the saddles and other equipment even more so. The uniforms, red and blue serge jackets, gray flannel shirts and blue trousers, were inappropriate for the Saharan climate, and the column met far greater difficulties than expected trying to pass the second cataract.

---

* In the words of one expedition report, "Water is water, and rock is rock, whether they lie in America or in Africa." The route suggested by most tacticians was inland from Suakin through Berber, thence to Khartoum; a brief punitive expedition led by General Gerald Graham had already administered a defeat to the Mahdists surrounding Suakin.

*   *   *

By November, all the players were in place: Wolseley's huge column
trekking slowly southward; the forces of Muhammad Ahmad concentrated around Khartoum; the hungry, fearful citizens looking up at Gordon
stationed on the roof of the governor's palace, peering northward through
his telescope, looking for help.

The journals kept by Gordon after the September departure of the
Europeans were smuggled out on one or another of the small steamers.
They arrived wrapped in bits of cloth and bore labels reading, "No secrets
as far as I am concerned." Once read by every schoolboy in England,
Gordon's Khartoum *Journals* are among the least pretentious memoirs
ever written. Filled with rages, insights, ironies, contradictions, jokes and
philosophic observations, Gordon's writing gives close scrutiny to a court-
yard chicken, the nature of religious faith, politicians and bureaucrats, and
his own failings; nothing escapes his notice, he lives in a very small world
and he knows every corner intimately.

The *Journals* are more than anything else transcripts of a monologue;
their range is encyclopedic; and, since we know how the story ends, a
little poignant: A month after the Europeans' departure, for example, "A
mouse has taken Stewart's place at table; she (judging from her swelled-
out appearance) comes up and eats out of my plate without fear."

• • • •

"The turkey cock has become so disagreeable that I had to put his head
under his wing and sway him to and fro till he slept. The cavasses thought
he was dead, but he got up and immediately went at me. The putting the
head under the wing acts with all birds, but it is the cock alone who gets
mesmerized by the chalk lines drawn in front of his beak. How do you
account for this?"

• • • •

"We are a wonderful people; it was never our Government which made
us a great nation; our Government has ever been the drag on our wheels. It
is, of course, on the cards that Kartoum is taken under the nose of the
expeditionary force, which will be *just too late*."

• • • •

"I believe Government can, now-a-days, get men to do anything by
means of money and honours (*not honour*), and I have a shrewd idea of
how this affair will end up here. However, it is not my affair, and I have
taken my decision."

• • • •

"It is very curious, but if I am in a bad temper, which I fear is often the case, my servants will be always at their prayers, and thus religious practises follow the scale of my temper; they are pagans if all goes well."

• • • •

"If they do not come before 30th November the game is up, and Rule Britannia. In this calculation, I have given every latitude for difficulties of transport, making forts, &c, and on 15th November I ought to see Her Majesty's uniform."

• • • •

"I dwell on the joy of never seeing Great Britain again with its horrid, wearisome dinner parties and miseries. How we can put up with those things passes my imagination! It is a perfect bondage. At those dinner parties we are all in masks, saying what we do not believe, eating and drinking things we do not want, and then abusing one another. I would sooner live like a Dervish with the Mahdi, than go out to dinner every night in London. I hope, if any English general comes to Kartoum, he will not ask me to dinner. Why men cannot be friends without bringing the wretched stomachs in, is astounding."

• • • •

"The people up here [in Khartoum] would reason thus, if I attempted to leave: . . . all this goes for nought if you quit us, it is your bounden duty to stay by us, and to share our fate; if the British Government deserts us that is no reason for you to do so, after our having stood by you . . . I declare *positively*, and *once for all, that I will not leave the Soudan until every one who wants to go down is given the chance to do so* . . . therefore, if any emissary or letter comes up here ordering me to come down, I WILL NOT OBEY IT, BUT WILL STAY HERE, AND FALL WITH THE TOWN, AND RUN ALL RISKS."

The last entry, dated December 14, 1884, ended with this warning: "NOW MARK THIS, if the Expeditionary force, and I ask for no more than two hundred men, does not come in ten days, *the town may fall*; and I have done the best for the honour of our country. Good bye."

It is difficult to spend an evening with the *Journals* and not feel an irrepressible anger on Gordon's behalf; yet despite the entries' stark honesty and self-revelation, at the end of the day a reader feels that Gordon must remain an enigmatic figure, since the only alternative is to view him as some sort of saint.*

At Ambukkol, where the Nile describes the gigantic question mark that ends at Khartoum, Wolseley halted the main column and dispatched a flying column on camels across the Bayuda under the experienced command of Sir Herbert Stewart. The column comprised the expedition's best young officers and men, and the drama of the race to Khartoum was focused on this relatively small contingent—which included young Lord Charles Beresford, who was developing a monumental boil on his bum, due to the camels, no doubt, and the hero of the Blues, Colonel Fred Burnaby, who had shown up as an unauthorized but entirely welcome combatant. Every man in the column felt he was on the brink of great glory. At Abu Klea, twenty-five miles west of El Metemma, they fought a fierce battle with the Mahdi's Ansar warriors. They barely escaped defeat, but in the melee, Burnaby was killed and Stewart was mortally injured. With the two best field commanders lost, command devolved to Sir Charles Wilson, an intelligence officer completely ill-prepared to lead an army in the field. Brimming with caution, Wilson managed to attain the river at El Metemma on January 19, but he couldn't quite decide what to do next. So he did nothing. He knew that time was running out, that the very nature of his command was predicated on speed of execution. He asked Beresford, the naval commander of the expedition, for advice, and, concerned with being in on the final rush to rescue, Beresford, normally a dashing young officer but at the moment unable to even walk, let alone sit a camel, suggested a few days' delay to allow for a little reconnaisance and reorganization. On the 21st, four steamers, dispatched earlier by Gordon in anticipation of the column's arrival, arrived and conveyed news of the perilous state of affairs in Khartoum. Wilson hesitated until January 24, when he finally decided to send a small force upriver to Khartoum. On

---

* For many, that's an uncomfortable notion. In fact, the life of Gordon apparently has a considerable capacity for generating disbelief. Shortly after his death, Lytton Strachey libeled him in his *Eminent Victorians,* and, as a result, Gordon was seen as a quixotic dipsomaniac for a generation or so. Subsequent research finally eliminated that blot, but occasional efforts are made to exhume the myth, as well as another, more fashionable one, alleging homosexuality, this one appearing in a book in which the author can't even be sure of the year of Gordon's death. That Gordon was neither an alcoholic nor a pederast nor a homosexual is apparently a continuing source of substantial disappointment. Almost certainly, Gordon died a celibate.

January 28, 1885, Gordon's fifty-second birthday, the British arrived in Khartoum—two days too late.

On the 26th, the receding level of the Nile had revealed to Muhammad Ahmad's generals a weakness in the city's defenses. His army had crossed the river in the night and easily overwhelmed the starving Egyptian defenders, who by this time were eating rats and palm trees. Gordon, according to most accounts, heard the commotion, ran to the palace roof to see the mad rush of Ansar warriors, retired to his chamber to put on his dress uniform, and emerged to meet a group of dervishes on the stair outside his apartment. He started to draw his sword but simply shrugged instead, and they got him. His head was taken across the Nile to Muhammad Ahmad for that face-to-face meeting in Omdurman, while Wolseley retreated back to Cairo.*

Khartoum. January 26, 1987: I spent the day loitering in the district surrounding the presidential palace, sometimes crossing the busy street to stand on the banks of the Nile. You can look down the river until the river disappears and see pretty much what Gordon saw, which is not much. A little to the left is Omdurman. In the middle of the stream is Tuti Island, where taxi drivers wash their cabs on the shore. Behind them, the dull, secular tower of the Friendship Palace Hotel rises above the scrub.

At night there were fireworks and celebrations throughout Omdurman. I bummed a car and drove through the jammed streets, stopping twice at makeshift outdoor theaters, where large crowds ate chicken and tomatoes

---

* The death of Gordon was quite a blot, you understand. Public shame and anger, big now in the press, a national trauma—England fails her favorite, and all that. The evening after he received the news of Gordon's death, Gladstone went to the theater, where he was nearly thrown out by an angry crowd. For weeks, enraged demonstrators gathered on Downing Street. After receiving the news in the middle of the night, a tearful Queen Victoria burst into a courtier's cottage, crying, "Too late!" Aside from members of the government and a handful of intellectuals, like the anti-Semitic Wilfred Scawen Blunt— who, when he heard the news, said he rejoiced—a deep and angry sadness consumed the nation. Dozens of biographies of Gordon appeared, each written in florid, hagiographic prose and destined to become school prizes for the good boys and girls of the country. (One of mine originally went to a young man named Plowright, from Putney, for "Good Conduct, Regularity & Diligence.")

The Queen severely rebuked Gladstone, who replied that the only mistake he had made was in sending troops beyond the Egyptian border in the first place.

Despite Gladstone's attempt to distract public attention from the fiasco by drumming up a new Russian threat, the episode was instrumental in finally driving him out of office. But he never relented; Gladstone had all the modern certainties, and he understood the childlike attention span of the public; in 1886, he was once again prime minister. But the Queen, at least, never forgot—and never forgave him.

while the triumphant dispatch of Charlie Gordon was re-enacted by grownups and kids. In one skit, Gordon had straight platinum-blonde hair and wore a red minidress over a pair of black flared trousers. It was all too atmospheric: Dust and clouds of smoke from the grills and the fireworks wrapped around Gordon's legs like dry ice as the Ansar approached. Gordon seemed to shout an insult at the dervishes, who replied with a loud Hurrah! and ran him through with their spears. (The other time I saw Gordon die, only a few blocks away, he was shot.) Sadiq al-Mahdi, Muhammad Ahmad's grandson, was in power, and his Umma party had come up with a good idea for a new national holiday.

Certainly Gordon's end was more memorable than that of his nemesis. On June 22, 1885, five months after his victory at Khartoum, the Mahdi suddenly died after a brief illness. Following a squabble among the various Khalifas,* the Khalifa 'Abdallahi ibn Mohammad emerged victorious and succeeded Muhammad Ahmad. It was a logical outcome. The Khalifa was to the Mahdi what Pancho was to the Cisco Kid: As the Chosen One's military adviser and administrative assistant in life and surrogate in death, 'Abdallahi was a spiritual and temporal sidekick. But he controlled the army, so, despite a steady diet of political intrigue, he managed to rule the Sudan during the Mahdist ascendancy, until his death at the hands of Kitchener's advancing British troops on November 24, 1899.

The Khalifa 'Abdallahi lived in the shadow of the Mahdi. Literally, 'Abdallahi lived next door to the Mahdi's tomb. The Khalifa's house is an extremely modest place—dusty, low and rambling, with something of an Old West feel to it. But when the Khalifa was living there, it was the center of a more or less typical fanatic-Islamic social scene, the sort one imagines in modern Beirut: Slatin Pasha was imprisoned right around the corner, while Austrian missionary J. Ohrwalder, a few nuns and sundry other hostages were stowed nearby.

At one time, perhaps in retaliation, 'Abdallahi's residence was used by the British as a post office, but now the Khalifa's house is a small museum sheltering odds and ends relating to the Mahdist state, including several artifacts that once belonged to Gordon, which are stuck in some glass-topped cases. Owing to my eccentric fascination with Gordon, I went to

---

* The Mahdist state was a theocracy in which, according to P. M. Holt and M. W. Daly in *The History of the Sudan* (1961; reprinted 1979), the Islamic fundamentalists dramatized their faith's origins. The three principal disciples of the Mahdi were the Khalifas; beneath them were the emirs (or amirs), most of whom were tribal leaders. Beneath them were the Ansar, or "helpers." Holt and Daly provide a thorough survey; A. B. Theobald's *The Mahdiya* (1967) is authoritative, comprehensive and highly readable. Theobald, by the way, speculates that typhus killed the Mahdi.

see what had fallen out of the great general's closet after the dervishes plundered the palace, but there wasn't much: a saddle and some other personal items, including a faded yellow jacket he'd once tried to give to the Mahdi. I hung around until it was dark and the floodlights went up on the great dome of the Mahdi's tomb.

I don't know what I expected to find. In my fantasy life—the source of my ongoing disappointment—I thought I would walk into the house of the Khalifa and maybe find the missing portion of Gordon's journals—the bit captured by the Mahdi when Stewart and the others were killed on their way to Cairo—stuck in the bottom of a fruit crate or something. (I had earlier entertained a similar delusion centered on the somewhat disorganized document collection at the Khartoum University library.) The curator at the museum would say, "That? Oh, I don't know. Some old letters, I suppose." I'd ask to borrow them, and he'd say, "Sure. Help yourself."

I admit, it became a bit of an obsession, finding the missing chunk of Gordon's journals. I searched out and bothered a good number of the Mahdi's kind and tolerant descendants, including his grandson—the poet Ishaq M. A. Sharif, not the prime minister—who patiently described his ancestors' cavalier regard for dead men's diaries, and I spent days bumping through the rough streets of the capital, venturing into odd neighborhoods in Omdurman, getting nowhere, of course.

One day I was grousing to a Sudanese acquaintance named Noor M. Noor about the difficulties of tracking down Gordon's lost diaries. Noor, as it turned out, knew an old-timer who knew another old-timer who knew the posthumous son of the Khalifa, born a few months after his father's death. The second old-timer told Noor and me that his father had told him that everything that had belonged to Gordon had been kept safe, since it was assumed all of Gordon's effects would have a ransom value for the British. Armed with a letter of introduction and a bad map, I drove out through Omdurman, out past the prison, down a street dominated by a brand-new, oversize purple stucco mansion to a small cul-de-sac where a vine-wrapped gate led into a small garden.

A gardener was pulling weeds and from somewhere inside the house, I could hear children. I asked for the Khalifa and was directed to a side door leading into the house from a concrete patio slab.

I expected to be met by a housekeeper. But there was nobody in the modest foyer. I had rehearsed the Khalifa's titles and was reluctant to be surprised and commit some capital gaffe. So I stood where I was and said, "Hello!" several times with increasing volume. From a room off to the right, I heard some Arabic, so I stuck my head around the corner to see if I could find someone to act as my host. Instead, there was an old man dressed in a white burnous sitting in an overstuffed chair next to a small cot. His broken leg was in a cast and propped up on a pillow on top of a wicker coffee table. Although the room was cool and dim, he was wearing sunglasses exactly like Roy Orbison's.

He said something in Arabic. Of course I didn't understand, and I quickly apologized in English.

"I told them I would send them the money. You didn't have to come."

He spoke in English, but I still didn't understand. "Excuse me, I'm here to see the son of the Khalifa 'Abdallahi ibn Mohammad. I have this letter." I held it out to him.

He glanced at it quickly. "This is the bill? You must give it to the housekeeper."

This went on for about five minutes. He was convinced I was from the electricity company, and he was adamant about not paying the bill on the spot. "You must give it in to the housekeeper."

I finally made the purpose of my visit clear. He admitted to being the Khalifa, asked me to sit down, summoned a young woman whom he identified as his new wife, and asked her to bring us some lemonade.

"The things you are asking about happened long ago," he said, "and so most of what I know I have learned from friends of my father and others.

"For example, I know that the Mahdi was very angry when he learned that Gordon Pasha had been killed."

I asked if that was because they were such kindred spirits.

"No, not at all. The Mahdi hoped to capture Gordon and exchange him for Arabi Pasha, who was a prisoner in Egypt." Arabi was the leader of the nationalist uprising in Egypt; the notion of the two Muslim nationalists working in tandem was intriguing to me. But not as intriguing as the missing journals.

"They were found in a safe in the boat," the Khalifa told me. "Later, the English sent them back to Cairo or to London."

Cairo or London? But he was certain: "After the war [in 1899], the British sent all of those things away. They are not here."

I was disappointed, of course, and started to take my leave when the old man suddenly said, "Wait! I remember something."

He hesitated for a moment. "Yes. Please tell the man at the British Society to send the rent money to me here, not at my other address."

Will do, I said, and left.

* * *

Nothing, apparently, was left of Gordon's Sudan. In fact, Gordon's Sudan had been substantially revised the day Khartoum fell. While a few isolated garrisons—notably those at Sennar and Kassala—bravely held out for a few more months, it seemed that all the provincial governors were dead or held captive by Muhammad Ahmad. All, that is, except Emin, holed up in Equatoria on the far side of the swamp. Just before Bahr al-Ghazal province fell, Lupton wrote to Emin to tell him about the bad news from Khartoum. Emin first tried to surrender, but it was too much trouble for the local Ansar commander to get to Equatoria. So, fearful of trouble in the north, Emin did the prudent thing: He moved south.

6.

If it be true that "whom the Lord loveth He chasteneth," I am surely of the elect.

—*Emin Pasha, governor of Equatoria, 1887*

THE SUDAN COLLAPSED around a handful of lucky survivors, all of whom had had a very bad year or two. Wilhelm Junker, a Russo-German scientist, for example, narrowly escaped the dervish noose as it closed around Bahr al-Ghazal and, after seeking refuge with Emin in Equatoria, had decided to make for the coast, only to find himself imprisoned in Bunyoro. He had talked himself out of that one and had beat a hasty retreat to Buganda, where Mwanga was busy roasting Christians, another close call. By November 1886, when he arrived on the doorstep of Frederick Holmwood, the acting British consul general at Zanzibar, he was bushed. It had been eleven months since he'd left Equatoria, and he had some stories to tell—especially about Emin, the singular scientist who held the last flickering flame of civilization on a darkening continent.

Holmwood had been waiting months to hear Junker's account. He'd been trying to follow the slow twist of Alexander Mackay and the missionaries in Uganda, and he'd received a copy of a breathless dispatch from Junker to a friend at the Church Missionary Society station at Msalala ("Send forth words of thunder that will open the eyes of all the world!"). Holmwood's enthusiasm for tales of derring-do and madcap martyrdom had already attracted considerable attention at the Foreign Office. For although Holmwood was new to Zanzibar, his transfer was already under consideration.* His predecessor, Sir John Kirk, would never have sent

* Holmwood was a target of Bismarck's, who saw in the diplomat anti-German tendencies. Bismarck's pressure, more than any other factor, eventually led to Holmwood's recall.

telegrams like this one, from Holmwood to Lord Iddesleigh, the Foreign Secretary, dated September 23:

> News from Uganda, 12 July. Junker left for Zanzibar. Terrible persecution broken out, all native Christians being put to death. Missionaries in extreme danger; urgently requests our demanding from King their being allowed to withdraw. Emin at Wadelai holds province, but urgently needs ammunition and stores. Objects, if he can avoid it, deserting the 4,000 loyal Egyptian subjects there. No time to be lost if assistance decided on.

Another lonely, loyal guy stuck up to his neck; Gordon all over again. Why, the government wondered, couldn't these Sudanese hangers-on just pack a bag and go home quietly? Reckoning that what the governor of Equatoria needed was the arrival of a supply caravan, the Foreign Office asked the War Office to draw up the necessary plans, to which Sir Henry Brackenbury replied that he was fresh out of ideas for delivering food and guns, to where? Equatoria: "Our interests there are not so great that we have ever made this a special subject of study." Two days later, Holmwood wrote to Baring in Cairo:

> Both Dr. Junker and Mr. Mackay strongly urge the necessity of the immediate relief of Wadelai, if it is not to be abandoned to the same fate as that which overtook Khartoum. . . . I would, however, suggest . . . that this would be a good opportunity for dealing at the same time with Uganda, the famous conduct of whose King has for many years been prejudicial to the development of the interior.

Holmwood went on to recommend a military expedition of 1,700 men, including porters, which, when joined with Emin's garrisons, would just about be able to deal with the problem in Uganda and put the empire in a choice position for later, more leisurely expansion.

In London, the War Office didn't think very much of Holmwood's plans: "A perilous undertaking . . . madness . . . useless . . . out of the question." Probably Holmwood would have done better to leave the Khartoum parallel out of his dispatch. "If a fierce persecution is going on at Uganda at this moment, it may not be prudent to send any servant of the Crown there," said Salisbury. "We might have to rescue or avenge him." Besides, wasn't this fellow Emin a German? "It is really their business," the Prime Minister said, without relief.

But word got around. Letters started appearing in the press as early as October 1886, and the public response was instantaneous. A dandy deuteragonist had wandered onto the proscenium; at last, there was a chance to write a new last act to the drama that had begun two years earlier in Khartoum. "A second Gordon," said the *Times* on December 15, extolling the "true heroism" of this man, Emin, the "noblest . . . of Gordon's lieutenants." Irresistible momentum for a rescue effort began to build, and finally letters from Emin himself surfaced. At last it became clear that what he wanted was not actually rescue ("I personally am in no hurry to return to Egypt"), but reassurance—wrapped in blankets, surrounded by ammo and packed in smoked ham. "I am still waiting for help," wrote Emin, "and that from England." It was all very exciting, very Gordon—except nobody could quite figure out who the hero was (Emin? Doesn't sound English) or where he was (although most Britons assumed Equatoria must be somewhere south, but not too far) or how to get to him to effect his rescue or his relief or whatever.

Here's a safe bet: Nobody born in the Prussian province of Silesia on March 28, 1840, was named Emin. Certainly Eduard Carl Oscar Theodor Schnitzer wasn't. His father was a merchant who provided a sensible middle-class upbringing for a bright boy who, by 1864, had attended universities in Königsberg and Berlin and was practicing medicine in Albania* and spending a lot of time on his tan: "I have turned so brown," he wrote his sister Melanie, "that I no longer look at all like a European, and the fez and clothing of course add to my foreign appearance." In my favorite photo of Emin, he looks like a French character actor, or a straight man in a Marx Brothers movie, maybe, with his long, sad face and his tiny glasses and his Shriners hat.

After seven years on his own, his life was starting to shape up, in a Byzantine sort of way. "I have passed through a great many trials," he wrote to Melanie in January 1872, "and so I was perhaps entitled to one year's contented and happy life, although I should never have dreamt of finding my life's ideal in a Turkish harem! Do not ask me what I have passed through and what I have done, nor reproach me for my silence. . . .

---

* Schnitzer was actually not qualified to practice medicine in his homeland; though he had received his M.D. from the University of Berlin, the Minister of Education decided he had delayed too long in applying for the official qualifying exam, and refused his petition to sit for it.

Much of the detail in this episode appears in *Emin Pasha: His Life and Work Compiled from His Journals, Letters, Scientific Notes and from Official Documents* . . . , by George Schweitzer (two volumes; 1898; reprinted 1969), with a disputatious introduction by Dr. R. W. Felkin, who later will be a brief acquaintance of ours, as he was of Emin's.

The most thorough work on the subject of this episode, though, is Iain R. Smith's *The Emin Pasha Relief Expedition, 1886–1890* (1972), a carefully wrought, precise account.

I am here* with Ismail Hakki Pasha and his family, and in spite of all we have passed through together we are quite well. . . . All my wants are provided for, and good fortune still attends me; I have gained a reputation as a doctor; I have acquired Turkish and Arabic to a degree of proficiency seldom attained by any European; and I have adopted the habits and customs of the country to such an extent that no one would suspect an honest German behind the Turkish name which disguises me (do not be afraid, it is only a name—I have not turned Mohammedan)."†

A month later, Melanie received a more illuminating report: "It is best to [live] in genuine Turkish fashion, for the present and future only! For nearly four months . . . I have had ample time for reflection, having nothing to employ me beyond a daily visit to the harem. Madame Ismail is a native of Transylvania, who speaks German, French and Italian, and is very kind and amiable. We are thus on good terms. She is probably between twenty-nine and thirty."

In August 1875, Emin showed up at his parents' house in Neisse with an entourage of eleven—Hakki Pasha's grieving widow, alas, her four children and a half-dozen Circassian slave girls. Six weeks or so later, on September 18, Emin decided to visit some old college chums in Breslau.

His family didn't hear from him again for almost fifteen years.‡

Emin drifted through Italy and the Levant, then to Cairo, then to Suez, where he joined a caravan of Syrian traders embarking for the Sudan. By early December 1875, he was in Khartoum, living in a warehouse, making a spectacle of himself among the tiny foreign community. As Carl Giegler Pasha, a European telegraph inspector, wrote, ". . . he introduced

---

* Emin gave his address as "Monsieur le Docteur Hairoullah Effendi . . . à Trebizonde." For several years previous, he had been a government medical officer at Antivari, an Albanian port. Although now a commonplace honorific, at the time, "effendi" was a title that carried official status. In terms of Turkish precedence, it was a rank inferior to that of bey and pasha.

† In a letter to his mother, written at about the same time, Emin tries to explain his new moniker: "Do not fear, I have not turned Mohammedan; but as the whole country [Albania] is Turkish, and there are only a few Christians here, who are all of a very low degree, I have adopted a Turkish name in order to avoid being continually pestered with all sorts of questions as to my origin, etc."
It seems likely that Schnitzer went by Hairoullah for some time. According to Schweitzer, he only adopted Emin when he replaced a medical officer in Equatoria by the same name. Whether this is true or not, I've chosen to call him Emin throughout.

‡ It took another six weeks for Mr. and Mrs. Schnitzer to get Emin's household out of their parlor.

himself to me, and to Friedrich Rosset [the German vice-consul] as a Turk who had been brought up and educated in Germany. He persisted in keeping up this fiction all through, notwithstanding the fact that he soon afterward presented his passport to Rosset, in which he was described as 'Dr. Schnitzer, a German' . . . much curiosity was aroused concerning the strange new-comer. As he was entirely without means, Rosset and I took upon ourselves to provide for his wants."

Emin was the talk of the town. He lunched with Rosset, dined with Giegler, played piano at the home of Hansal, the Austrian consul, and beat everyone in chess. ("He was," Giegler noted, "the merriest and maddest of the party.") When his new friends finally persuaded him to get a job, he opened a medical practice and was soon self-sufficient.

It didn't take Gordon, then governor of the Equatoria province, long to get wind of the presence in Khartoum of some new talent, and in May 1876, Emin was summoned to Lado, where Gordon offered him the post of chief medical officer.*

Two years later, he was governor. Gordon, having put Equatoria on a paying basis, had suddenly resigned, then just as quickly had accepted the post of governor-general of the entire Sudan. Under Gordon, Emin had been entrusted with tricky diplomatic missions—including one to Mutesa in Buganda, where a contingent of Egyptian soldiers had been imprisoned. His success had impressed Gordon, who, when he became governor-general, made Emin a bey and gave him his old province to govern.

Much of Equatoria is a swampy, disease-filled netherworld inhabited by undiscovered Knicks—Dinkas, Nuers, Shilluks and other long-legged Nilotic tribes, who worship their cattle and live hovering above water in huts built on stilts. But, like Gordon, Emin found pleasure in Equatoria. He was a remarkable chap, perhaps the smartest man to ever seek refuge in the botanical excesses of Africa. He spoke languages by the dozen; he was an accomplished naturalist and corresponded with prominent museums in Europe, often donating invaluable specimens; and he was a fellow of several learned societies. In the middle of a very untidy part of the planet, Emin was a paragon of neatness. His stations were clean and orderly places, much admired by travelers, like Junker, and missionaries,

---

* Gordon thought Emin was weird, and wondered why he "pretends to me that he is an Arab by birth and religion." Nevertheless, with all other Europeans in the Sudan otherwise employed, he quickly put Emin to work and later came to relish the exploits of his "doctor," calling him at one point "my Mussulman priest."

like R. W. Felkin, who stayed with Emin at Lado on his way to Buganda (where, against Emin's advice, he was determined to establish a mission). According to Felkin—who later became instrumental in first presenting the case for the relief of Emin—the German seemed genuinely concerned about his province and its inhabitants; Emin expanded Gordon's administrative network, making his own improvements along the way, and, to his visitors at least, it seemed, could do everything except govern effectively. He was infuriatingly indecisive, and often subjected his orders to the chaotic abuses of democratic debate; his subordinates—as well as his superiors—often mistook his ambivalence for deviousness, and thus his deviousness was often mistaken for treachery. Among Emin's many peculiar characteristics, the one for which he was most noted was his myopia. Even with his thick spectacles, he was nearly blind; he cheerfully wandered his damp domain squinting into the middle distance.

As the situation in the north grew more perilous, however, Emin grew more cautious. At one point, he received a summons to travel north to submit to the newly triumphant Mahdi; he was packing his bags to go and was prevented only by the threat of mutiny from his northern garrisons— who mutinied anyway when he changed his mind and ordered the withdrawal of the garrisons from the northern portion of the province in order to relocate his capital from Lado to Wadelai, some thirty-five miles north of Lake Albert, on the Ancholi frontier. The troops—convinced he was going to sell them into slavery—turned him down and decided to stay where they were. A separate, ad hoc administrative district was thereby established, permanently dividing the province (and consequently reducing the effectiveness of the loyal garrisons in the south).

By July 10, 1885, Emin was entrenched in Wadelai—a much more healthful neck of the woods—where he was joined by refugee Europeans on the lam from the dervishes. In the south, Bunyoro and Buganda were at each other's throats again, and escape in any direction seemed quite out of the question. Junker had already left for the coast (journeying from Lado to Zanzibar in January 1885), but together with Vita Hassan, a Greek pharmacist and provincial official, and Gaetano Casati, an Italian wanderer, Emin made a small corner of Equatoria safe for himself. Isolated and forgotten, Emin wrote letters to anyone he thought might be able to receive them, and waited for something to happen.

In England, the chance to regain a little lost honor drove everyone (except, that is, the members of Salisbury's government) to distraction, and even on the Continent, there was a sense that this was the perfect nineteenth-century adventure. There was a public consensus that Emin must be helped. In meetings, in churches and in the press, the name of Gordon was invoked countless times, with an easily anticipated effect: A great swell of European passion led to the formation of an Emin Pasha relief committee. Under the guidance of Sir William Mackinnon, a pious but adventurous merchant who, in addition to "saving" Emin, was also interested in forming the sort of enterprise that later became the IBEA, the committee raised some £20,000, half from the dizzy government of Egypt. Fortnum & Mason donated boxfuls of gourmet treats to the proposed effort, and other commercial concerns, eager to garner publicity, followed suit with guns and ammo, clothing and the like. Leaders were discussed: The English nominated Henry Morton Stanley—"Bula Matari" (the Rock Breaker) to his friends—the man who had presumed to meet David Livingstone.

Another, better-qualified candidate had been put forward by the Scots—Joseph Thomson. To those with an understanding of the difficulties of African exploration, Thomson was a solid, thoughtful choice, but the public expectation was for a more militant sort of man; the mood of the country was still deeply affected by the softness of the government in dealing with the Gordon tragedy. Thomson, a gentle man who had traveled through various parts of Africa in peace, making friends as he went, was a victim of his own success.

Stanley, on the other hand, was the Rambo of explorers, with a reputation better suited to prevailing sentiment. His expeditions—small armies, really—cut through Africa with mean efficiency, blasting away at troublesome native settlements, flogging porters to death, leaving his expeditions' sick and lame to die on the trail and the deserters hanging in the trees.

In the movies, Spencer Tracy played Stanley, but it was all wrong. Stanley was an insecure egomaniac, a bastard born John Rowlands in 1841 in Wales and dumped by his mother's family on the doorstep of the local workhouse, a grim Dickensian fantasyland. He put up with it for nine years, until, at age fifteen, he finally beat up the man in charge and took off for America, sailing as a deckhand on a packet boat bound for New Orleans. There he met a kindly cotton merchant named Henry Morton Stanley, a name that had a certain charm for the boy. The man promised to take Stanley "for my son," and for the next few years, Stanley happily wandered the American South learning his new father's business.

In 1860, the elder Stanley died, and his namesake enlisted in the Confederate army. He fought at Shiloh, was wounded and taken prisoner. He escaped, then deserted and joined the Union army, caught dysentery and was discharged. He returned to the sea, working for a time as a merchant sailor, then joined the Union navy and deserted again. It was clear by now that Stanley was cut out to be a journalist.

Eventually he ended up at James Gordon Bennett's *New York Herald,* where he covered Indian wars and gold rushes, building a grand reputation as a colorful and ambitious correspondent. When the British declared war on Abyssinia in 1867,* Stanley followed the troops into battle and retired ahead of them, filing scoops through a bribed telegraph operator in Egypt. The following year, as a reward, Bennett sent Stanley on a round-the-world string of assignments that ended with the order "Go after Livingstone." He also gave him a huge expense account.

Stanley hated Africa—and showed it—but he found his man. You know the story: Dr. Livingstone, I presume; the famous missionary dies; nobody believes Stanley, but it turns out to be true, and presto! Stanley is the definitive African explorer, crossing the continent and discovering things, harvesting the condemnation of Parliament and aboriginal-protection organizations for his penchant toward slaughter, creating King Leopold's amusingly named Congo Free State, writing bestsellers and talking to church groups and college kids, which is what he was doing when he got word that he was to save Emin.

If you look at a map of Africa, it makes pretty good sense that if you want to retrieve a man living on the headwaters of the Nile, you start from someplace around Zanzibar and head inland. That was the route suggested by Thomson and others, and it was the route everyone assumed Stanley would take. But Stanley had a better idea. As he was contractually bound to King Leopold II of Belgium, and as Leopold badly wanted to prove his right to annex Equatoria to his new colony, Stanley figured the best way to reach Emin was to sail to Zanzibar, pick up some porters, then sail around the Cape to the mouth of the Congo and follow it through Leopold's preserve† to the Aruwimi River, up the Aruwimi to Yambuya, then through the jungle to Lake Albert, up the lake to Wadelai, no

---

* The loony Emperor Theodore had imprisoned a batch of resident Europeans, including the British consul, after he fancied he'd been insulted by Queen Victoria. Sir Robert Napier led a huge army into Ethiopia, where, at the battle of Magdala, he killed Theodore and restored order. Alan Moorehead's *The Blue Nile* (1962) recounts the story vividly; Stanley's account is *Coomassie and Magdala* (1874).

† Although it was recognized by the Berlin Conference in 1885, the Congo Free State was not yet a Belgian colony. Rather, it was the private estate of King Leopold II, who, despite his ruthlessly exploitative policies, couldn't turn the property into a profitable venture. In 1908, the Belgian government assumed colonial jurisdiction, and the Congo Free State subsequently became known as the Belgian Congo. Shortly after independence in 1960, the name of the country was changed to Zaïre.

problem, then out to the east coast and to Zanzibar. One of the principal reasons Stanley gave for his decision was that the Zanzibaris would be less inclined to desert the column if they were headed toward home anyway.

Such was the strength of Stanley's reputation and will that virtually no one questioned this extraordinary strategy, even after it was revealed that, for the provision of additional porters for his column, Stanley would have to rely on the good offices of one of the most notorious slavers in all Africa, one Hamed bin Mohammed el-Marjebi, better known by his Land of Oz nickname, Tippoo Tib.*

As if to increase the drama inherent in his expedition, Stanley convinced himself that Emin was an "ideal governor," who, with his faithful soldiers, was bravely holding out against the fanatic hordes of the Mahdi. Time, he decided, was of the essence in the relief of the pasha, and he made his preparations on the run, quickly assembling a staff of nine Europeans from the hundreds of applications the committee received.† After stops in Cairo and Zanzibar, Stanley arrived at Banana, a village at the mouth of the Congo, on March 18, 1887, with nearly 700 Zanzibaris and Tippoo Tib. He was met there by thirty-five of Tippoo Tib's wives and five dozen camp followers, and together they all set off up the Congo to Equatoria. It was, cabled Holmwood from Zanzibar, "in every way the most perfectly organised expedition that has hitherto entered tropical Africa."

At first, everything went swimmingly. Using river steamers, the column reached the cataracts at Matadi, more than 100 miles inland, by March 21. From there, the column was to march overland the nearly 200 miles to the capital, Léopoldville (now Kinshasa). With the addition of porters recruited locally, the expedition now numbered nearly 1,000 men, divided into various companies, each with its commanding European officer. It was all very military, and on paper it seemed that Holmwood might have been right about its perfect organization. In practice, however, things soon

---

* Say it out loud, a truly musical moniker. The son of a Muscat trader, Tippoo Tib had become the most powerful Arab in central Africa, and had worked with Stanley before. He lived in a large house next to the English Club in Zanzibar Town. After slavers had ransacked the provincial capital at Stanley Falls, he was offered the governorship there with a salary of £360 per annum, a European assistant and license to "be at full liberty to carry on his private trade in any direction and to send his caravans to and from any place he may desire." Although he thought the salary was a little low, he accepted. The appointment was part of the comprehensive agreement worked out between Stanley, functioning, in respect of the appointment, as Leopold's representative, and Tippoo.

† Stanley's expedition was the space shuttle of its time. Everyone wanted to go along, and some were willing to pay as much as £1,000 for the privilege.

became confusing. The column was scattered all over the countryside, with essential loads of food and shelter often in the wrong places. The European officers all took sick, and Stanley himself came down with dysentery. Frustrated at the chaotic conditions, Stanley took to berating his officers publicly, accusing them of nonsensical conspiracies and subjecting them to humiliations—once ordering the African porters to take no orders from any officer other than himself and to tie the Europeans up should they give the porters trouble—that made it impossible for them to command their men. It was the rainy season, and the route was frequently blocked by swollen streams that, despite the presence of a collapsible steel boat, had to be swum, thus causing the loss of valuable loads. The area had been reduced by famine, and the column was often unable to supply itself with enough food. Men began to die and desert, and the morale of the officers plummeted.

Arriving at Léopoldville on April 21, Stanley determined that if the expedition were to approach the schedule he'd set (which called for a rendezvous with Emin in mid-June), he'd have to change his plans. After commandeering several boats belonging to local missions, Stanley found that, with his collapsible, the *Advance*, he could muster a fleet of only eight vessels and barges—not enough for all the loads to travel by river the 1,000 miles to the next staging area, at Yambuya on the Aruwimi. So he decided to divide the expedition into two main groups—an advance party and a rear column. The first group, with most of the loads promised to Emin, would move quickly toward Equatoria, while the second would travel more slowly, carrying the bulk of the expedition's stores. In exchange for additional porters, Stanley had agreed to supply Tippoo Tib with ammunition—a precious commodity. But those loads and others would be left behind in Léopoldville and at another settlement, Bolobo, some 180 miles upriver from the capital. The officers and men remaining were to make their way slowly to Yambuya, where Stanley would leave a rear column of 271 men while he took the rest with him through the forest to Lake Albert. It was going to be a very slow go.

Stanley's main column arrived in Yambuya on June 15. Tippoo Tib had already gone to Stanley Falls with one of Stanley's officers, where he was attempting to enlist porters but finding the task impossible without the payment of the ammunition promised by Stanley. The tribes in the vicinity of Yambuya were extremely hostile—as they had been when Stanley had last visited the area in 1883—and food and supplies were scarce.

Stanley lingered in Yambuya for nine days. On June 24, he issued some vague instructions to Major Edmund Barttelot, his first officer (with whom he had had frequent, violent arguments), suggesting that Barttelot should try to figure a way to get the rear column on the march after the Léopoldville and Bolobo contingents arrived, but that if he couldn't, he should wait until Stanley returned from his meeting with Emin. His last words to Barttelot were, "I shall find you here in November when I return," suggesting that Stanley doubted that Tippoo Tib would be able to deliver the necessary porters to the rear column. (Stanley's failure to secure the rear column's position was later roundly criticized. Indeed, it was a typical Stanley maneuver; he never consulted with his officers on important tactical matters, preferring instead to issue orders, however vague, and leave his subordinates to sort out the details. In this case, Stanley was clearly preoccupied with his imagined deadline for reaching Emin, and the fate of the rear column seemed to be too complicated to fully consider. So he simply left them behind, knowing that if something went wrong, he could always put the blame on Barttelot or someone else.)

The area between Yambuya and the equatorial lakes is occupied by the Ituri rain forest, an impenetrable, dark and dangerously primeval world that covers some 50,000 square miles. It is an unimaginably humid, fetid hell filled with disease, where thick vegetation blocks the sun, and life rots in a dark and steamy bath. No European had ever traversed the forest before, but through Arab raiders it was known to be inhabited by very few natives; those that were there had been thoroughly terrorized by slavers who had made brief forays into the jungle, then quickly withdrawn, leaving a frightened and decimated population in a state of murderous terror at the sight of any intruders.

All expeditions in Africa depended for their success on their ability to trade with natives for food and other essentials. Stanley's party encountered only destroyed villages, where no food was to be found. The rain was torrential. Booby traps laid across the paths crippled the porters, while invisible armies of Pygmies showered the column with poisoned arrows. Sick and wounded men—including some Europeans—were left in the careless custody of Arab caravans or simply abandoned in the forest to die. Soon Stanley was in peak form, killing natives for their canoes, torching villages if the inhabitants seemed reluctant to part with what little food they had, making maximum use of his Maxim gun, hanging and flogging porters who disobeyed orders, and blaming everyone else for the mess he'd got himself into.

Stanley was not entirely without compassion, however. At one point in his narrative, *In Darkest Africa,** he surveys what remains of his column: "Over fifty were yet in fair condition; 150 were skeletons covered with ashy grey skins, jaded and worn out, with every sign of wretchedness printed deep in their eyes, in their bodies and movements. These could hardly do more than creep on and moan, and shed tears and sigh." How, he wondered, would they carry their sixty-pound loads? Still, it was a learning experience: "Deep, deep down to undiscovered depths our life in the forest had enabled me to penetrate human nature with all its endurance and virtues."

On December 13, 1887, the 169 survivors of Stanley's march from Yambuya arrived at Lake Albert. More than 200 men had been murdered, left for dead or deserted on the trail. Stanley had sent word to Emin that he would arrive at the lake in August. He was only four months late, yet Emin wasn't there to be rescued, and Stanley was put out. "A governor of a province," he wrote, "with two steamers, life-boats, and canoes and thousands of people we had imagined would be known everywhere on such a small lake as the Albert, which required only two days' steaming from end to end. He could not, or he would not, leave Wadelai." It wasn't just the rudeness of the governor that irked Stanley; he was extremely worried by persistent rumors that Emin had contrived to rescue himself. If that had happened, it could be somewhat embarrassing.

Stanley's preoccupation with reaching Emin vanished. Now it was the Emin Pasha relief expedition that was badly in need of relief. Since Emin hadn't shown up to provide it, Stanley hoped that Barttelot, left at Yambuya with the rear column, would. The advance party retreated a small distance from the lake to a village called Ibwiri, where they made a permanent camp, named Fort Bodo by Stanley. With the advance party taken care of, Stanley began considering what he should do next.

The expedition was spread across the map. More than a hundred men were being abused by Arab slavers in their camps; others were in small parties strung out along the expedition's route. A large body of men, the rear column, was presumably en route to Lake Albert from Yambuya, although how Stanley had expected Barttelot—whom he reviled and had effectively abandoned—to make a successful march to Lake Albert when Stanley had blown the job so badly, is a testament to his frightened optimism. After taking a month to think it over, he fell ill (gallstones); the European officers of the advance party took the opportunity to put in a crop of corn and beans in the fields surrounding Fort Bodo.

---

* Written in fifty days in Cairo on the way home; published in two volumes in 1890. The narrative is a careful denial of incompetence and cruelty, filled with omissions and lies and libel of the dead. A book that mirrors a career.

By April 2, Stanley was well enough to again visit Lake Albert, this time with happier results: Emin had heard of their previous visit and had left a letter informing Stanley that he should stay where he was and send word to him. Emin would then steam to meet him. Stanley was overjoyed; he might still be able to rescue Emin, provided, of course, Emin could first rescue him.

Stanley made a camp at the southern end of the lake and dispatched one of the European officers, A. J. Mounteney-Jephson, to Emin's nearest outpost, at Mswa on the eastern side of the lake, where the young Englishman was politely received by the equatorial garrison. For Jephson, it was somewhat awkward: "I felt awfully dirty in my old worn out suit of Tweed beside the smart Nubian officer and even beside the servants who were all dressed in suits of fresh white cotton cloth which Emin Pasha's people weave." Five days later, Emin arrived, and, after assembling a cargo of grain and livestock, Jephson, Emin and the Europeans in Emin's care—Casati and Vita Hassan—set off for the rendezvous with Stanley.

"At eight o'clock [April 29, 1888]," wrote Stanley, "amid great rejoicing, and after repeated salutes from rifles, Emin Pasha himself walked into camp, accompanied by Captain Casati and Mr. Jephson, and one of the Pasha's officers."

It was a golden opportunity for Stanley to re-create his dramatic meeting with Livingstone, but, alas, one can only presume so much. " 'Ah,' " he says he said, instead, " 'you are Emin Pasha. Do not mention thanks, but come in and sit down. . . .'

"At the door of the tent we sat, and a wax candle threw light upon the scene. I expected to see a tall, thin military-looking figure, in faded Egyptian uniform, but instead of it I saw a small spare figure in a well-kept fez and a clean suit of snowy cotton drilling, well-ironed and of perfect fit. . . . There was not a trace of ill-health or anxiety; it rather indicated good condition of body and peace of mind."

Stanley uncorked three small bottles of champagne and drank to his own good fortune. He had made it this far; now all that was left was to persuade Emin to be rescued.

The next day, Stanley began pressing Emin to return with him to the coast. But alas, "the Pasha's manner is ominous," Stanley wrote. "When I propose a return to the sea for him, he has the habit of tapping his knee, and smiling in a kind of 'We shall see' manner." Emin, in fact, had never intended to evacuate his post. Even the official letter from the khedive, presented to Emin by Stanley, had said, "You are absolutely free either to withdraw to Cairo, or to stay where you are with the officers and men."

The garrisons were united in their opposition to evacuation. For the enlisted men, Equatoria was home; the bulk of Emin's soldiers were local recruits. As for the officers, they had served in the province for much of their careers; they had taken wives and were determined to stay with their families. The Egyptian clerks, who ran the province's bureaucracy, were roundly despised by everyone, but they too had no wish to leave Equatoria. "If they will not go," wrote Emin in his journal, "I presumably shall stay as well . . . so far as I can see at present, all the gentlemen of the expedition are particularly bent on getting me to withdraw to Egypt or to England, and it sounded almost comical to hear Stanley say, 'If Major Barttelot hears you are not coming, he will, I fear, shoot himself. He is a very impetuous man.' "

The two men talked at each other for days—or, rather, Stanley talked. Emin simply repeated that he would first determine what his followers desired, then would act to implement their wishes. Stanley didn't hear him. Emin must return, he maintained. When Emin continued to insist on consulting his garrisons, Stanley made other suggestions. Emin could establish his province elsewhere—at Lake Victoria, perhaps, under the flag of the IBEA. Or he could remain the governor of Equatoria, but as part of King Leopold's Congo Free State.

Stanley's position wasn't particularly strong. After all, he owed his survival to Emin's assistance, and the relief he was to have brought Emin had been left in Yambuya or scattered along the expedition's route. Nevertheless, the argument went on for weeks, with Stanley's temper growing increasingly strained. Emin would not be moved.

It had been almost a year since Stanley had left Barttelot in Yambuya; he had promised to return the previous November, and he was eager to learn of the fate of the other half of his expedition. Besides, the rear column had all the good Fortnum & Mason groceries, along with the bulk of the supplies and matériel promised to Emin for his relief. Finally, on May 24, Stanley set off for Yambuya, leaving Emin and Jephson to poll the troops and thereby come to a decision about whether or not to evacuate.

It wasn't any easier going than it had been coming. Emin had given Stanley some Madi carriers to help him back to Fort Bodo, but a few hours of Stanley was enough for them and they deserted en masse; Stanley had to wait until Emin could retrieve them for him.* The next day, Stanley "discovered" the Ruwenzori mountains—Ptolemy's "Mountains of the

* Since the column would need additional porters to complete the passage out to the east coast, Stanley suggested that while he was away, Emin might "take advantage of the period of our absence to make some slight chains for a set of ten carriers with neck rings."

Moon"—just as Jephson, with Thomas Parke, the expedition's doctor, had discovered them earlier and notified Stanley of their existence.*

On June 16, Stanley finally departed from Fort Bodo, leaving fifty-nine men behind to wait for Jephson and Emin, who were to assist in relocating them to a station closer to Lake Albert. The march through the jungle was predictable: death, desertion, poisoned arrows, floggings. Already Stanley was apportioning blame for the disaster he felt must surely await him: It was Tippoo Tib's fault for not supplying free porters, or it was Barttelot's fault for not moving the column by making repeated marches with the small number of carriers he had. Or maybe it was the fault of one of the other European officers left behind. When he finally got to within ninety miles of Yambuya, he had still heard not even a rumor; it was going to be bad, he knew. Somebody was going to pay. Finally, on August 17, 1888, Stanley saw the expedition's Egyptian flag fluttering from a post on the riverbank.

"About 200 yards from the village we stopped paddling," he wrote, "and as I saw a great number of strangers on the shore, I asked, 'Whose men are you?' 'We are Stanley's men,' was the answer delivered in mainland Swahili. But assured by this, and still more so as we recognized a European near the gate, we paddled ashore. The European on a nearer view turned out to be Mr. William Bonny, who had been engaged as doctor's assistant to the Expedition. Pressing his hand, I said, 'Well, Bonny, how are you? Where is the Major? Sick, I suppose?' 'The Major is dead, sir.' "

The camp was a gloomy wreck. Unburied bodies, scattered loads, sick and dying porters. Bonny, the sole European survivor, told Stanley of the rear column's nightmare year at Yambuya, about the general demoralization as the column realized they were stranded, and how within nine months, a third of the men were either dead or seriously ill. There was no food in the vicinity of Yambuya, and the natives had become increasingly hostile. Barttelot, despite his military background, was an inexperienced leader; he did not care for the Zanzibaris, and he had been frequently sick with fevers that led to paranoia. He had been shot after a quarrel with a porter. The longer Bonny talked, the better the story got. It involved

---

* Stanley held to his claim of discovery, ignoring Jephson's later protests and Parke's calm denials. Since the Europeans had signed contracts forbidding their writings to appear in print until well after Stanley's account had been published, and since Stanley's book was by far the most widely read, the discovery of the Ruwenzori has been given to Stanley. After receiving a letter from Stanley notifying Emin of his discovery, the governor replied: "Allow me to be the first to congratulate you on your most splendid discovery of a snow-clad mountain. It is wonderful to think how, wherever you go, you distance your predecessors by your discoveries."

murderous intrigues, gunfights, cannibalism and cowardice. Bonny, severely addicted to opium, had been the low man on the totem pole at Yambuya, and now he was getting back.

The fate of the rear column is well documented.* The cause of the disaster is simple: The rear column didn't leave Yambuya because it was impossible to do so. Stanley had not been able to supply river transportation for the expedition, and he had not been able to provide Tippoo Tib with the ammunition he needed to be able to pay for the porters Stanley wanted him to recruit. The officers at Yambuya, in great peril, simply followed the orders Stanley had given: If they could not leave, they were to wait. The rear column became an overlooked detail.

Incapable of taking responsibility, Stanley panicked. He wrote letters to everyone, sprinkling blame around like fairy dust. To a dead officer, he writes a letter accusing him of desertion. In his book, he viciously flogs the officers of the rear column in purple passages punctuated with exclamation marks, as if he cannot believe such stupidity. He rewrites the history of the expedition to exculpate himself; his slander of his subordinates is deeply offensive.

But what seems to have made Stanley angriest was that the officers of the rear column, having heard repeated rumors of Stanley's death, had dispatched his personal wardrobe, a case of Madeira and the Fortnum & Mason goods down to the coast in order to reduce the number of loads. He is, he writes, reduced "to absolute nakedness. I am so poor as to be compelled to beg a pair of pants from Mr. Bonny."

During Stanley's absence, Equatoria disintegrated. The garrison officers, always on the brink of mutiny, had been expecting that Stanley's column would deliver precisely what had been promised—supplies and ammunition to enable Emin to continue as governor of the province. The sorry spectacle of Stanley's ragged band, itself so desperately in need of help, set off a chain reaction that resulted in a general insurrection. Rumors of treachery spread north from the lake, and the situation grew dangerous. Far from believing that the garrisons had been recalled by the letter

* Most of the European officers of the expedition published memoirs. For contemporary accounts, see W. G. Barttelot (editor), *The Life of Edmund Musgrave Barttelot, from his letters and diaries* (1890); J. S. Jameson, *The Story of the Rear Column* (1890); J. Rose Troup, *With Stanley's Rear Column* (1890); Herbert Ward, *My Life with Stanley's Rear Guard* (1891); D. Middleton (editor), *The Diary of A. J. Mounteney-Jephson* (1969); T. H. Parke, *My Personal Experiences in Equatorial Africa* (1891). Tony Gould's excellent *In Limbo: The Story of Stanley's Rear Column* (1979) is among the more recent contributions about the disaster at Yambuya.

brought by Stanley, the Egyptian and northern Sudanese officers and clerks assumed that Stanley and Emin were in collusion to betray the khedive, that the letter was a blatant forgery and that Stanley's real aim was to sell them to Christians or into slavery.

Jephson was stunned. Emin's troops hadn't been paid for more than eight years, and it had been more than five years since the last steamer from Khartoum had appeared in Equatoria. Yet their officers, many of whom had been sent here as punishment, refused to believe the khedive wished them to leave the province. Although the rank and file seemed genuinely devoted to Emin and appeared to distance themselves from the actions of their superiors, they, too, had no wish to relocate. At station after station, Jephson and Emin found a near unanimous resolve among the officers and clerks to stay where they were. At Dufile, the situation was highly volatile; the governor's party was imprisoned by rebels. The group was then freed and sent south only after the intercession of Selim Bey—an officer respected by both sides but unswerving in his loyalty to both Emin and the khedive. But an invasion of Mahdist forces instilled in Emin's rebellious troops a wonderful sense of obedience; Khartoum had become alarmed by the presence of a European expedition in the south. (The invasion also had another benefit: It offered proof to the rebels that Khartoum really had fallen and that they could expect no help from the north.)

Even after suffering these indignities, Emin was still unwilling to leave (although he was entertaining the notion of establishing an IBEA outpost near Lake Victoria). After serving so long in Africa, Emin, a naturalist first and a governor second, had little taste for the anonymity and meaninglessness he saw awaiting him in Europe, and, like Gordon at Khartoum, he declared he would rather stay than be the sole object of a rescue. "I protest against the fact that the expedition has come to 'rescue' me," Emin wrote. "In all my letters to Europe I only asked for help for my people and never mentioned myself personally."

However, by January 16, 1889, Stanley and the rear-column survivors had struggled back through the Ituri and arrived at Lake Albert; he was in no mood for Emin's uncertainties. He resolved to rescue the pasha by force, if necessary, and sent a letter ahead to Jephson ordering him to make clear to Emin "the bitter end and fate of those misguided and obstinate people who decline assistance when tendered to them."

On February 17, Emin met with Stanley and Jephson at Stanley's camp. Emin had with him a contingent of sixty-five soldiers and officials, including Selim Bey. A huge man, Selim Bey was revered by his comrades, ferociously loyal to Egypt and Emin, and the only officer capable of ensuring the cooperation of the others. Selim had brought word that other soldiers, still in Wadelai, were willing to follow Stanley out to the coast. On February 26, Selim Bey set off for Wadelai with an assurance from Stanley that those who wished to evacuate the province could come with him. Emin, by this time, was simply acquiescing to events as they unfolded, and events were more and more controlled by Stanley.

Soon more than 1,000 people had gathered near the southwestern edge of Lake Albert, and Stanley set April 10 as a firm departure date. Selim Bey wrote from Wadelai explaining that he was encountering difficulty in completing his part of the evacuation and asked for more time, which Stanley, on the edge of paranoia, refused.*

On April 10, Stanley's column started for the coast. Of his original expedition, less than one-quarter of the men were still around. Instead, there were 1,500 camp followers and others (including only 126 of Emin's men); in addition, Stanley's slave raids had rounded up 500 men from local villages who were forced to act as porters. This policy occasioned vast desertions, and further recruits were impressed along the way. Stanley's column proceeded to the east coast as a huge slave caravan, leaving behind burned villages and deserting slaves. Stanley's treatment of Emin was rude and insensitive, at best, yet when Stanley and the other officers fell ill a month into the march, it was left to Emin and Vita Hassan to nurse them back to health. And when Selim Bey—who had assembled some 200 officers, soldiers and clerks—once again asked Stanley to wait, since traveling through the countryside made hostile by Stanley's raids was impossible, Stanley again refused. So Selim Bey, pursued by rebels now in possession of Wadelai, could do little more than flee a short distance to the west, where, with his soldiers and camp followers, he planted the Egyptian flag and waited for relief. In the end, Selim was joined by hundreds of other Sudanese askaris—along with thousands of their followers—as Equatoria collapsed.

Finally Emin had had enough and told Stanley he wished to proceed on his own. Stanley responded by holding Emin prisoner to prevent him from leaving Stanley's command. By December 4, 1889, the column finally reached Bagamoyo on the coast; less than half of those who had set out from Lake Albert were still accounted for. Only a fraction of those who had left from Banana were still on hand.

Emin was surprised at the reception that awaited him in Bagamoyo. In

* Stanley was convinced that Selim Bey was hatching a plot to steal the expedition's weapons, and resolved to abandon him. There is no evidence of such a plot, however, and most other contemporaries—including not only Emin and others on the scene, but also Lugard—claim Selim Bey was loyally trying to follow orders and bring his men to the departure point, where Stanley had promised to meet them and escort them away.

the harbor, ships' cannons boomed salutes; telegrams were read from the Queen and from the Kaiser. A lavish banquet was put together by the representatives of the English and German East Africa companies.

At the banquet, held in one of the few two-story buildings in East Africa, Emin was dazzled and apparently in a good humor (the Kaiser's telegram had been especially cheering). He drank champagne, talked with guests, expressed his thanks for their good wishes and wandered into another room, where he mistook a large window for a door and fell onto the street below, cracking open his skull.

Two days later, Stanley left for Cairo to write his book. He never saw Emin again.*

Frederick Lugard, the IBEA's Uganda adventurer, considered Selim Bey's Sudanese askaris "the best material for soldiery in Africa."† They had served under both Gordon and Emin, and if their record of loyalty was a bit irregular, so were the conditions of their service. Selim Bey, however, was ill inclined to serve under another flag, and it was only after protracted negotiations that Lugard finally persuaded Selim to accept a command. Lugard, who had been highly critical of Stanley's treatment of Selim, was delighted:

> It was a sight to touch a man's heart to see this noble remnant, who were fanatical in their loyalty to their flag and their Khedive, scarred and wounded, many prematurely grey, clad in skins and deserted, here in the heart of Africa, and I do thank God . . . that it has fallen to my lot to come to their relief as well as that I have been able to secure so fine a body of men for the Company's service.

The transfer of command was accomplished to the accompaniment of the blare from dented bugles. "It was impossible not to feel a thrill of admiration," Lugard wrote, "for these deserted soldiers, as they carried past flag after flag, torn and riddled in many fierce engagements with the

* Emin's fall wasn't fatal. After spending several months in the hospital, Emin entered the German service, and on April 26, 1890, he left the coast to lead an expedition back to the equatorial lakes. Once on the trail, he conceived the fantastic idea of pushing on through the Congo to the Cameroons. Disregarding messages ordering his recall, he left most of his expedition behind and the following spring finally reached an Arab camp on the Congo River. On April 23, 1891, he was murdered by slavers. For years afterward, however, African travelers claimed to have seen Emin or to have heard rumors of his continuing odyssey.

† Both Miller and Perham—in addition to Lugard, of course—provide interesting details of Selim's ragged army.

Mahdists." In early October 1891, Lugard turned back toward Lake Victoria. He had gone at the head of some 400 soldiers and porters; he returned at the head of a column of 800 soldiers, their camp followers, concubines, slaves, wives, kids—altogether some 10,000 destitute, barefoot, dusty souls—establishing garrisoned forts as he slowly progressed.

By the middle of 1892, Lugard, with Selim Bey's assistance, had completely pacified Uganda. The warring factions were still at odds with one another—but at least they were also at peace. The kabaka reigned over a tranquil kingdom. Unhappily, the IBEA had decided to abandon the place by the end of the year, and it seemed that all Lugard's efforts had been for nought.

On June 9, 1892, a surveying party under the command of Captain J. R. L. Macdonald, R.E., arrived in Uganda, having completed a preliminary survey of the railway that had been proposed to link the bush outposts—including Nakuru—between Lake Victoria and the coast. Leaving a trusted aide, Captain J. H. Williams, in command, Lugard joined Macdonald's caravan and set off for London to plead Uganda's case. While by now he had little use for the IBEA, Lugard was convinced that England should rule in Uganda.

The trip to Mombasa was a foretaste of what awaited Lugard in London. Macdonald, an ambitious and jealous officer, despised Lugard and belittled his success in Uganda; in fact, Macdonald eventually abandoned Lugard during the final stretch to the coast.

Lugard arrived in London in October 1892. Politically, the situation was glum: Gladstone's anti-expansionist government was back in power and the IBEA had already committed to the evacuation of Uganda. Lugard received important backing, however, from an unexpected quarter—Lord Rosebery, the influential Foreign Secretary, who was at odds with the government's hands-off policy toward eastern Africa. By threatening to resign, Rosebery managed to extend the government subsidy to the IBEA until the end of March 1893.

Lugard's battle began with some severe skirmishes to clear his own name. Before his return, the Catholic missionaries in Uganda had written to the Quai d'Orsay and their church fathers that Lugard had committed atrocities against those of their faith and had deliberately encouraged civil war and the murder of Catholic converts. In Parliament, opponents of the movement to retain Uganda used the French accusations as the basis for appointing a commission to investigate the charges. Unhappily, Macdonald was named head of the commission.

On his return, Lugard first dealt with the French accusations. He wrote three comprehensive rebuttals to the charges and buttressed their arguments with two lengthy letters to the *Times*. Slowly public favor began to turn his way, and when he began a series of whistle-stop appearances across the country, it was clear from the crowds in the halls that public opinion had been won over completely. On November 24, 1892, the government sent a commission to Uganda under the guidance of Sir Gerald Portal, British consul in Zanzibar, who, it was thought, was a firm supporter of Rosebery's and Lugard's views.

Portal, however, backed the condemnation submitted by Macdonald, and Lugard once again was called to account. Fortunately, however, other developments came to Lugard's aid. First, there was a letter from Bishop Alfred Robert Tucker, an important leader of the Church Missionary Society, casting doubt on Macdonald's impartiality; second, Macdonald had placed a pro-French, German propagandist, Eugen Wolf, on his commission and had been censured for doing so by the government; and finally, Macdonald had stupidly disarmed the Sudanese troops and arrested Selim Bey because he wrongly suspected his complicity in a mutiny. The Macdonald report was ignored; England stayed in Uganda.

The Sudanese troops were re-formed as the Uganda Rifles. Although among the very best soldiers in Africa, they were poorly treated and poorly paid; their leader, Selim Bey, had been banished*; and new, British officers, none of whom spoke Arabic, were never left in command long enough to garner the respect of their troops. Poor rations led the troops to plunder, and their uniforms were rags. Morale sank, and disciplinary problems emerged. Finally, in September 1897, during a local uprising, the Rifles were, as a result of a bureaucratic bungle, marched nearly to death. Their consequent rebellion started at the Eldama Ravine boma in what is now Kenya, just before Lord Delamere arrived there on his last major hunting expedition, at the head of a caravan of ivory-laden camels and in the company of a really first-class taxidermist. Delamere marched on into the Kenyan highlands; the Sudanese lit out for the bush. It took the British until February 1898 to suppress the troublesome garrisons that had served Gordon, Emin and Lugard.†

* Selim Bey died in Naivasha as he was being transported to the coast after his conviction. Lugard and most other knowledgeable observers strongly protested Selim's treatment and considered his conviction to be very wrong.

† Renegade bands of Emin's Sudanese soldiers remained a minor security factor in the area between Uganda and Equatoria until well into the twentieth century.

PART THREE

FOOD
FIGHT

7.

One thing these governments [in Africa] are good at is starving their people. Most of them are incompetent, and all of them are corrupt. But, by God, they sure know how to create starvation. They starve them much faster than we can feed them.

—A United Nations agricultural-development specialist in Nairobi

I'M LIKE YOU, I want my Third World green and full of documentary animals, great jumping gazelles and wide-eyed antelopes wearing lions around their necks. I want the soft percussion of *Graceland* in a Walkman and the sweet wet of jungle enthusiasm.

Well, I'm here to tell you that you can stand in the middle of the Sudan's Sahara and see what seems like a third of the Third World, and there's nothing there but the heat and the wiggle of a faraway horizon. You can drive miles through the hot, bright vacancy of the Sudan, and aside from your face in the rearview mirror, you see nothing. Good thing nobody's home, you say, they'd all be hungry. Then a speck on another hill moves in and out of focus until it grows up and turns into a Land-Rover carrying two relief workers out beating the bushes for the isolated and the starving, part of a survey, part of a program. This is their turf, so to speak, and they're worried about me and my program until I explain I'm going noplace, doing nothing and that I'll be back in Khartoum before dark. Good, good. See you there, right.

Like clockwork, they show up at a "cocktail" (fruit punch and a lonely fifth of mysteriously foggy quasi-gin) party in Khartoum's embassy-filled New Extension, where many diplomats, relief workers and other foreigners live. The chatter is slow and cynical. ("Hell is the Sudan filled with Nigerians," a tractor salesman tells me.) It's very crowded, but nothing's happening here; I want gossip and I'm not getting any. The two Land-Rover riders nod at me carefully, as though anything more forward might involve them in conversation. The Sudan is dry—no legal hooch noplace—so the rampant home-brewing fad is a principal subject: Last week's meeting of the KGB (Khartoum Guild of Brewers), held at the home of an oil-company pilot named Lou, is generally considered to have been one of the best. There's desultory talk of an old scandal surrounding the expenditure of several thousand dollars in relief funds on "really first-class" household furniture by a now-departed Englishwoman, and some idle patter about moving on to Mozambique, the next big theater in the war against hunger. A young woman, barely mentioned in a then-current issue of *Time* magazine as part of a story about international aid, mixes through the crowd, desperately querying visitors in an effort to find a copy of the magazine to send home; she is followed everywhere by two lean and hungry mechanics who clearly have tapped a private source of liquor before turning up here.

The New Extension is neither, really. It's not a neighborhood of paved streets and California-style split-levels, or anything. Rather, it's a hodge-podge of rutted, dusty streets and oversize concrete residential vulgarities. This particular house, like most others, is surrounded by a high wall. Unlike most others, it is modest in size and design. Inside, where party-goers and the weather have made it hot and humid, curios from the bazaar in Omdurman clutter the corners, dull rugs and wooden platters inlaid with surrogate mother-of-pearl hang on the walls; the furniture is rental-type stuff—modern and beige. The punch bowl has been placed in front of the air conditioner, so that virtually everyone in the house stands in a six-foot circle of semiarid breeze. Outside, it's hot and dry on the dusty veranda, where two young Canadians—Development majors, no less—corner a stranger and tell him a very great deal about an irrigation project in El Fasher and a misplaced girlfriend in Winnipeg. A medical-supply salesman stands in the scrub-filled yard and chats with a pasty-faced Dutchman about business.

While there may be some desperate dinner dates here, rumorwise this party's a bust. It takes a topic of compelling substance to shake out the gossip. The weather, of course, isn't even worth a shrug, and not everyone has an opinion on a pending Soviet trade agreement or allegations of bureaucratic corruption in the international development community. You need something potent, so you haul out the real relief story of the year, the food fight to end all food fights, a fly-by-right fancy or fiasco relief project called Operation Rainbow and its champion, the director of the Sudan office of the UN's World Food Program (WFP), a forty-year-old, movie-perfect, hemi-Italian, aristo-activist named Staffan Domingo deMistura. In a lot of ways, deMistura is the ideal twentieth-century version of Chinese Gordon, either a confusing, misunderstood man of goodwill or a Machiavellian misfit in Khartoum. Try deMistura and Operation Rainbow and you get a bumper crop of innuendo and calumny. "He's the leading man in his own film," a Brit tells me between highly personal allusions; a woman ventures intimate and improbable guesses, while someone else condemns his unforgivable arrogance. Everyone takes a shot: He's a high-living social butterfly, a wheeler-dealer, an egomaniac who disregards orders, puts his own concerns ahead of his mission and has been fired from every relief agency he's worked for. That's one side. Here's another: DeMistura is a powerful antidote to official lethargy, a brilliant tactician with a genius for PR, a hardworking saint who sacrificed a marriage on the altar of charity work, a man with a clear sense of priorities who is willing to buck the system when the system doesn't work, the forerunner of a new generation of relief activists. Take your pick, there's nothing in between. Nobody says, "Hmm, interesting chap doing a curious job of work."

His latest brainchild, Operation Rainbow, was one of the most troubled and troublesome emergency food-and-medicine airlifts in recent memory. Prevented from flying supplies into the famine area in the south by conflicting claims of authority from officials in Khartoum and their rebellious counterparts in the south, where a civil war was raging, deMistura's project relied on a combination of publicity and guilt manipulation to defeat the stubbornness on both sides. Like deMistura, Operation Rainbow had a lot of detractors, most of whom claimed the plan had congenital defects: It cost too much money, and it didn't work, and it made every other relief worker's life a little more difficult. But Operation Rainbow also had some influential backers, and to them it was the essential courageous gesture, one that not only saved countless lives but also made military criminals accountable for their crimes.

It's easy to get the gossip going by mentioning Rainbow and deMistura because both are very much on the minds of worried relief and development specialists, angry government officials and a community of surprised, delighted, furious or mystified diplomats. They're all concerned, with acute justification, that something very much like it might happen again.

Charity starts at home, and by the time it gets to Africa, it's a bureaucratic mess. One sort of assumes that by sending in a few dollars, somebody goes out and buys a bag of semolina or something and gives it to a starving person in Africa. In fact, just sorting out the problems of emergency food distribution itself is confusing enough. According to one U.S. relief expert, "Africa is floating on an ocean of rotting food" provided by a variety of charities, organizations and agencies; there are nearly 100,000 relief and development "experts" in Africa today. A lot of the food and medicine gets more or less permanently warehoused because distributing the stuff is too tricky; big chunks of the inventory are missing from time to time and turn up in markets or other, much more unlikely places. In the Sudan, the relief and development business represents not only the best instincts of the generous Western bloc but also an interesting assortment of failings—diplomatic niceties often go unobserved by those consumed by righteous fervor, and inefficiency flourishes on a level normally associated with the defense industry. Advanced agricultural equipment is shipped to natives who have trouble jump-starting their donkeys; in regions where people are starving and where food shipments have been delayed forever by hypercautious government officials, T shirts bearing the slogan of one charitable effort or another arrive by the truckload. An ex–Peace Corpsman told me the one about the 5,000 toothbrushes sent by an American service organization to one particularly hard-hit famine area; he said he assumed that if they brushed after every meal, the toothbrushes might last forever. In Khartoum, ninety-odd sometimes cooperating, sometimes competing international and governmental agencies and a welter of non-governmental organizations (NGOs) and private voluntary organizations dedicated to relief (that is, the emergency distribution of food and supplies) and development (the long-term strategic planning necessary to avoid situations that call for relief) have carved up the map like Victorian visionaries. They not only provide field jobs for a burgeoning group of disaster specialists, but also stimulate a false economy (one based on bartered emergency food supplies), erode governmental authority by riding roughshod over the bureaucratic infrastructure, create new academic disciplines for modern college kids and generate enormous profits for contractors, truckers, suppliers and friendless mercenary pilots.

Emergency relief and long-term development are the only surefire growth industries in Africa; the market is huge and getting bigger every day. For example, it isn't difficult to quantify the disaster in the Sudan. The numbers are everywhere: The Sudan is running a trade deficit in excess of $1.25 billion; exports in 1985 declined by more than $150 million, to $554 million; the nation's official international debt is approaching $10 billion (unofficial estimates put the figure closer to $13 billion) and in 1985 the country fell into arrears with a number of creditors (overdue loans and obligations total more than $3 billion), despite receiving more than $400 million in concessional loans and grant assistance; the Sudan's unmet $200 million obligation to the International Monetary Fund caused the IMF in February 1986 to suspend that country's eligibility to use IMF resources; inflation reached 70 percent in 1985, and the country's budget was in the red by a half-billion dollars; the exchange rate is lame, with the official rate pegged at £S3.3 to U.S.$1 and the black market rate at £S5.0 to U.S.$1. The United States gives more money to the Sudan than to any other country in Africa, save only Egypt; in 1985 the U.S. government granted $200 million in economic aid, and the same amount in famine and drought relief funds. Meanwhile, the insurgency in the south has caused Chevron Oil, one of the largest investors in the Sudan (the company spent nearly $1 billion in 1985 in oil exploration) to suspend its operations; other investors are discouraged from putting much hope in the Sudan because of bureaucratic bungling and obstruction, apparent instability in the face of an intense civil war and the almost complete lack of skilled labor. For 1987, the UN's Food and Agricultural Organization, which oversees the World Food Program, pledged $7.1 million of the estimated $47 million needed just for emergency food aid (an additional $9.5 million was needed for medical relief to help save an estimated one million children threatened by cholera) for poor Sudanese and refugees in the area, where more than 1,000 children die every day and where the heinous government in neighboring Ethiopia pursues policies designed to kill its citizenry wholesale, stimulating the massive displacement of populations. Refugees from Ethiopia are entering the Sudan at the rate of 3,000 per day, and by the middle of 1985, had already reached 1.5 million. The United Nations estimates that 11.5 million Sudanese—nearly half the population—are seriously affected by ongoing "substantial food deficits" and are "unable to maintain themselves and their families without external support." Some 1.8 million people are in urgent need of shelter items and basic clothing.*

In Africa—and especially in the famine-belt countries of Ethiopia, Chad and the Sudan—emergency programs designed to meet short-term goals live on and on in a bureaucratic limbo. But Operation Rainbow was different from all other relief efforts. Faced with growing starvation in the south, where a guerrilla insurrection led by the Sudanese People's Liberation Army (SPLA) exacerbated a conflict between the necessity to rush food and supplies into a famine-stricken area and the insistence of the

---

* Most of these figures are from various UN documents, the sort that litter the offices of people like deMistura, who routinely ignore them. "Numbers mean nothing," deMistura told me. The real measure of disaster in the Sudan, he said, is impossible to come by. "It's something you sense. You can feel it."

central government in Khartoum to maintain sovereignty over the rebellious south, Rainbow was intended to shame both sides into an agreement. To do so, it employed Mother Teresa, a small army of journalists, a DC-8 painted like an old hippie bus, and some of the most ambitious development officers in the area.

Operation Rainbow is long dead. It had an insect's lifespan—a week or two—and a giant budget—something well over $1 million. If you heard of it in September and October 1986, when it was in the news, you've forgotten it by now (although you may perhaps hear of it—or something quite like it—again). Yet in a part of the world where malicious, intransigent or naive governments are best moved with a polite nudge and a quiet suggestion, where relief is spelled with an endless number of acronyms and where emergency food projects are a major growth industry, Operation Rainbow was an exquisite rarity—at once a textbook example of everything you should never do to feed starving people and a clear-cut case of doing exactly what was necessary when nothing else would work.

DeMistura's office is overrun with monkeys, memos and maps, and he's very busy. He has, he says, little incentive to talk to journalists these days. He has had it with publicity, and besides, he thinks now it's time to lay low. "I am behaving myself," he says wryly. "I am polite. I write memos."

It's a façade, of course; deMistura is possessed of about as much reticence as Charo. "If you get him on Rainbow, he really gets going," one Westerner advised me. And he does get going: The conversation moves from slow inquiry to an angry monologue, fueled by deMistura's certainty that whatever Rainbow's failings, at the bottom line it was a success.

"In the Sudan, Operation Rainbow became a major issue," he told me. "And that was the whole purpose. It *had* to become an issue. I mean, the south had to be recognized as an emergency area, and those who did want to stop the food should take the courage and say so, if they wanted to do it publicly. That's why the original part of the idea was to use the press, if I may say so, as a weapon to counterfight missiles and political pressure—i.e., the public opinion. And use the press in its most open, most public and most aggressive way possible. No other weapons. I had no missiles."

I suggested that perhaps loading an airplane full of journalists, flying them to the south and daring the SPLA to shoot the plane down wasn't much of a deterrence—that airplanes full of journalists might be considered legitimate targets virtually anywhere.

"Yes, that's so," he said. "But there was two things: First, almost all the journalists wanted to be on the first Rainbow flight, but at the last minute decided that their companies wouldn't insure them. And second, that's why Mother Teresa." It was necessary, deMistura claimed, to have a lot of journalists around in case the SPLA shot down Mother Teresa. He would have had Bob Geldof there, too, he added, "except I didn't think of him.

"So I had sixty-two press people, and I said, 'Gentlemen, you are not press people as far as I am concerned. You are part of a team, you are colleagues, you are our pressure group, and if the Rainbow Operation will succeed, it will be thanks to you and then you will have a story . . . because everything seems to be against the fact that this plane should leave. But you can make it [leave]. We don't have missiles, we have you.' "

And to me: "Well you know, by the way, I'm half Italian, half Swedish, but anyway—they made a big issue about the fact that this new generation, or this new UN official, made it possible, but in fact it was many of us together."

While deMistura claimed that Rainbow had averted wholesale death in southern Sudan, he also acknowledged that it had polarized the development community—many of whom disputed the operation's effectiveness—and had deeply embarrassed the host government. Nevertheless, he would do it again, he said; if necessary, he would resign rather than sit on the sidelines while timorous officials quietly pursued the prolonged protocol of famine relief.

As a high-level official of the World Food Program, deMistura is driven around in an air-conditioned car by a UN chauffeur, a circumstance that, like some others in his life, causes him some unease, especially around strangers like me. On an afternoon drive from Khartoum to his home, deMistura explained to me and a visiting UN Development Program (UNDP) official that the car with driver was something they *made* him use. It was crazy, he said, how bureaucracies can find ways to fritter away money. On the other hand, he recalled what a comfort it was to have such conveniences at hand when he first arrived in the country. "I was so depressed," he said. "The suffering here is tremendous." Not only that, but the UN hadn't done a very good job finding him appropriate quarters, so his first few weeks were spent in a frustrating search for a place that he could call home, one that could afford him the refuge he said he needed from the trying job of feeding the starving all day long. As deMistura talked about his house search, we passed through southeastern Khartoum's dusty neighborhoods. No yardwork here, no yards, just the big brown of the Sahara and all these ad hoc houses, some of concrete, some of mud, some of crates and cloth, all of them somewhat weird. Whose idea was it, I thought, to build a town here, of all places? The British, natch. The Arabs had been happy as clams with cluttered Omdurman. The English apparently could not stand the idea of a colonial outpost that didn't bear at least a spiritual resemblance to Leeds. ("Believe me," one diplomat told me, "the Brits are fascinated by the Sudan. They curse it here every day of the week for twelve months, nonstop. Then when they go back to London and we all meet for oysters and white wine at Victoria Station, all they want to do is get back to the Sudan. I mean, if you had a room four meters by three meters in the middle of London, you don't think you'd dream of a place like this? And the snow and the rain and the taxis and buses that never come?" Sounded fine to me.) The driver plowed on through what amounted to a giant vacant lot—the streets were quite arbitrary—until deMistura announced that we were almost there.

"I took one look at this," he said, gesturing at the world outside, "and said, 'No, it will be impossible.' Yet, I was lucky."

Yet, he was. We pulled into a thicket of trees and parked at the end of a shady drive. From there, a flagstone footpath led to yet another coppice. A dog showed up, followed by a couple of tall, thin, burnoused servants. "What do we have for lunch?" deMistura asked them. I went ahead with the UNDP man, past an open-air bar-and-kitchen pavilion, which sported a thatched roof like a prop at Trader Vic's, to a shady lawn, where a table beneath a wide umbrella had been laid for lunch. Another pavilion, housing a bath, stood to one side, and a small, two-story house was fifty yards or so directly in front of us. Beyond that was the Blue Nile, with more of the mud-and-minaret sprawl of Khartoum on the other side, all golden and just right in the afternoon sun. Suddenly Italian baroque music filled the trees in the surrounding gardens, and an older servant appeared with a jug of ice-cold lemonade.

Our host reappeared and took me on a brief tour. "I was lucky to find this," said deMistura. "It was a tennis club, I think, and they had to abandon it very quickly. Everything was just as it is." Except the arboreal Vivaldi, which had been installed by an Italian anthropologist friend. "But, of course, it needs a girl, no?"

Oh, of course. I thought of many, many single women, mid-thirties, cabbing it to shrinks on New York's Upper West Side, who might find feeding the world's hungry a rewarding calling, provided real estate like this came with the package. He was ahead of me: They show up, stay for a while, but then something happens and they're gone.

In and out of the bath, big as a city apartment. Upstairs, downstairs in the little house. Out on the terrace overlooking the river. Time out for a fisherman who lugs a gigantic Nile perch out of a dhow, climbs up the twenty-five-foot cliff to the yard, hands the fish to deMistura and descends again to his boat. "Lunch," said deMistura, looking the fish over. "Lunch," this time a little louder, a little more insistent, until some servant shows up to take the fish off his hands. Then around the gardens into a little grove of trees, where some aluminum-frame tents had been pitched. A small group of men and a boy sat around a fire tending a pot.

"It is my own village," said deMistura, laughing. "They lived nearby, but I said, 'No, you can live here.' They do work for me." He turned to his subjects, nodding and offering a few words of Arabic. Many happy smiles all round.

I mentioned that he seemed to have a lot of people working for him. "Yes, but of course. It is my own small contribution to the economy, you see?"

We returned to the UNDP man, who had spread papers out on the table. He and deMistura went over a few odds and ends, mostly about the logistics of moving food (a recurring conversation among relief people; obtaining food is never a sweat, delivering it is). The fish reappeared, surrounded by lemon slices. As we ate, the radio crackled and the UNDP man fielded questions from a subordinate concerned about arriving specialists. At the other end, a young woman's voice sounded strained and there was urgency in her voice. She was at the airport, but she couldn't make out how many specialists there were to be on the UN's chartered aircraft. Six? Was it six? Or was it more? The UNDP man urged her to look at the paperwork, but events were unfolding too quickly. Finally, she had the number, and it didn't sound good.

"My God! There are *sixteen*!" Big trouble.

"Oh," said the UNDP man, nonplussed. "Sixteen, right."

"But we only have the Volkswagen bus," the woman explained. "Don't you see?"

"See what?"

The woman was exasperated at the UNDP man's apparent stupidity. "We can only get nine in the bus, at most."

The UNDP man and deMistura looked at each other. No expression showed on either man's face; they were waiting for the arrival of significance.

Finally, the UNDP man clicked on his mike. "I have it," he said.

"Yes?" There was a slight softening at the other end, a hint of relief.

"Make two trips."

After a brief pause, the woman, much calmer now, came back: "They really should make it clear, things like this. It would save a lot of bother."

Friday is Sunday in Khartoum, and I didn't really expect deMistura to be at work. I wandered into the UNDP complex—down the street from the Khartoum zoo, a terrible sight—and was surprised to see him at his desk. He had news, or rather, he had a new idea: a fifty-man strike force that he could summon at any time to combat starvation. The rules, he thought, would be simple: If your country is suffering from famine and needs help pronto, you call deMistura's rangers. They arrive within maybe forty-eight hours, and twenty-four hours later, dinner's ready. The only catch is, they won't be bound by any troublesome local laws or bureaucratic or diplomatic niceties. If you want protocol, call Chicken Delight. He signs me up.

"It could be something, really, Denis. Something exciting."

I asked if he was bored.

"No, no. Not really." But he seemed to want to talk adventure and history, so we chatted through the afternoon, mostly about his aspirational Swedish-Italian father and his own career with the UN: his slow rise to the top echelon of the Food and Agricultural Organization and his subsequent resignation, which enabled him to return to the field. He tells stories about famine fighting in Chad and Vietnam, and especially about his good idea previous to Operation Rainbow, a flamboyant relief effort mounted in Ethiopia in January 1985.

"I called it Operation San Bernardo," he said. "The idea was, like, those dogs. Also, I wanted a name that was a neutral name, and what is more neutral than a Swiss dog?

"The idea was to drop food to starving people in the Ethiopian highlands. Wait. I'll get a magazine article."

He disappeared and came back with an Italian newspaper supplement. Inside were color pictures of military Hercules C-130s dropping boxes on a mountainous plateau.

"The principle behind it [San Bernardo] was the following: People were hungry and they were able to get to a camp, but they were starving there because nobody could reach them. I came to the conclusion that we could try to reach them. There was difficulty in reaching the highlands; not even a Land-Rover can get up there. They used to get up there on donkeys, but they had been eating all their donkeys. So the idea was, why can't we do air dropping there, like we do in war zones?" It seemed logical. After all, planes from a half-dozen different air forces were converging on Addis Ababa, carrying food and emergency supplies.

"But that was part of the problem," he said. "The problem was that the planes belonged to several nations and they don't work together and they are all military aircraft. But why couldn't we put them together?

"That was the unique feature of it. For the first time since the Second World War, we managed to put together the military air forces of NATO and Warsaw Pact in a joint military operation—with one small detail: Instead of throwing bombs, they were throwing food."

To pull off the operation, deMistura had first enlisted the support of the British. "The British ambassador told me, 'We don't have a budget for that.'

"I said, 'Well, you do training of air dropping in England, don't you? So just transfer that part of the military budget to here, and you will have a large amount of money to train them in a field way, instead of training them on golf courses in England.'

"The next step, I went to the [West] Germans. I told them the RAF was doing an air drop, and he told me the Luftwaffe could do a better job.

"Then I went to the Ethiopians and said, 'Look, you are under pressure for your resettlement program [a murderous social-political exercise that has cost perhaps millions of lives]. Why don't you show your goodwill. You can show that you really care about your people in the highlands.' And they said, 'Fine.'

"Then I went to the Russians, and this was more complicated. The ambassador—a very powerful man, dead now—said to me that they didn't do those kinds of things. But I said that it would be strange that a brother country in trouble will receive help from the RAF, and the Luftwaffe, but not from you. I said, 'You've got twenty-two aircraft and sixteen helicopters. Let them do the job, and you supervise and coordinate it, then I can claim that without you the airlift could not be done.'

"And he said, 'Yes, you can do so. But use the Polish air force.' It worked.

"I have a picture of a Russian M19 [*sic*] helicopter flying with a Polish pilot, a British copilot, a German navigator, and inside was an Italian doctor, myself and a load of Canadian wheat. And that was the UN, and that's what the UN should be, in my opinion.

"In other words, let them argue at the UN General Assembly, let them make major issues and conferences, but when you go down to an emergency, technical people from all over the world should be able to join in. In San Bernardo, we reached 850,000 people with 4,000 tons of food."

For the next few hours, deMistura unloaded photos of the operation, recalling names and pointing out details. (A photo shows a dropped bag of grain exploding as it hit the ground. "See?" he said. "There is immediate food distribution.") "It was a great thing, honestly. Because it was in a country that was close to the East but hungry enough to be close to the heart of the West. It should be something that is repeated. You know, in life and in politics what counts is precedence, and one day, when they tell me, 'Well, this cannot be done,' I can say, 'Well, listen, in 1985 it *was* done.' "

Eventually, we got around to how his long absences in the bush had destroyed one marriage, but how he feels compelled to try one more time. He carefully avoids reports of his running battles with his superiors, first at the Food and Agricultural Organization for his handling of Operation San Bernardo, then at UNICEF, for reportedly allowing a flotilla of relief barges on the Nile to be used by the Sudanese government in violation of an agreement made with the rebels in the south. He doesn't touch on yet another convoy carrying food to the southern provinces that had barely left Khartoum when it was commandeered by the Sudanese military. He is defensive about allegations that while many of his projects have a high profile, they also have a low performance. Operation Rainbow, for example, consisted of only nine flights (perhaps 350 tons of food, max) and cost something in excess of $4,000 per ton, a phenomenally high price to pay.

"It doesn't matter. It was not a matter of money."

On one level, Rainbow was a simple enough project: In a country torn by a north-south civil war, it became necessary to get emergency supplies to starving people in the southern part of the country from stockpiles in the northern part of the country. At first, prospects for quick relief seemed good, at least on the surface: The Sudan harvested the largest grain crop in its history in 1986, and enormous amounts of relief supplies were still on hand from the country's last bout with famine in 1982.

But relief efforts in a country fighting a civil war can be tricky maneuvers, and the dilemma faced by deMistura and his colleagues was simply another episode in a civil war that has split the Sudan since well before independence, in 1956. The citizens of the Saharan north, always secure inside the Egyptian sphere of influence, have only one thing in common with the people of the south—the Nile. The southerners, divided from the rest of the Sudan by a nearly impenetrable swamp, are long-legged giants, tribesmen who live in a wet and verdant suburb of the central African rain forest. Unlike their Arabic, Islamic rulers in Khartoum, the southerners are quite black and worshipers of one variety or another of the Christian God or their local tribal deities. The long-running civil war went into remission during the military rule of Gaafar Nimeiri, who came to power in 1969, but revived in 1983, when Nimeiri, nearing the end of his rule, introduced an exaggerated version of shari‘a that allowed for public executions, amputations and floggings in punishment of even minor crimes. (You're better off making your own liquor: One Italian visitor, attempting to bring booze with him into the Sudan, got sixty lashes, while resident foreigners who take up moonshining are almost never prosecuted.) The imposition of Islamic law was a red flag to the southerners, who took one look at each other, said, hey, we aren't Arabs, and went back into revolt. That left the northerners, who have long had little use for the Dinkas, Nuers, Shilluks and other southern tribesmen, worried about protecting their desert half. "I know there are Arabs who go to sleep at night worrying about being engulfed by blacks from the south," one senior diplomat told me. "You cut away all the crap," he added, "and you'll find the northerners care very little about the southerners."

Over lunch one afternoon, Douglas Manson, a veteran of UN development efforts in southern Sudan, gave me his view of the history of the UN's attempt to feed the hungry there. After the signing of the Addis Agreement in 1972, which resulted in a cease-fire in the civil war, Manson had been posted to Juba, where he was assigned the task of establishing a UN presence. "We had no office, no accommodations and no staff, apart from myself," he recalled. "In those days, we were mostly concerned with refugees from all over the place.

"After a slow start, we got the teams and we started working closely with the government on what amounted to collecting the incoming refugees, equipping them with seeds for the first crop—a hoe-and-shovel type of thing, really. Preparing them to look after themselves. Many of them were people from neighboring countries, but there were lots of people who just fled from the troops—one side or the other—and they couldn't make out Anya Nya* [a faction of the southern guerrilla force] from the army or government. They had to be convinced to come out, but it eventually worked out very well. By the time I left in '75, there was a high

---

* The name, according to P. M. Holt and M. W. Daly in *The History of the Sudan* (1961, 1979), comes from the name of a poison concocted from "snakes and rotten beans" (the text actually says "beams" but that couldn't be it, could it?). The group started in 1955 as a bunch of mutinous soldiers, just before independence. Early government attempts to crush it gave it an enhanced credibility, and Anya Nya quickly transformed itself into a rural guerrilla movement until it was disbanded following the Addis Agreement. These days, there's a sequel group, called, in the best new tradition of Hollywood, Anya Nya II.

executive council established in Juba, and many of the Anya Nya commandos became, if you like, cabinet ministers. We had doctors and teachers and agriculturists of all sizes and shapes, and we were proceeding extremely well in those days toward an effective program of development.

"I think the UNDP's operation there was successful because we were able to provide a focal point for all the nongovernmental organizations, who sometimes have a hard time slipping themselves into the scheme of things. But the NGOs can take a $2,000 investment and buy, for example, chains that would harness a plow to a bull that had never been harnessed before. Now the UNDP is not terribly interested in a $2,000 project; the UNDP is mandated to come up with a program in cooperation with the government. But these NGOs took the money and they were extremely successful, especially with the Dinkas and the other people who are cattle-oriented. To make it easy, we brought in trained bulls from Kenya and paired them up with untrained bulls, and within a couple of weeks, you had another trained bull, and then we paired them off again, and we went on like that.

"But one thing I noticed about government officials and ministers is that they had no idea of appropriate technologies. Let's say we're talking about sugar and sugar refining and sugar production. They [the officials] want a sugar refinery built where you can push a button and sugar comes out in one-pound bags ready for market. The truth of the matter is that there is a demand for packaged sugar cane in the southern region, and you can use a variety of methods to produce sugar for that market. It would be brown and lumpy, but it's still sugar and if you historically take three teaspoonfuls, it's all the same.

"Middle-level technology, appropriate technology, was seen by government ministers as a second-class way of development, that other people had bigger things. . . .

"Then everything changed," he said, referring to the renewed hostilities. "We've closed down in the south now. We evacuated the place in '86. We're absolutely closed."

Manson had the large, open face of a farmer, and despite his frustration, laughed readily at the absurdities of African circumstances. He had returned from Juba that morning, and was on his way to retirement in Canada. "And about time," he said.

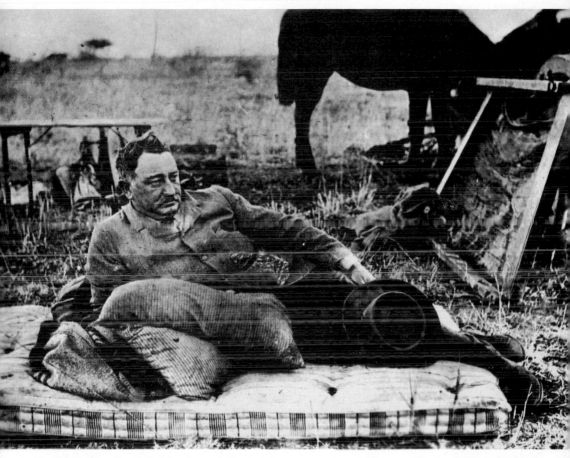

Cecil Rhodes, the definitive imperialist, resting on a mattress in a meadow in Africa.

David Livingstone, the
African-born explorer and
missionary, and the object of
Henry Morton Stanley's famous
presumption.

Henry Morton Stanley in
an early photo. Despite his
popularization as a gentle
purveyor of civilization by
Spencer Tracy in the film
Stanley and Livingstone,
the quick-draw champ of
Africa was a ruthless
egomaniac.

MAP OF EQUATORIAL AFRICA SHOWING ROUTES OF STANLEY'S JOURNEYS

MAP OF STANLEY'S ROUTE FROM YAMBUYA TO KAVALLI

STANLEY'S ROUTES.

Major General Charles George Gordon. "A little off his head," wrote Lytton Strachey, one of the earliest in a long line of Gordon's odd detractors. In *Eminent Victorians* Strachey branded Gordon a dipsomaniac; subsequent profilers have discovered new and more perverse frailties. Any virtues General Gordon may have possessed do not suit the temper of modern times.

Beryl Markham hovering far above New York's Mayor Fiorello La Guardia as she receives the keys to the city following her transatlantic flight in September 1936.

Karen Blixen, left, discussing her literature with Marilyn Monroe at a February 1959 luncheon.

Elspeth Huxley, a longtime resident of Kenya, is one of East Africa's best-known writers and the biographer of Hugh Cholmondeley, Lord Delamere.

Karl Peters, "a model, if stern, colonial administrator," according to Adolf Hitler, a later admirer.

Emin Pasha at home in Equatoria.

Patrick Shaw in his office in the Starehe School.

Left: Lord Delamere, center, with Prince George, left. The incredibly persistent and somewhat clumsy settler-king of Kenya, Delamere had a taste for the big gamble that paid off; more than any other settler, he is responsible for the development of East Africa.

Below left: Ian Douglas Smith, the last prime minister of Rhodesia, at home in Harare. In 1987 he was thrown out of parliament as Zimbabwe moved toward a one-party dictatorship.

Below right: Staffan deMistura holding his lunch.

Frederick Lugard, later Lord Lugard, whose "dual mandate" became the model for British colonial administration in Africa. This photo was taken shortly before he joined the London Fire Brigade.

8.

Whoso diggeth a pit
shall fall therein: and he
that rolleth a stone, it
will return upon him.

—*Proverbs 26:27*

AT SOME POINT, you stop and ask yourself why, after trying to get along for a century and not succeeding, the Sudanese in the north don't let the Sudanese in the south go their merry way? Why don't they just let their arbitrary nation divide in two like some amoeba and live happily apart? After all, as it stands, the country is surrounded by the member countries of the weird alliance: Uganda, the Central African Republic, Libya, Ethiopia, Chad and Zaïre. Only Egypt and Kenya qualify as nations in the modern sense of the word. Why do the Sudanese insist on fighting inside their borders when all around them are the slum states of the twentieth century?

I went to Equatoria once in 1979, stayed for a cup of coffee and left. There must be something to it, the southern part of the Sudan, to make it such a treasured part of the nation. My ostensible mission was to see the most recent Sudano-Egyptian effort in the province because it sounded to me like something of which Ismail would have approved. But I also wanted to see what made civil war make sense in the Sudan.

In the south, the task for the Egyptians and the Sudanese was daunting: digging the longest canal this side of Mars through the biggest swamp on earth. They certainly had the tools for the job: a 2,200-ton paddle-wheel excavator that could churn through 9,000 tons of mud and dirt each hour. According to my information, a bewildered, ragtag bunch of Dutch, French, Egyptian and Sudanese engineers were said to be steering this monster machine through the bogs and marshes of northern Equatoria.

When they were finished, the lives of millions of people who depend on the ancient patterns of the Nile would be irrevocably changed.

The idea was to produce a V-shaped channel 170 feet wide and thirteen feet deep across a giant swamp called the Sudd, which would connect the southern portion of the Nile with the Sobat, one of the Nile's principal tributaries. Called the Jonglei Canal, the project was to be the first of a series of schemes formulated by the government of Egypt, with the compliance of then-President Nimeiri's Sudanese government, to "reorganize" the Nile from Alexandria, on the Mediterranean, all the way to Lake Victoria. Huge control dams would be built, which would add 500 billion cubic yards of water to Lakes Albert and Victoria. Key tributary rivers would be rechanneled, and water levels in other, secondary storage lakes would be closely regulated. The natural flood cycles of the Nile would be eliminated forever.

Just what benefit this would give the Nuer, Dinka and Shilluk tribesmen of Equatoria had become a matter of extended debate. Supporters of the overall project, known as the Nile Waters Agreement, promised that millions of acres of desert and swampland would become arable and that dozens of new industries would spring up once the Nile had been tamed. Opponents charged that a tragic environmental debacle was in the making. They claimed that the region's fragile ecosystem would be destroyed, the tribesmen of the southern Sudan would be driven from their traditional homelands, and hundreds of already threatened species of wildlife would perhaps be made extinct. Shortly after the plan was announced, an American diplomat stationed in Khartoum wrote to a colleague in Washington about possible protest over the project. "Although we are not very much involved with the Jonglei itself," he wrote, "it will be so important to the Sudan as a whole that it is likely to have a bearing on the entire economy of the region. . . . However, it will not surprise me if the environmentalists and their allies make an issue over the anticipated dangers of the project. . . . I think it is likely to elicit more interest than elephant tusks." The diplomat ended his dispatch somewhat acidly: "If you like the Alaska pipeline, you'll *love* the Jonglei Canal."

No matter which side was actually right, the Nile Waters Agreement would have broad political implications and was, in a way, just the latest attempt to annex the southern Sudan to Egypt's Mediterranean sphere. For if successful, the project would enable the Egyptians to carve out for themselves an area of African hegemony that would extend to Kenya, Uganda, Zaïre and beyond, significantly shifting the entire Middle East power balance. The Sudan, bordering as it does on the Red Sea oil routes, is already one of the most strategically important regions on the African continent; if, as the Sudanese hoped, the taming of the Nile could help them to create arable land on a vast scale, there would be still further impact on power relationships in Africa and the Middle East, and the political repercussions of the Nile Waters Agreement could eventually reach as far as Moscow and Washington.

Remarkably, in view of its enormous potential importance, the Jonglei Canal had received relatively little international attention. Occasionally, a Western journalist like myself would make a foray deep into the Sudan to report on the progress of the canal, to gawk at the huge German-built ditchdigger, or to interview the Nilotic tribesmen, who posed obligingly with their cattle as they explained the benefit derived from rubbing the ash of cow dung into their skin (it keeps away the bugs). But in the Sudanese and Egyptian press, there was hardly a word—despite the fact that the Nile Waters project was the most expensive Egyptian undertaking since the Six-Day War, the rough equivalent of an environmental Star Wars program. In fact, for perhaps obvious political reasons, the canal's impor tance to Egypt was rarely acknowledged by Egyptian officials, who preferred to let the Sudanese do the talking. One high-ranking Egyptian minister, for example, assured me that he had never heard of the Jonglei project and, appearing not to trust my pronunciation, asked me to write out the name of the canal on my notebook so he could read it. "Where is this canal?" the official asked.

"In the Sudan."

"And who is building this canal? The Sudanese?"

"Yes," I replied, "with participation by Egypt."

The official carefully examined the ceiling of his office and whistled softly in amazement. "Fantastic, these things we do," he whispered reverently.

Sudd is an Arabic word meaning "obstacle" or "blockage." That it is an obstacle is the only thing certain about the swamp. Beryl Markham, who flew over the Sudd several times in the '30s, called it the "one place in this world worthy of the word 'sinister.' " The provinces of Bahr al-Ghazal and Equatoria, which lie south of the Bahr al-Ghazal and Sobat rivers, constitute the lower third of the country. The black tribesmen of the region, animist and Christian in religion, for more than a century have been bound to the northern two-thirds of the country by Samuel Baker's and Ismail's ambitions. The notion that the country is held together by the Nile is extremely dubious; the Bahr al-Jebal, as the Nile is known in Equatoria, flows to the north, then turns back on itself in the swamp; the country to the north is a matter for speculation among most of the southerners, who have never been there, couldn't speak the language if they went, look and behave nothing like their Muslim countrymen and have been taught by a hundred years of history not to trust what they do know about the north. The swamp is an absolute border; nobody—neither the Sudanese authorities, the environmentalists, the UN Development Program nor the engineers who were working on the canal—can determine with any accuracy the size of the Sudd, the amount of rainfall it can expect over a long period, or the amount of water lost in the swamp through evaporation, drainage and transpiration. The best estimates are that the swamp covers a yearly average of 40,000 square miles, an area approximately the size of Ohio, gets as much as four inches of rain in a single afternoon during the monsoon season, and loses through evaporation and seepage about 55 billion cubic yards (or some 850 billion gallons) of water each year. At least 3,200 square miles of the Sudd are always covered with water; the marsh sustains a dense jungle of floating vegetation, 20 percent of it papyrus, which grows up to twelve feet high along the edge of the river's main channel. Where the land is not continually flooded, marsh flowers and tall grasses grow; on higher ground, fig, bassia and tamarind trees root, and herds of zebus and Longhorn cattle graze in the lush foliage. Wallowing in the mud and roaming through the reeds are giraffes, buffalo, gazelles, antelope, zebra, lions, black and white rhinos, hippopotamuses and elephants.

Critics of the canal were convinced that much of the Sudd's extraordinary vegetation and wildlife would vanish once the project's drainage process began. They also charged that the effort would create tribal conflict in an area already racked by wars, intensify the epidemics that already afflicted the local population, create deserts out of seasonal grazing lands, and present enormous environmental problems in the lakes and rivers that feed the Nile. They contended, too, that the scheme would be ruinously expensive.

Advocates of the project answered that those concerns were unimportant when weighed against the potential benefits. They said the canal would save at least 170 billion cubic feet of precious water now being lost to the Sudd; reduce the size of the swamp by 20 percent, thereby opening up an additional 3.7 million acres for grazing and agriculture; give jobs to people whose only paycheck in the past had been a sack of beans and a chicken; allow for a reliable water source for cattle, the abiding preoccupation of the Nilotic people living in the Sudd; substantially reduce disease, especially malaria; and make possible, for the first time in history, year-round overland transportation between the relatively prosperous north and the impoverished nomadic tribes in the tropical south.

I chose to visit the Sudd while a number of interesting things were happening elsewhere in the Sudan. It was Ramadan, the month of fasting for Muslims, and anyone who could find the slightest excuse for going on vacation had fled the cities. It was also the middle of the monsoon season, which meant that the whole world south of the tenth parallel had been called on account of rain. Finally, Sudanese workers were threatening a general strike against the government. While students were stoning cars in Khartoum and Omdurman, Nimeiri was shuffling and reshuffling his cabinet, hoping for a pat hand, and the entire civil service had phoned in with an acute case of coup fever—some five years too early, as it turned out.

In the midst of this, I bribed my way onto a DC-3 carrying fuel pumps and tinned carrots through the monsoon to a development area near the canal site. I'd met the pilot the evening before, and stayed up to drink with him through the night; by the time we got past all the others to his current wife, who was at the time in Florida, it was time to fly. It was a long drive to the airport, and once off the ground, time stood still. Finally we made a three-point landing on a mudded-out airstrip near a messy collection of Quonset huts and shacks. Nothing was happening. Inside one hut, a group of men sat on benches staring into the air, looking at some place short of the far wall. Nobody was in charge.

The pilot and I looked at each other, tried a few times to start a conversation, and finally, with a mutual shrug, made tracks for the plane, which, thanks to an Italian despot, had been made empty.

When I got back to Khartoum, I asked a minor official in the Ministry of Irrigation why nothing was happening on the Jonglei project.

"Maintenance, maintenance." He spoke brusquely, as if he had to rush off to a board meeting and didn't have time to deal with idle chatter from a foreigner.

"What kind of maintenance?"

"Mud; it's the rainy season."

"How long has this maintenance been going on?"

"Almost two months." Now he was starting to sound embarrassed; he was softening.

"Two months?" I tried to sound shocked. "For maintenance?"

He squinted at me conspiratorially. "Maintenance," he repeated. "Also, maybe too much bhang." (Bhang is the local marijuana.) At last he smiled: "In fact, mostly I think it's just too much bhango."

Actually, I learned later that during the rainy season, when the Sudd is an endless muddy morass, the huge earthmover broke down often and sometimes was out of action for weeks at a time.

Maintenance, mud and too much bhang have been the least of the problems facing those who, from time to time over the course of this century, have proposed building a better Nile through the swamp. The idea was first mooted in 1898, but it wasn't until 1938, when the Egyptian government presented the Sudanese government with a summary of its studies, that a systematic development program for the Nile Basin was finally formulated. A 1959 revision, which followed the Sudan's independence in 1956, established the Joint Technical Commission for Nile Waters and determined the share each country would receive of the river's bounty. Currently, Egypt receives 75 percent, while the Sudan gets 25 percent, or 650 billion cubic feet, per year. Under the terms of the agreement, the benefits from any subsequent development programs that increased the Nile's discharge would be split fifty-fifty.

Unfortunately, while experts were planning the future of nature in Africa, the Sudan was being ravaged by the first round in its current civil war. Through the 1950s and '60s, the conflict between the north and the south intensified, and by the time the war ground to a tentative halt in 1972, as many as one million southerners had been killed in the seventeen years of fighting.*

The peace agreement did not end southern suspicions, however, and when the government announced the Jonglei Canal project in 1974, Nimeiri's enemies in exile put out the rumor that two million Egyptians would be settled in the south to operate the canal and safeguard its security. This provoked riots and demonstrations throughout Bahr al-Ghazal and Equatoria, and several people were killed before troops could put down the disturbances. At that, Nimeiri dispatched Abel Alier, a

---

* The 1972 treaty gave the south limited autonomy, but left the government in a precarious position. When Nimeiri felt compelled to meet the increased demands of northern fundamentalist Muslims, the repercussions were felt in the south, where Islamic law and the like were of no interest, and, to the southerners, represented an abrogation of the treaty. The politicians in the north are at least cosmetically sympathetic to the anger felt by the southerners. The imposition of Islamic law "must be changed," one senior Umma party official told me. He added that the only constraints to an immediate repeal of the shari'a came from fundamentalists, many of whom provided important backing to the Umma party. "We must find a way to ignore them," the official said. "It will be very delicate." Indeed, the method by which the civil war is ended is crucial—the balance between the north and south has always been delicate—and will almost certainly determine the future of parliamentary government in the country.

key southern leader who had been taken into the government as vice-president, to squelch the rumors and underscore the government's determination to go ahead with the project. For a time, the ploy was successful. Alier is an American-educated Dinka, a member of the largest and most rebellious tribe in the south, and even today a symbol of confidence to the people he once led. Alone among southerners, Alier has been able to keep some level of communication open between both sides. In 1974, Nimeiri needed him to bang a drum, and Alier obliged. Addressing the south by radio, Alier concluded his speech by declaring, "If we have to drive our people to paradise with sticks, we shall do so."

The drive to paradise involved traveling on some rough roads. Securing southern support for the canal scheme was only the beginning of the government's woes: They next had to find the cash to meet the Sudan's share of the project's cost. For financial aid, Nimeiri turned to the Saudis and Kuwaitis, who, along with several Western guarantors, agreed to underwrite the Sudan's share. The Egyptians, meanwhile, made an early decision to underplay their role in the project; from the official point of view, the Jonglei was a Sudanese project in which the Egyptians happened to cooperate. After the Camp David accords, Egypt's role was nearly written out of the script, leaving the Sudanese government some room to maneuver. One high-ranking Sudanese official said at the time, "We are in an awkward position at the moment. But we are committed to this project, and our Arab neighbors know that for us it is not a political project but one that is essential if we are to have enough food. You can quarrel all you like, but you must eat."

The Egyptians had their own reasons for initiating and supporting the project, of course; clearly, they expected to get more than extra water out of the deal.

"The canal is more important as part of our foreign policy than it is as an agricultural or irrigation project," one Egyptian official told me.

Dr. Osama el-Baz, then first under secretary in the Egyptian Ministry of Foreign Affairs, agreed in terms that Disraeli and Gladstone would have understood: "We must make our nation secure, and in the twentieth century, security no longer means just the possession of arms. The Nile Basin has a greater significance on a global scale than ever before. Its stability and security is important to us, and, ultimately, to the rest of the world." Certainly, Egyptian policy toward the Nile had changed little.

"The whole question of the Jonglei has become very sensitive," said Gassim Osman, then an under secretary in Sudan's Ministry of Irrigation. "At the beginning, the project was seen as part of our problem with the south. The south was initially very suspicious; they thought it was a project that would only benefit the north. But finally we have made the people of the south see that the project is for their benefit, too."

"It is assumed that the tribes are happy and that altering their life patterns will make them less happy," Alier told me. "That isn't true; they *aren't* happy. . . . I know because I am from that region. I grew up there and I know what it's like. I'm the only member of my family who *doesn't* live in the Sudd—and I am convinced that the project will bring more benefits than disadvantages. We aren't dealing with the problems of industrialized societies; the Sudd isn't New York or London. The problem here is that these people can barely survive. They haven't yet been pulled out of the Stone Age. Here the problem is that these people can only hope that the will of God will help them overcome the atrocities of nature."

Hello? Is there an echo here?

By 1987, the canal was still a partially completed ditch; the foreigners had gone home and the giant trencher was rusting away in the tropical damp.

9.

Away your proud grandeur of the recent past
You're nothing now but a name
With shameful garb striding the blast
And voicelessly singing in utter shame.

—*From "An Epitaph to Stalwart Sudan,"* *
by Ishaq M A Sharif

ONE OF THE ARGUMENTS put forward by the advocates of the Jonglei Canal is that after the swamp has been drained, the south will prosper because of easier access to the north. But if the increase of commerce in the Sudan was a long-term nightmare, the seemingly simple process of getting food from one place in the north to another in the south was a profoundly complicated short-term headache. The emergency situation in the south existed as early as April 1986, by which time a great number of southern towns and villages were feeling the effects of the civil war and the enormous influx of refugees from the past year's horror spot, Ethiopia. Western aid sources quickly mobilized under the banner of the Food and Agricultural Organization's World Food Program (WFP), only to have things break down under the weight of local politics. By late summer

* The full text of Sharif's poem:

O! Stalwart Sudan where is your bust?
That ancient monument to a golden age,
Which your barren waste one wore in trust
During dustier times and in your secret page.

Your Book of Hours is done and torn,
As are the leaves of meaningful time.
And long before this drab day was born,
Your illumined manuscripts had lain covered with grime.

1986, the Sudanese government in the north was arguing over matters of sovereignty with the rebels of the Sudanese People's Liberation Army (SPLA) in the south. Matters came to a head when the SPLA discovered that civilian flights were being used to resupply government garrisons; they issued a number of warnings that after August 15, any aircraft operating in the south without SPLA clearances would be destroyed. On August 16, despite the fact that Sudanese military aircraft were in daily operation in the south, the SPLA aimed a SAM-7 missile at a civilian airliner and blasted it from the sky near Malakal, killing all 60 aboard. Suddenly, deMistura and the other advocates of airlifting food to the south were filled with a renewed sense of caution.

The situation dragged on through the final days of the summer. Along with his colleagues, deMistura became increasingly frustrated by the deadlock and began suggesting publicly that both sides in the civil war were using starvation as a weapon. "You'll never see a starving soldier," he pointed out. It didn't matter to the SPLA; apparently feeling that they had blown the battle for international hearts and minds when they shot down the airliner, they continued to refuse permission for relief flights in the Texas-size area. Western diplomats estimated that as much as 90 percent of the southern provinces was under the control of SPLA guerrillas.

By early September, the UN estimated that as many as two million southerners faced starvation, and that the number was growing quickly. The rebels swore they would snag any airplane that attempted to fly into the area from the north unless the towns that they controlled also were

---

This bright day is dead for ever more
And your once brave spirit is a grave
Which whistling winds with drifts galore
Do cleanse of all value and lave

Away your proud grandeur of the recent past
You're nothing now but a name
With shameful garb striding the blast
And voicelessly singing in utter shame.

To all the deaf and dumb of mankind
They shrug disdainful shoulders and listen
To the dry murmur of withered grass resigned
That dead souls in cold may glisten.

After first reciting it aloud, then giving me a copy of the poem, the author was at great pains to make clear that it was written during the darkest days of Nimeiri's regime, when the Mahdist Umma party was banned and most of its leaders were in exile. Presumably Mr. Sharif does not mean for it to apply to the Sudan today, which is now under the leadership of his nephew, Sadiq al-Mahdi, his faithful Ansar and the Umma. Mr. Sharif is himself a grandson of the Mahdi.

provided with relief and unless almost all the food was channeled through their own relief agency. The government said no airplane carrying relief supplies would be given permission to fly if the aircraft might also deliver food to rebel-held positions or if food was distributed by SPLA officials.

Finally, deMistura conferred with Peter Feith, the Dutch chargé d'affaires in Khartoum, and John Koehring, the director of the U.S. AID mission in the Sudan, and presented his blueprint for what he called "breaking the wall" that the two sides had erected to prevent food from reaching the south. He would initiate a series of relief flights that would generate more and more attention until sufficient food and airplanes could be assembled to alleviate the emergency. To do that, he needed every ally he could find. He got the Americans, the Dutch, the Canadians and a number of other Western governments; he also wanted the assistance of the most powerful nongovernmental organization in Khartoum, World Vision, but that wasn't so easy.* While World Vision wasn't averse to doing deals to make sure relief got to the people who needed it (in April 1986, World Vision successfully negotiated a quiet agreement with the SPLA that allowed 1,700 tons of food—more than five times the amount moved by Rainbow—to get to Wau, one of the hardest-hit areas), they weren't alone in keeping Rainbow at a comfortable distance. Most agencies took one look at the prospect of importing five dozen hacks and a saint to a completely impoverished Islamic nation and decided to be counted out. "We would be crucified if it got screwed up," another relief director said. "And frankly, Operation Rainbow held out every good prospect of failing miserably." The operation was viewed as too dramatic,

---

* World Vision is one of the largest, richest international relief charities on the planet: In 1986, they toted up $237.4 million in donations that averaged just $35 each. From their Southern California base, they send food and supplies to virtually every international trouble spot—often accumulating enemies on the way, such as the diplomat who told me that he felt that since their TV campaign had used two-year-old footage, it was misleading; besides, he said, he felt uncomfortable attending meetings with people who concluded every conference with an earnest handshake and a call for the blessings of the Lord.

Nevertheless, in the Sudan, World Vision represented a substantial potential resource for the Rainbow consortium. Thomas Staal, World Vision's Sudan director, got deMistura's call one morning, but the plan for Rainbow, he said, made him "nervous." As an NGO, World Vision was on its own; there is no Foreign Service for good causes, and if the government, already irritated at what it considered the excesses of some relief organizations, thought World Vision was more trouble than it was worth, it would be gone. (I later saw World Vision's request for staff visa extensions sitting on a desk in a security office at the Ministry of the Interior. They were covered in dust and obviously bound for misplacement.) Besides, along with other officials of NGOs, Staal felt that the political stalemate between the north and the south had created a very volatile situation for everyone working in the Sudan, and what he called "confrontational" operations like Rainbow would only rock a dangerously leaky boat. "We wished them well. We were really rooting for them," he told me. "But we decided to keep it [Operation Rainbow] at arm's length."

too circus-like, too aggressive to work in an arena that has traditionally relied on moral suasion. "I'm still not convinced it was a success," she added. "After all, they blew a lot of money."

Despite these reservations, deMistura was committed. While clandestine meetings with SPLA officials in Addis Ababa delivered some limited assurances, he and the others knew that publicity would be the key to getting both sides to back down. As he later told me, "Everybody needs public opinion." So he lured five dozen journalists—representing virtually every major news agency—to Khartoum to cover the relief flights, offering them the chance to be on the first flight into the emergency areas. And just in case the SPLA or the government thought American TV correspondents were too tempting as targets, he also invited Mother Teresa.

By the end of the third week in September, deMistura was promising a flight every morning and canceling it every afternoon as negotiations with the SPLA dragged on. Reporters got desperate, and all across America highly detailed stories about the export earnings and the continuing financial problems of the Sudan began appearing in newspapers as editors sought to justify the several thousand dollars it takes to keep a journalist in Khartoum. The bar at the Hilton, which serves orange and grapefruit juice in a bewildering variety of ways, became a sort of press center; the telex operator told me that she thought it was good there was no alcohol at the bar, since she was sure "all the reporters would turn into drunks" waiting for the whimsical telex connections. (I was a victim of the communication gap myself; when the telex still hadn't coughed after two days, I asked what the problem was. "The satellite," a helpful young man told me. "Ah," I said, somewhat dubious, "the satellite. Um, what's wrong with the satellite?" The man shook his head like a NASA veteran and said simply, "You know. No spare parts.") The pressure on the relief consortium started to build, and deMistura's superior, a UN relief veteran named Winston Prattley, who, after thirty years with the UN, had only a few weeks to go until retirement, finally reached his breaking point: The atmosphere that deMistura had created for Rainbow had finally pushed him and other more traditionally minded relief officials to the brink. Not only had deMistura made acute embarrassment of the Sudanese government a crucial ingredient in getting Operation Rainbow off the ground, but many in the relief community questioned whether the operation was really necessary at all. "As a logistical operation," Prattley told me, "it had no hope, really, of supplying the needs of the population, which came to be met, as I expected they would be met, by trickles that came across the Ugandan border and otherwise over a period of time. Any little droplet of that was equal to an Operation Rainbow flight." To Prattley, the exercise smacked of self-publicity. "It was an act of exhibitionism," he said, claiming that deMistura had manipulated the press and, in a later conversation with me, dismissing him as a "very sophisticated, multilingual cowboy" with only one goal: "He wants to be famous. That's all." Prattley muzzled his wunderkind and told reporters not to talk to deMistura anymore.

The battle that took place between deMistura and his superior became a transatlantic preoccupation. At UN headquarters in New York and at the Food and Agricultural Organization's headquarters in Rome, everyone familiar with the enormously popular Prattley, an accomplished veteran, and the somewhat suspect deMistura followed the daily flow of cables like installments in a soap opera. "We were all rooting for Winston," one senior UN staffer told me. "We knew deMistura was a kook." (When it became known that I was talking to officials about the deMistura-Prattley conflict, the curtain came down quickly.)

By September 26, when the first Rainbow flight was due to take off, Prattley was in Rome, trying to get the World Food Program to withdraw deMistura. "Quite aside from Rainbow," Prattley explained, "I had been asked, on behalf of the [Sudanese] prime minister, to do just that [obtain deMistura's recall] because they did not like the way he had been embarrassing the government in front of the media—and he did that flouting the many instructions I had given him. The whole thing was a gung-ho—well, it had a cast of thousands."

The first Rainbow flight was due to leave Khartoum at seven o'clock that morning. Mother Teresa was up and ready to fly, and the reporters were ready to watch. Suddenly, Prattley received a telephone call in his hotel room in Rome "from a very responsible person," he told me, "formerly high in the government of the Sudan and now aligned with the SPLA," reiterating telex messages that had been received at WFP offices in Addis Ababa, stating that if the airplane took off, it would be shot down.

Prattley conferred with his superiors at the WFP headquarters at the Food and Agricultural Organization in Rome and they decided to cancel the flight. The cargo and Mother Teresa were taken off the airplane—which had been parked at the Khartoum airport for two weeks at the rate of twenty-five grand per day—and the journalists all went back to bed.

"Winston Prattley gets a call in his hotel in Rome at three in the morning," a high-level diplomat said to me later. "How do you think the SPLA got his number?"

Back in Khartoum, the widespread suspicion was that Prattley had

finked to the SPLA, although Prattley denied such an allegation as "ridiculous," pointing out that contacting him would have been easy for anyone
determined to do so. Whether or not that's true, he did cable Kamil
Shawki, the Sudanese High Commissioner for Relief and Rehabilitation,
and suggested that deMistura had overstepped his duties in involving
himself in direct meetings with the SPLA and in his jockeying of the
Rainbow mission. He should, Prattley suggested, be made persona non
grata by the government and thrown out of the Sudan.

But as Prattley was telegraphing his pitch, deMistura literally moved
his office into Shawki's Relief and Rehabilitation Commission (RRC) and
helped the high commissioner draft a reply that at once praised deMistura
and condemned Prattley, and declared that if any persona was going to be
declared non grata, it would be Prattley.

According to Prattley, the cancellation of the flight had been a severe
embarrassment to a high-ranking government official who, Prattley said,
was eager to cover his own involvement in negotiations with the SPLA.
"[The official] was running for cover," Prattley claimed to me later, "and
also deMistura was afraid he was going to lose his job, and they cooked up
a plan between them they thought would suit both parties."

By the second week in October, Mother Teresa had gone home and
there weren't enough reporters left in the Sudan to cover a barroom floor.
The successful inauguration of Operation Rainbow on October 12 was
noted by a couple of stringers for Reuters and UPI. After nine flights and a
million dollars, Operation Rainbow faded into the mist. Within weeks,
other flights, other operations (one, my personal favorite, was called Eros
Bow by the Sudanese RRC, who replaced the WFP as flight coordinators)
to Juba were routine. In a way, deMistura had done his job too well: The
flights that were supposed to carry groceries to hungry natives also con-
tained the odd pallet of military hardware.

What follows is a sad and somewhat skewed account of a dispute that
seriously disrupted the WFP's campaign in the Sudan. The reasons for its
lamentable quality will be obvious, but the reason for its awkward retelling requires some explanation.

First, the allegations that follow are those of the principals—both very
high-ranking UN officials—and should be clearly seen as something other
than documented fact. Needless to say, my attempt to recontact deMistura
came to nought, while my best efforts to find independent corroboration
of the story of the conflict between Prattley and deMistura were thwarted
by UN senior staffers in New York. (One official, sympathetic to Prattley,

was very eager to help and was attempting to provide me with information; when her superior discovered her efforts on my behalf, he ordered her to refuse to cooperate.) Second, as far as the UN was concerned, Prattley and deMistura were parts of a well-oiled, highly efficient relief machine.

Nevertheless, the conflict between Prattley and deMistura revealed more than just the inevitable fallout of the UN's clumsy politics. It also revealed something about the nature of the combatants. During the time I spent with deMistura, he was careful about his characterizations of Prattley; he had the air of a generous victor. Prattley, however, seemed to me to feel injured, and so his accusations had a particularly harsh bite. The clash had become personal at an early stage, apparently, and, at least for Prattley, it continued to be so. I was unable to speak with deMistura and obtain his reactions to Prattley's comments. However, based upon my prior conversations with deMistura, I'm certain he would deny these allegations.

Prattley, a soft-spoken New Zealander with a major general's mustache, had worked in international relief all his life; his appointment was trumpeted in the *UN Chronicle* as an expression of "the secretary-general's concern about the emergency in the Sudan." Prattley, according to Bradford Morse, director of the Office of Emergency Operations for Africa, was "one of the most senior field officials of the United Nations." Before being posted to Khartoum, Prattley had been the resident representative of the UNDP in Bangkok; before that, he had served as coordinator of the UN Border Relief Operation designed to ease the refugee problem along the Thai-Cambodian border; he had also worked for UNDP in Pakistan, Sierra Leone, Nigeria, Uganda, Zambia and Iran. He was, a New York–based UN staffer told me, "one of our best." Operation Rainbow certainly caught him unawares, occurring, as it did, as he was packing to go home and into retirement.

In the world of famine busting, most personal and political clashes have the dynamics of quilting-bee quarrels. But this one was different. This one had some interesting nuances, some resonances of a bigger power struggle.

According to Prattley and sources at the UN in New York, deMistura wasn't the son of an Italian-Swedish aristocrat, as he claimed. "His father was an Italian-cum-Albanian," Prattley said. "The Swedes told me that his Swedish was pretty poor. He's a clever man, anyway, and he is multilingual and has a lot of charm and he convinces a lot of people, but I never felt too comfortable with him."

To Prattley, deMistura was walking point in a battle that had been raging between Edouard Saouma, the director of the Food and Agricultural Organization (FAO), and the WFP's number-one man, James Ingram: "The man who deserves any credit for dealing with the emergency is not deMistura. He came when it was over. It was Alan Jones, his predecessor, who is now in Nairobi. He was a real professional of fourteen, fifteen years in the WFP. DeMistura's a Johnny-come-lately. He'd only been there, literally, weeks.

"There was something strange about the whole thing. You see, he was part of the [leadership] of Edouard Saouma, and Saouma threw him out of the FAO."

I asked Prattley if he thought deMistura had actually resigned from the FAO cabinet in order to work in the field, as he had claimed.

"No," said Prattley. "He was thrown out as a consequence of his activities in Ethiopia. He went out there with his FAO hat on and disobeyed Saouma's instructions, as he disobeyed mine."

According to Prattley, James Ingram was "at war" with Saouma, and because deMistura knew the "inside secrets" of the FAO cabinet, "Ingram took him on and stuck him out there [in Ethiopia] to get him out of the way. But he also wanted to use him to engineer his defense—or attack, as you want to see it—against Saouma."

It was clearly difficult for Prattley to air this sort of linen. But he managed: "I don't want to cause a kind of stink and make it look as though I'm rancorous about this. I'm agitated—not agitated, that's not it, no—I'm *annoyed* with deMistura, but it's a pettiness that as far as I'm concerned is not worth the attention. He will reap his harvest, of that I'm quite sure. And, more particularly, his boss, Ingram, who's using deMistura to help him in his manipulations against Saouma, who is coming up for reelection as director-general of the Food and Agricultural Organization shortly. . . .

"DeMistura had nothing to do with organizing the major emergency operation. That's why he wanted to make a splash—although the tide had gone out on the emergency. He wanted to jack up the southern situation, and he eventually escalated it out of all reason, primarily by engaging the attention of the media—excessively, in my opinion, for the nature of this work. . . . He's clever. That's his forte.

"I mean, $4,000 a ton [the cost of food carried on Rainbow flights] is an outrageous waste of taxpayers' money, to spend that rate per ton to try to relieve the needs of hundreds of thousands with one little airplane. . . .*

---

* An overloaded DC-8 can manage to carry thirty-six, maybe thirty-seven tons, if all conditions are right. The nine flights of Operation Rainbow, then, might have carried 330-odd tons. The final figure, however, was closer to 250 tons. The estimated cost of the operation was in excess of $1 million.

He wants to be famous, that's all. He thinks the UN is too bureaucratic, too bogged-down with too many old fogies—he's referring to people like myself, I suppose. . . . To deMistura, it needs individual entrepreneurship, you know, the sort of Reagan style: a gun slung low on each hip, quick on the draw and not too worried about the sheriff."

Prattley and his sympathizers are fond of pointing out the Malakal barge operation as more typical of a deMistura effort. It was, in the words of Prattley, a "madcap" operation, in which deMistura—who, at the time, was not yet working for the WFP, but was instead under the control of UNICEF, for whom he was in the Sudan to administer a mass immunization program—made an agreement with the SPLA to allow two barges filled with food to pass through their lines to recipients in the south. The SPLA agreed to a hands-off policy, but the Sudanese government got wind of the deal and insisted that the barges wouldn't move unless they were allowed to attach additional barges to the small UNICEF flotilla. By the time the barges left the north, there were seventeen or eighteen of them, all under the UN flag, but some were carrying weapons to besieged government garrisons in the south. The SPLA, said Prattley, "was furious." And deMistura "had double-crossed Alan Jones [who had been] dragged into it unwittingly."

According to Prattley, deMistura had "sold himself" to UNICEF to do the immunization program, which, as Prattley pointed out, "has nothing to do with starvation or emergencies. But this [the immunization program] was not dramatic enough for him and he switched his attention to this Malakal operation in an attempt to become famous. It really did jeopardize the whole UN emergency operation at the time."

Prattley's most damning charges against deMistura—corroborated by at least one knowledgeable UN official—related to allegations of deMistura's connection, apparently through Ingram, with international arms dealer Adnan Khashoggi. Not only does deMistura's long-sought riverside paradise allegedly belong to Khashoggi, but, according to Prattley, deMistura may have more significant ties to the arms merchant. "He's an operator," Prattley told me. "He had been surreptitiously—even when he was working directly under my control with WFP—[trying] to organize all kinds of mysterious private operators to airlift out of East African countries into the south [of the Sudan] without the knowledge of the government or even myself, until rather late in the piece, when I squashed the whole thing, because it was illegal. He is prone to do this kind of thing. I'm inclined—and I may be very naive about this—to give him the benefit of the doubt. But there are people who are linked with the south—I mean southerners—and some people in Khartoum claim—maybe out of jealousy, I don't know—that he's involved in arms supplies and that sort of thing as well. Certainly that wasn't part of the Rainbow operation. Rainbow may have been intended as a cover for those other illegal flights which he was trying to organize and which I intercepted."

On the other hand, if Prattley's right about deMistura's role as a political tool in Ingram's fight against Saouma, Prattley might have suggested to Ingram that he was an even more formidable weapon. One longtime colleague told me the story of how Prattley once stood up at an important meeting, when Saouma was addressing the gathering, and angrily demanded to know why one of the FAO's men in Southeast Asia had been selling tons of donated rice on the black market. "Saouma was enraged. He simply walked out of the meeting. And you can be quite sure he never, ever, forgot Winston."

Meetings of relief officials often resemble pieces of fluorescent theater in which the leading players sit in summer-suit perfection in rooms resembling Holiday Inn conference suites and discuss traffic conditions on the road to hell.

In Khartoum, the players at one typical performance include a brilliant woman (BW), a tactician long of wind and experience but short of patience, maybe fifty-five and quite striking, really; a young hotshot (YH) with great hair, very much taken with the whole notion of having graduated from some Euro-university two months ago and now plotting rescues and relief; and a seasoned vet (SV), a gray-haired gent who seems to view his role with some cynical concern. The problem at hand is how to move tons of food from places like Kitale, in Kenya, near the southeastern border of Uganda, and El Obeid, in Kordofan, to emergency areas in Bahr al-Ghazal and Jonglei provinces.

BW: So I had those 3,000 tons of maize in Kitale, and I'm going to do a cable tomorrow saying to release the final 1,000 tons to Sudan Aid and start procurement on the second lot. I think Mohammed feels he can get it through.

This is the first thing said at the meeting. There seems to be a certain set of assumptions at work here. I had been invited, but told that while there was no objection to my recording the meeting, I could not use anyone's name or mention any specific nationality. I tried to interrupt to clarify some of the names BW had used, but was ceremoniously ignored.

SV: He can at least try, for a change.

YH: I should say so. He should try. The other route seems to be open.

SV: No, the road is a little complicated now. [To YH] Haven't you heard about it? The Zaïre road is the worst, because you have to pay so much to Zaïre.

BW: It's outrageous. But the other road to the west of Nimule [the border crossing on the main Juba-Kampala road] is open at the moment. Now, I have also got an engineering report, complete with colored, glossy pictures, on how much bridge work and road grading have to be done to get those roads fixed up. So I turned that over to the engineering office, because I wondered about World Vision going into southern Sudan and doing road and bridge repairs, because World Vision has a tendency to underesti mate how much it's going to cost, and said, you know, Look at the cost estimates and the pictures and tell me how far off they are and how much it's going to cost to fix it up. I should get that report by tomorrow.

SV: It might work . . .

BW: It might, but, you know, it's Uganda.

YH: I sent a ten-page cable about it to . . .

SV.   Oh, a ten-page cable. Ten pages.

YH: . . . outlining strategy and sending off the logistic plan and saying where the Americans were sitting in each, the U.S. AID. Now, let me give you my problems with . . .

BW: B —— is writing the contract to go down to Malakal, as though the trucks were going around the corner, as though it were a risk-free voyage.

YH: . . . so what was I going to say? Oh, then I give the logistic plan, then I said what the Americans should do.

SV   (to BW): Did you swap the grain in Wad Medani for the grain in Ed Dueim?

BW: Yeah, so the present barges will load up with Sudan Aid and take as much as they can, and there'll be another 1,000 [tons] waiting for them farther along. Now, luckily I had diesel fuel, so I gave them forty tons. The next thing, Lutheran World Service comes in and says they want another forty tons to run their tractors in Malakal, because last year they had that big success [developing large chunks of acreage just outside the war-torn town and allowing 60,000 displaced people to farm the land], so this year they want to enlarge the program. So, you know, my boss still isn't used to my wheeling and dealing, and, you know, you have an hour or so to make a decision on something of these things or you miss a bargeload or whatever have you. So, I got that off, too. Now I had eighty tons of fuel on the barges and whatever food they could carry. So I go to the meeting with the governor of Upper Nile [an especially pitiful southern province], and he said he would arrange to unload the food.

SV   (skeptically): Right.

YH   (by now, completely befuddled and sorting through a stack of papers): Where? Is there something on this?

BW   (ignoring him): Well, I'll believe it when I see it.

SV: But he may. You know, it's his constituency. Likewise, the governor of Central Province [not otherwise identified] is going to be there protecting his merchants, and the barge owners are going to gouge whoever will pay the most. How much did they pay, loaded and unloaded, in Malakal?

BW: You know, who wins that fight is up in the air, I think I've done everything I can there. Next, I'm told I have 4,000 tons of sorghum in El Obeid and I've given an allotment to the RRC [Sudanese Relief and Rehabilitation Commission] for 1,500 and told B —— to do the contract with the transporters for 1,500, expandable to 4,000 on satisfactory performance, so that they only have to advertise once. Now, you are aware that B —— wrote the contract with the EEC [European Community] that says the EEC has to pay for the petrol for the army escort.

SV   (looking at me): No, I'm not aware of that.

BW: I don't know who let that go by. I was sick when I saw it. I said, let me see the documents.

SV: [Kamil] Shawki [Sudanese Commissioner for Relief and Rehabilitation] can bloody well arrange for the military escort.

YH (to me): Are you using our names?

SV (to YH): No, he said he wasn't.

BW: Because if it hits the EEC papers that there's a free license for contractors to pay for military escorts and the EEC pays the contract, well . . . And you know another thing those boys [the EEC relief officials] have done? They're really stupid. They're paying the RRC for the transport contract instead of paying the contractor themselves, so the RRC can take a cut off the whole thing. I mean, let me tell you . . .

SV (to me): You must be careful. The situation is . . .

YH (earnestly): The plight of the poor is appalling.

BW: Look at Wau. The military controls the prices of food there. It's a stranglehold, really. They control all the sugar and the coffee exports. You know, the majority of the coffee is smuggled and sold for £S1,000 per bag. The price elsewhere is only £S250.

SV (to me): Who can report it?

BW: No, there's an ominous silence when things like the Italian rice convoy happen.

I asked what the Italian rice convoy was.

BW. It was a typical situation, the sort of thing that happens everywhere in Africa. The Italians donated some rice to help the effort, and a convoy was organized to take it to the south, where it was needed. The [Sudanese] military took over the convoy and stole the rice.

SV: It'll turn up in the marketplace.

BW: Anyway, I don't trust B —— .

SV: No. He's not . . .

YH: He's not an international humanitarian kind of man . . .

BW: He's a businessman working for a company, a construction company, and there is no concern for relief.

SV: Yeah, you know the RRC is attempting to put stipulations on the contract to take food to the south. The stipulations to my mind will prohibit any respectable contractor bidding on it. Now, if you don't call that outright obstructionism, I do. I've asked them for a draft contract to be reviewed by my contracts officer, and I'm going to see if I can't get some of the stuff changed and made more lenient, because I don't know who in their right mind would ignore risk. If they say the chances are one in thirty of having your truck blown up and losing your investment, you know, that has to be figured into the margin.

YH: Definitely. Right?

This is how they do deliveries along the more southerly stretches of the Nile, where insurrections, swamps and monsoons conspire to create a teamster's nightmare. They pile up a big load of food, guns and money, then stack part of it in an airplane that was bought cheap and is so worn out it won't matter if it turns into metallized roadkill some rainy afternoon, and fly it south from Khartoum, where the government of the Sudan lives, out over the Sahara to dinkyvilles in the swampy south, where government is a matter of violent negotiation.

To see how relief flights operated in the Sudan, I had signed on as a loadmaster—a stewardess for boxes, really—on a very old DC-8. My job, in theory, was to make sure that the aircraft was loaded properly—and with the prescribed food and emergency supplies only, thank you. But then an army tractor pulling a two-ton pallet of radios or grenades or what-have-you pulls up to the airplane; a soldier shouts an order and a pallet of cooking oil or tuna or something is hauled out of the fuselage and replaced with something that goes bang in the night.

Private cargo flyers, like the ruthless chap who owns this DC-8, can sometimes miss the fine print. A typical cargo cowboy, he had contracted to deliver food and supplies to the south: "Relief flights," he told his crew, neglecting to note that the contracting party was the Sudanese military.

What, I asked the RRC's Kamil Shawki, had gone wrong? Why had the situation in the south deteriorated to the point where emergency relief operations were necessary at all?

"As a developing country, we didn't know better," Shawki told me. "Besides, the country is bankrupt and coming out of autocratic rule [imposed by Nimeiri]. . . ."

Dealing with Operation Rainbow had been a trial for the new Sudanese government (the only freely elected government in Africa, by the way).

The sudden rush of emergency experts had not only embarrassed the government, it had caught it completely by surprise. "I was a UN expert for fifteen years," Shawki said. "I had to *drag* the government in."

Shawki couldn't quite figure out if Operation Rainbow had been a good thing or simply another international evil visited on an unsuspecting and innocent nation. At the beginning of our chat, he told me that "Operation Rainbow was ill-fated and accomplished very little." But later, he decided that maybe "it had saved lives" after all, and that, truth to tell, it had been his idea all along. When Shawki had seen the need for an emergency program for the south, he said he had been the first to move: "I raised $1.5 million in the first three weeks. Then it fell into the clutches of inefficiency." And from that point on, Shawki said, it was a financial disaster that required "the proper analysis, costwise."

The foreign experts, Shawki told me, had overstepped their roles. "It's difficult to tell whether these people [deMistura, local U.S. AID Director Koehring, and the Dutch chargé Feith, the Rainbow donors] were ill-intentioned or not," Shawki noted darkly. "People forget their principal missions."

According to some international relief workers, Shawki may well have forgotten his. I asked one Western official who worked closely with Shawki whether or not Shawki felt any local pressure to get aid to the south as quickly as possible. Suddenly, the rich smell of fish filled the air—

"No," he said, "it's all just lip service. Shawki needs his empire, and in order to have his empire he must have a continuation of the relief effort. Now, whether or not the relief gets there is no concern of his. He can always come up with a plausible excuse about military activity or a bridge falling down."

Rainbow certainly irritated some Sudanese government officials, who saw it not as a grand gesture to overcome institutional lethargy but as an insult to the sovereignty of an independent state. Souvenirs of Rainbow are everywhere in relief offices in Khartoum; everyone has a snapshot or something. It's one of those things that happened once, and, as far as Kamil Shawki is concerned, it isn't likely to happen again.

What would happen, I asked him, when April brought the rainy season and the roads became impassable and the SPLA came crawling out of the weeds to choke off the southern towns once again?

"I have hope that the military and political situation has improved and will continue to improve," Shawki said. The second anniversary of the coup that toppled Nimeiri was coming with the rains in April; it was widely suggested that the present Sudanese government of Prime Minister

Sadiq al-Mahdi would use the occasion to announce a deal granting the southerners a measure of the autonomy for which they had been fighting. But no cease-fire was announced, and if there was a contingency plan in place, I never heard about it.

And neither did anyone else. Almost every foreigner in the Sudan agreed that the south would be in trouble again before May 1988, political solution or not. "It's going to require another Rainbow," one relief official told me. "In April and May people are going to be pretty bad off," he added quietly. "It's getting worse instead of better."

PART FOUR

HIGH
AND
MIGHTY,
FAST
AND
LOOSE

10.

You can do anything you want here and nobody's going to call the FAA. Because there is no FAA. And there's no phone.

—*Helicopter pilot Gene Wilkie, Kinshasa, Zaïre*

DENYS FINCH HATTON came up with the idea of using an airplane to hunt elephants; for him, it was a fatal notion, but Beryl Markham made a living at it for a while and it makes sense to me. In fact, better than flying for hunters, I like the idea of airplanes for African sightseers. You think, swell, I'll get up there, not too high, say two, maybe three thousand feet or so. See everything from there.

But the right tool for the right job, I always say. The job was to look for some waterfalls along an overstated fault line running through the heart of Africa: This was a few years ago, when I was first getting acquainted with Third World freighter pilots. If you want to find geological landmarks in the jungle, seems to me like the right tool would be an airplane, like the old DC-6 George Pappas* used to cart cargo to Lubumbashi in southern Zaïre, out beyond the rain forest and near the Zambian border. But Pappas got confused, flew the plane jeep-style and almost killed me for the first time.

The whole episode had started like a zany remake of *The High and the Mighty*. In the real thing, you recall, young Robert Stack gets cold feet, loses his nerve, and it's left to the tested veteran, John Wayne, to carry the ball. He calms the edgy flight engineer, and, with only one of four engines on speaking terms, forces Stack to bring in the big bird—a DC-4, wasn't

* For obvious reasons, I've changed a number of names in this chapter and deliberately disguised some other details. For example, there's nobody I know named George Pappas.

it?—narrowly missing the coastal bluffs. Stack ends up with the credit, but he, and everyone else, knows it was the Duke who did it.

In Pappas's remake, playing maybe 1,500 feet over Lubumbashi, the grizzled veteran misplaced the airport. It was there, just a second ago, and then like crazy magic it was gone. Pappas led the DC-6—a plane as big as a DC-9—through a slow waltz of banks and curves in search of the strip. He scolded the copilot, who had been running the show and had to take the rap for flying past the airport; now the copilot sat angrily staring straight ahead. Pappas made no effort to calm the edgy flight engineer, who had the disagreeable habit of repeating twice everything he said in English. "Where the hell's the airport?" Pappas screamed at his two Zaïrian crewmen.

The copilot peered coolly into thin air. Not his job. The flight engineer tried to ameliorate the situation and said, "It will be here, it will be here."

Pappas didn't believe him. And, because Pappas didn't believe him, I didn't either. I wanted to. But then we started climbing, an admission of failure, I felt, and the string of buildings that defined Lubumbashi—once everywhere below us—now was someplace else.

Better luck on the second circle: gas stations, bars, a paved road. Pappas ordered up a fresh batch of flaps as the runway came into view. There was a small cluster of pink trucks and white Land-Rovers on one side of the runway, a prefab terminal building on the other, and off the far end was a French Mirage fighter stuck in the mud. Red, twelve-foot-tall anthills, hopeless patches of brown grass and thin, khaki-colored brush covered the sandy fields surrounding the runway.

The plane was met by an American delegation, representing the U.S. consulate and led with resolute cheerfulness by a woman, fiftyish, short hair, the painfully permanent smile of diplomats and Unitarians creasing her face; she had come to bid welcome to some household effects—drapes, ironing board, canned goods, John Denver's *Greatest Hits,* the works—belonging to the Palomes, newly of Lubumbashi, formerly Elisabethville. The Palomes's private cosmos, crated, weighed three tons. The balance of the freight had caused some consternation, we learned. The manifest was, as usual, vague enough, and when the telex arrived, announcing that 8,500 kilos of Teacher's was on its way, the Americans thought "Peace Corps" and the local education man thought "chaos," but only the guy from the liquor distributor was right, and the whiskey disappeared into the pink trucks; the Palomes were crammed into the Land-Rovers. The whole deal took maybe two hours.

Off to town for spare parts and a quick hustle, Pappas and I begged a ride from the diplomatic lady and made a fruitless search for a conservationist-pilot named Roger Minne, who might have a part Pappas wanted. Minne, in addition to flying antipoaching patrols in Zaïre's game parks, runs a bakery on the main street in town. He was out. We went instead to the bougainvillea-covered house of the American woman, where Pappas tried to fast-talk her into a regular weekly flight contract. We sat on her comfortable porch chatting, ants the size of toys everywhere, high-rise anthills in her front yard; she gave us lemonade, a long, polite smile and a ride back to the airport.

Pappas walked around the airplane, checking the gears and tires until the two crewmen sauntered out from the small building that served as a waiting room. Behind them was a tall, thin man with sandy hair, wearing a white shirt and khaki trousers, and behind him was a crowd of well over a hundred aspiring travelers, each bearing one or more cardboard boxes and each complaining that Air Zaïre had canceled its flight that day—and every other day for the past week. The copilot and the flight engineer cleared a small area near the props, and the crowd jostled there in the Kansas-summer heat shouting for passage like a game-show audience while Pappas talked to the skinny guy in the khaki trousers.

"This is Klaus," Pappas said, presenting the man to me. I think his name was Klaus. In any case he was German. "He's a German," Pappas said. "Works for the diamond company."

"No more," said Klaus, pulling his hand out of his pocket. He unwrapped a handkerchief containing a small pile of stones. Pappas laughed, the German climbed aboard, and Pappas, ignoring the wailing crowd, returned his attention to the landing gear. Finally, he seemed ready to mount up.

"I have five seats," he said authoritatively without looking up. He stood and turned to face the potential passengers, but instead found himself looking down into the cold eyes of a short, stern-faced, fatigues-clad military officer who had been standing six inches behind him. The officer carried an automatic rifle and an Asterix coloring book. "I have five seats," Pappas repeated. Then, pointing at the soldier, "And one of them is for *you.*"

The others fell to squabbling, each trying to outgesture the others. Pappas, who spoke French like a farmer reading the words aloud for the first time, listened to the hard-luck stories with patience, his sweaty countenance artificially but appropriately magisterial—no mean feat for a man who looks alarmingly like a cross between Vincent Price and Eve Arden. Finally, after careful vetting, four were chosen—all women, and all with astonishingly large breasts. I couldn't figure out why they had been selected before others who I thought looked more deserving—the elderly, some pregnant women, some kids. "I have a rule," he explained without being asked. "First, you choose 'em by the size of their guns. Then you choose 'em by the size of their tits."

Back in the cockpit, Pappas waved away questions about the extraordinary scene at the airport. For him, it was a typical flight, and, typically, a profitable one. Even though he'd make the return flight to Kinshasa virtually empty, he'd earn well over a thousand dollars for his day's work. The German, Klaus, lounged in a makeshift bunk near the cockpit bulkhead; I started to wander back to the passengers, who were secured to some old airliner seats in the aft of the aircraft with rope, but quickly realized that I would probably skid on the roller bearings that covered the cargo floor and become a source of in-flight entertainment. Instead, I retreated to the cockpit and stood behind Pappas's seat and talked to Klaus about diamonds and the business of flying until Pappas interrupted us with an idea. "Ask him if he remembers the waterfalls he was telling me about," Pappas shouted over the engine noise. He unfolded a navigational map and handed it to me to pass to Klaus. "Ask him where they are." The German climbed down from the bunk. "I want to look for them," Pappas explained.

Klaus circled an area to the north, shrugged, handed the map back and returned to the bunk. "I never have seen them myself," he said.

An hour later, Pappas was standing up in the cockpit, shouting something at his copilot. Out the window, trees screamed by as the plane ducked into a horseshoe chasm at the end of which a waterfall made a thousand-foot drop from deep jungle and disappeared into vapor and mist. The copilot suddenly stood up, too, forcing Pappas to sit down in order to use the rudder controls. "Chickenshit!" Pappas yelled to the copilot. "Sit the fuck down!" The copilot, however, had his headset off and was looking behind his seat for a misplaced shoe and didn't want to hear. The flight engineer was in full repeat mode and kept screaming "American people! American people!" for some reason, and from time to time would look up, then cover his eyes like a kid at a horror movie. I was thrown to the back of the cockpit and looked down the fuselage at our lucky passengers, who were straining against the ropes and looking out the window in terror. The coloring book was on the floor halfway along the cargo floor, and one woman was crying.

The German passed me on his way to the back of the airplane, and I saw him take a cartoon-style tumble as I pulled the cockpit door closed. Better, I thought, that the passengers shouldn't hear the driver shouting and cursing, might get the wrong idea.

We ducked in and out of canyons like cheery barnstormers. At the end of each canyon was a waterfall, and at each waterfall Pappas would shout, "Look at *that* one!" as if it could be distinguished from any of the others. During one lull, the German reappeared. He heard me screaming and asked if I was scared. Before I could answer, Pappas cursed, the airplane seemed to stand still, then fall, and the German went sliding across the freight floor again.

In front of the airplane, the ground dropped away like a giant step down, and Pappas went down with it, over the edge, over a small village of thatched huts. Only a few feet below us, an old man dropped the hoe he was holding and fell into a fetal curl, his hands over his ears trying to block out the stereo napalm. For him it was over in a second—the airplane climbed very slightly and disappeared into myth, maybe a cautionary fairy tale, a horror story for children. Or maybe the whole incident would become the basis for an angry letter to a local parliamentarian. In any case, the old man would be struck by the silence that would follow our indiscreet passage, and it would end.

But for us, the party rolled on over the flat, thick jungle. The copilot tried to smile but couldn't, and the flight engineer was strangely silent. Our world was in Pappas's hands, and Pappas was transported, looking now for more villages or for wildlife, I wasn't sure. At 200 feet and 225 m.p.h., some fool yelled, "Look, lions!" and the plane banked sharply in search. I held on and looked out the pilot's window to where, down below, animals of some sort—definitely not lions—evacuated a clearing. The rain forest, at high speed and up close, filled the cockpit windows first on one side, then on the other, and after a while it was all over. Pappas grew bored with the chase, lectured the sheepish copilot, gave a navigational order and climbed out of his seat and up into the bunk. The German edged into the cockpit and asked what was going on. "Going home," Pappas said wearily. He paused, then smiled. "When I start doing that stuff, I just can't stop."

The German nodded sympathetically as if he were listening to the confessions of a schoolboy. He started to say something, but Pappas was already asleep and didn't stir until Kinshasa reappeared four hours later, ten thousand feet below us.

That was the first time. The second time, it's 1985. I was scouting the dangerous perimeters of small business and suburban romance when I got a call from Pappas. He had a new deal, a DC-8 this time, flying bulk loads of civilization from Europe and South America to everyplace in Africa and beyond. But there was a new wrinkle: Freight brokers were asking him to fly weapons from Tel Aviv to Teheran; did I think that was news? Which is how I found myself in a flying Dumpster that reeked of twenty-five years of bad beans, 14,000 feet over an African civil war, spiraling downward in a tight corkscrew through the clouds, looking for an isolated runway cut off by ambitious and well-armed chaps who would have loved to stuff and mount some really big game, like this garbage truck here.

We had all been through it before, but believe me it never lost its freshness. In what amounted to cockpit choreography, the flight engineer and I were on our feet, looking over the shoulders of the nervous pilot, hoping to God we were in the right place—there was no way to know for sure, since the radio beacon wasn't working and the weather made it impossible to see the ground. The idea was to come out of the clouds over a troubled Angolan army outpost called Saurimo in the northeastern corner of Angola, and not over anyplace else, since everyplace else was a rebel UNITA outpost. Flying into Luanda is like flying into Lincoln, Nebraska. Lights, beacons, guys chatting to you on the radio, little trucks that say FOLLOW ME on the back escorting you to a parking place. Flying into Saurimo, on the other hand, is like playing pin-the-tail-on-the-donkey, and for all we know, we were way off target.

It happened again, just like the other four times. We poked out of the clouds in the wrong place, *everybody* said so, the DC-8 shuddered, the flight engineer shouted some numbers, the copilot shouldered some levers and up we went again, into the clouds, into hiding. This is no way to travel, I said to myself, you see so little of the countryside, the people and their quaint folk ways.

Pappas, of course, had backed out at the very last minute, just before takeoff, and was back in Brazil with somebody named Brigitte.

II.

We import everything by air. We even import
Kitty Litter.

—*U.S. embassy staffer, Kinshasa, Zaïre*

FIGURING OUT HOW TO BE in the right place at the right time is the secret
of survival for men like Pappas and the other expatriate pilots, who
command a ragtag air force of beat-up cargo planes that, in many ways,
holds a continent together. For in Africa, where nothing much moves
unless it flies, they run their one-man airlines the way Mr. Butterfield once
ran the Overland stages. They tote rice and guns, Xerox machines and dry
goods in and out of places nobody else wants to go— often with what
seems little regard for their own safety. Pappas, for example, was known
around Kinshasa as "The Gross Greek" because of his habit of flying
airplanes loaded several tons over their maximum limits, among other
reasons. "It's just a matter of time," warned one of his pilot acquaintances.

"Bullshit," said Pappas. "It could be worse. I could be flying over-
weight in war."

In fact, in the remarkably tight-knit community of freight flyers,
Pappas is almost a war virgin. His own military career spanned just those
several months in Central America while El Salvador and Honduras
slugged it out, ostensibly over a soccer match. But for most of the others,
World War II, Korea and Vietnam provided an abundance of practical
experience.

Jim "Black Bart" Fore, for example, flew in Laos and Cambodia for
Continental Air Transport—one of Air America's CIA affiliates*—until

* Air America was probably the most successful of all state-run airlines; at its peak, it
had the largest commercial fleet in the world. Started by General Claire Chennault—

149

he was shot down on the China border, and, according to the story, narrowly escaped death by popping out of the emergency hatch on his DC-3 moments before impact. Fore started by flying B-17s over France during World War II. In his Southeast Asia days, Black Bart earned his nickname by the monochromatic quality of his wardrobe—black flying gear; a long, black scarf; black shades; a pair of pearl-handled, black steel pistols he carried in his belt. By the end of the '70s, he looked like Burl Ives and was known as "Bicentennial" Fore—he dressed only in red, white and blue—and flew out of Cairo in one of Pyramid Aviation's DC-3s to oil-exploration camps near the Libyan border.

Or Captain Robert Grider, a stiff-backed veteran of seven wars—"Four of them on both sides"—whom I met after he arrived in Zaïre to help put together a couple of old Convairs, and who had had the misfortune of flying into Malta's Luqa airfield while running guns to Biafra. The Maltese confiscated his unmarked Lockheed Constellation and imprisoned him and his crew. They staged a successful escape (I think Grider is still wanted in Valletta), but the Maltese got custody of the airplane, sold off the engines, towed the hulk off the tarmac, put down the passenger steps, painted BAR AND RESTAURANT on the side and opened it for business. Grider was appalled when I told him about it.

Or the young copilot from the wealthy American family who came to Africa to log some first-officer hours and ended up with a copilot gig on a DC-3 flying out of Chad. On his first night in Ndjamena, though, he apparently got real drunk, went off with a whore and wound up at four in the morning with his throat cut and his wallet missing. "What he missed in wars," one of his colleagues noted, "he made up for in one night." Unable to face what they considered a rather terminal blotch on their son's résumé, the family hired a famous detective from Texas to get at the truth of the matter. The detective decided that the kid had died for his country, the victim of a tragic political assassination suffered while in the employ of a CIA-front airline, and got the family to attempt a lawsuit.

Or the veteran Dutch pilot known around his home field for habitually

---

commander of the Flying Tigers during World War II—Air America flew for the intelligence service until the collapse of the war effort in Vietnam, when, after a heroic episode evacuating Saigon, the company was sold off piecemeal. Known for its derring-do (Air America's motto was "Anything, Anywhere, Anytime") and its dubious cargo manifests, the airline employed some of the most colorful pilots of the postwar generation, men like Fore with names like "Radar" Milan, "Shower Shoes" Wilson and "Earthquake" McGoon. For an entertaining and affectionate account, try Christopher Robbins's *Air America* (1979).

trying to take off in his Cessna 172 with the concrete tie-down block still attached to the tail of the airplane (frustrated airport officials finally fined him for unauthorized towing). On a contract for a TV news organization, he flew a camera-and-sound crew down to Dakar to see the finale of the Paris–Dakar trans-Sahara road rally, and on the way decided to skirt the beaches of what used to be the Spanish Sahara but is now the scene of a bizarre war between Morocco and the Polisario guerrillas. The Polisario shot down the airplane, then lined up the survivors on the beach and killed them.

They aren't bush pilots, the laid-back Piper jockeys who cruise the pipeline in Alaska, nor should they be confused with missionary pilots, whose planes are bought with charity but who often charge an arm and a leg for a ride to those most likely in risk of losing an appendage anyway. In equatorial Africa, especially, the independent cargo pilot is often the only component of a transportation system that otherwise doesn't exist. Highways are a threatened species in Africa (in Zaïre, for example, there were some 90,000 miles of passable roads in 1960 when the country obtained its rather abrupt independence from Belgium; by 1980, after two decades and a quadrupled highway budget, there were only 6,000 miles left, according to an International Monetary Fund report released that year). At the same time, the cyclic disruptions occasioned by a turbulent climate wreak havoc not only with the roads but also with river navigation: Waterways shrink and expand quickly and unpredictably. Railroads have become mechanically obsolete, and many are no longer in operation. (I met a Belgian who had spent twenty-eight years working on the Zaïre railroads. He said it was "like making a career out of building sand castles.") Moreover, all forms of ground transportation are subject to prodigious amounts of theft; most shippers allow for one-third of their consignments to go astray, and the resulting compensatory increases in price force many products out of the market.

Cargo pilots are left a pretty clear field. "The pilots here," one Zaïrian businessman told me, "are like sharks. They make excuses and wait until we need them very badly, then they raise their rates. It is very difficult, very expensive." (And very questionable: One pilot told me that 90 percent of the cargo he carries on his flights is, one way or another, contraband; his friend put the figure even higher.)

So, Donald Douglas's greatest hits of the '30s (the DC-3), the '40s (the DC-4), the '50s (the DC-6 and -7) and the '60s (the DC-8),* along with

---

* There was a DC-5, a high-wing job. Douglas made five of them and sold them to the Dutch air force, which crashed them all.

stray Britannias, Electras, Constellations and the odd 707, support entire economies, keep industries, governments and guerrilla movements alive, provide logistical support for a welter of development projects and supply gainful employment for a gang of desperate, high-risk entrepreneurs who, back home, would be stuck in the suburbs teaching the finer points of aviation to Beechcraft kamikazes.

Together, they constitute an ad hoc Luftwaffe of seat-of-the-pants, fiercely independent small businessmen whose chaotic, hard-currency, cash-in-advance network of freight runs stretches from Malta to the Cape of Good Hope. "Anything goes here," Gene Wilkie, a chopper pilot, told me. "You can fly light or heavy, early or late, high or low. Just get your money up front."

You meet them in bars in Kinshasa, Kisangani or Khartoum and listen to them talk about flying for both sides in a half-dozen civil wars. Hang around for a while and they'll present you with a realpolitik more cynical than you'd hoped. Nearly every airplane owner has a pressing problem: how to transport rocket fuel from South Africa to a West German–built Libyan base hidden in a satellite shadow, or how to negotiate the deviously circuitous flights* that will take Iron Curtain hardware or Israeli rockets from Warsaw or Tel Aviv to Teheran. Commiserate with a broker who can't find anybody to tote military cargo from Havana to Lima or from New England to Johannesburg via Kinshasa. Or sign on as a loadmaster and transport weapons on relief flights from Khartoum to Juba, or watch American taxpayers feed the Cuban army in Angola.

If you're a normal kind of fellow, Pappas is the kind of man you meet by accident—on a train, maybe, or in a hotel lobby. In fact, I met him by accident myself one night in a hangar at Kinshasa's Ndjili airport. I was collecting interviews with cargo cowboys, and Pappas had been highly recommended. I had had a little trouble tracking him down, however; I'd been told he was in Goma, on the eastern border of Zaïre, and he had been, but wasn't by the time I showed up. Then I heard he was in Cameroon or had gone home to Canada. So when I finally arrived in

---

* A favorite route: Tel Aviv to Cyprus, then Cyprus to Mombasa. In Mombasa, file a flight plan to Bombay, but turn left just past the gulf. Iranian air force jets meet you at the border and escort you in; they've been alerted by the Israelis, and they're expecting you. In view of Iran's resemblance to the Hotel California, they suggest that you use no American crew members.

Kinshasa one evening and spotted his DC-3, I was relieved. I sat chatting
with some amiable mechanics in a hot hangar waiting for him to arrive
in his DC-4, trying to work out an E.T.A. He finally taxied in and discharged the Zaïrian national military soccer team through a belly hatch
and down a rickety aluminum stepladder. That was two days before
Christmas, 1979.

On Christmas Day,* President Mobutu Sese Seko addressed his nation
on TV and radio. The presidential address was somewhat rambling, but
the overall subject was Zaïre's somewhat conceptual currency, conveniently called the zaïre. The black market, he suggested, was rampant,
and, worse, people were hoarding their cash—in one sweep the year
before, the President said, his treasury inspectors had found millions
and millions of zaïres stuffed in the nation's mattresses—and it was
often impossible to pay the civil service because of the lack of cash. In an
effort to qualify for an International Monetary Fund (IMF) credit line,
Mobutu announced that effective immediately, all the zaïres in circulation
above a single (in other words, all the fives and tens; there was nothing
bigger) were no longer legal tender. It would be necessary, Mobutu said,
to take the money to the bank and get new, differently colored notes. He
allowed until January 1 for all the transactions to be completed, and put a
ceiling of 3,000 zaïres (about U.S.$1,500 at the official rate; maybe
U.S.$475 on the black market and falling fast) on all transactions. To
make certain that no money hoarded in Europe or elsewhere in Africa was
brought into the country, he sealed the nation's borders and prohibited
domestic flights.

The country's fragile economy convulsed dramatically. The black market exchange rate, which, on December 24, had stood at about 6.5 to one,
collapsed and revived at only a slightly lower rate forty-eight hours later (it
would eventually work its way above thirty). Employers had no money to
pay workers who went off to spend several days standing in bank queues.
The InterContinental and Memling hotels, both filled with visiting foreigners deprived of the ability to leave the country, took on a distinctly
Iranian gloom. Word soon circulated that Mobutu had neglected to import
enough new, improved currency from his printer in Munich; Kinshasa
itself had only half the amount needed to meet the anticipated legitimate
demand; the provincial towns, in many cases, had nothing at all, since the
government wouldn't allow domestic flights. I saw two planeloads of the
stuff arrive at Ndjili just the day before Christmas, so I tended to believe

---

* Christmas was outlawed by Mobutu, who replaced it with his own birthday. While it
no longer enjoyed legal status in Zaïre, the holiday was still celebrated by the sizable
Christian community.

the rumor that even the small amount of money minted hadn't been distributed. There was a logistical problem there someplace. In many bush towns and settlements, the barter economy revived with vigor, and produce and cigarettes became hard currency. In the capital the situation grew more confusing as New Year's Day approached. Without money for food, people began rioting; gendarmes and soldiers refused to quell the disturbances unless they were paid first, and once they got their money, they initiated a series of apparently random assaults on the people waiting in bank lines, carefully weeding out any Europeans before wading in with their truncheons. I sat on a wall opposite a bank with a woman who worked for a foreign-owned construction company and watched the action for a while. Gradually, a small group of white folk surrounded us. "Not a very good show, is it?" asked an Englishman.

At night, rumors of combat and death wafted through the *cité*—the crowded, immense and vague jumble of tin-and-cardboard shelters, home to more than a million—on clouds of tear gas. As the deadline neared, the city's bank managers, fearing for their lives, checked into the well-protected InterContinental and watched Charles Bronson movies that had been flown in before the emergency started. Alas, on New Year's Day, it was announced that an error had been made: The new ten-zaïre note—the largest and most popular bill—had been printed in the correct new color but from an old plate, one that showed Mobutu in a necktie. Since neckties had been outlawed by Mobutu during his last big purge of Europeans, the ten-zaïre notes were made worthless, and the government said they would have to be returned to the bank and redeemed for an even newer version at a date which would be revealed later. This created an enormous run on fives and ones, which the banks could not satisfy, since they were a little short on cash themselves. The currency crisis was made even more awkward by the fact that by the time the black-market rate had climbed to thirty to one, a dinner for two at an average restaurant in Kinshasa cost about 3,000 zaïres—a stack of singles about fourteen inches high.

It all got a little confusing. The American embassy statements grew increasingly alarming, and the unannounced arrival of a Sabena flight from Brussels only fanned coup rumors. Military hardware from all over the country turned up on the streets of Kinshasa, and at the bar in the InterContinental, two stranded black African diplomats, slightly tipsy, began seriously suggesting to me that the British be hired on a contractual basis to come and run Zaïre—along with Uganda and what was then the Central African Empire. One of the diplomats said the local situation reminded him of an old saying: " 'It's every man for himself and God save us all, said the elephant as he danced among the chickens.' How else," he added, "can you explain one of the richest men in the world behaving this way?"

Pappas seemed relatively amused through the crisis. One particularly stupid and dangerous night we went out drunk and caroused in his red pickup truck, surveying the disturbances and following a tank around the *cité* until we got sidetracked by two Belgian mechanics waving to us from a dilapidated sidewalk café. Before we could get out, a small solicitation of whores advanced on Pappas's truck.

"Who are they?" I asked.

"Never seen 'em before in my life," said Pappas, trying desperately to get the pickup into reverse. He was too late. They threw themselves at his window, crying "Papa" in unison.

It was cute. He actually pretended they weren't there and, while he waited for the two Belgians to distract them, discussed the current unrest: "Hell," he said, "if they can't fix a truck, how can they expect to fix a country?"

At the time, Pappas was fifty-six years old and already white-haired. He was the chief pilot, chief mechanic and proprietor of Kinshasa's largest privately owned "airline"—a pair of DC-3s, the DC-4 and the DC-6 in which we had gone looking for waterfalls. He'd been in Zaïre for just two years and had amassed some $2 million—not bad for a guy who had landed in Africa on the run from a batch of law enforcement and tax agencies and an angry wife.

The older you get, the less likely you are to run into people that your mom would call "bad influences." To someone like me, Pappas is a bad influence. What I mean is, I want a wife and kids, a good job with some security and a reasonable amount of responsibility, regular checks, a little yardwork, a tight pennant race. But I'm lapping forty, and I've never quite got the hang of it; I get bored, hence stupid, and fall prey to the odd chance, the risky choice that usually never pays off. Pappas, on the other hand, was a guy who did nothing *but* take chances, a consummate gambler, a permanent refugee who made it his job to keep jumping and keep landing on his feet. He was, in short, the sort of happy chappy I'd like to be, given sufficient testicularity. To make matters worse, he had made me an offer: "This is where it all happens," he said one day, pointing to a bumpy, patched stretch of African runway. "Stick around, you'll have a good time." Not me. Three months later, I was back in New York, begging for jobs.

And six years after that, I'm in L.A., working on my life-style, when the phone rings. It's Pappas talking hi-jinx on the Dark Continent. A week later, I'm sweating off weight over Saurimo, Angola. Bad stuff.

For Pappas, it's a day at the office, literally. Somehow, I thought, this wasn't quite what he had in mind. There he was, sitting in a tiny office in an obscure Brazilian airport the size of a modest K mart, surrounded by the paperwork incidental to operating a big and expensive jet. It had gone wrong in Zaïre, he told me. The government had taken as much pressure from the IMF as it could stand and had finally done the unthinkable—it had stabilized the currency, and for Pappas, "Everything just went to shit." Worse, he seemed very uncomfortable, although he thought he was probably making more money now than before. The trouble was, he wasn't his own boss anymore. A jet airplane, you see, is a little like a Broadway musical: It needs a lot of investors to get it off the ground. Just filling the gas tank on a DC-8 costs twenty grand or so, and a cycle—one takeoff and one landing—runs about $500 in wear and tear on the brakes, tires and gears. Pappas's business now was all numbers—in a pinch, the DC-8 could carry thirty-six tons of freight, but he often had to factor in an extra cycle and a tech stop (for fuel); $1,000 per flight hour for crew pay and engine wear, not counting fuel and insurance; and another $300 per average flight-hour just for overflight permissions from the countries along the airplane's flight path. Fuel varied in price wildly: In some European airports it could be had for as little as 65¢ per U.S. gallon, while in many Latin American and African countries, the price was often more than $2 for the same gallon, and the DC-8, loaded, consumed 7,200 kilos of fuel each hour (around 2,400 gallons, depending on the temperature and altitude), sometimes more. He tried to reckon how much extra he could make with a 747 but figured that a jumbo like that would cost nearly $10,000 per flight-hour, and he wasn't sure there was enough cargo to and from Africa to make that kind of nut. It was all a lot more trouble than he'd had to deal with in Zaïre, but apparently it had its upside. "I'm still ahead of the game," he'd often remind himself wearily.

Pappas was born in the '20s in Australia to a family that suffered through all the well-described trials of the Depression. His father disappeared early—just after the family emigrated to Canada—leaving him alone with his mother, his grandmother and a sickly elder sister. By the time he was thirteen, he had quit school and was soloing in a rickety Taylorcraft. Within a few years, he was flying for a local crop duster in the northern Great Plains, and by 1954 he was married, with six sons and a daughter. He had found a warmer climate, too, working summers in the Deep South spraying the rice crop, and winters working for what he called "a cowboy-and-Indian outfit" in Venezuela that, in theory, supplied the gold miners in South America with tinned goods and spare parts, but in reality had a more lucrative ambition.

"I think it was car smuggling," he said. "The guy [who owned the company] thought he could get rich smuggling Thunderbirds. He'd go up to Miami, buy some year-old T-birds, then run them down to Venezuela.

"It didn't work out very well. He was always arriving in Caracas with bullet holes in the cars, and we got stuck in the mud with striking regularity."

The experience caused Pappas to formulate one of his ever-useful maxims: If you're going to live on the run, it pays to have a ready supply of airplanes. If you never quite thought of meeting the exigencies of life that way, maybe it's because your life hasn't been a series of quick and essential departures, as Pappas's has been. Pappas has flown planes for right-wing governments and left-wing governments, for Texas ranchers and American movie directors; he's flown for money and flown for the hell of it, and more than once flown for his life. He's been winging it, as it were, for a long time, and for a long time, the runways and landing strips of the world have been black holes through which a handy fellow like him can slip into another dimension, suddenly invisible.

It worked after he watched helplessly as a kid walked into his crop duster's spinning prop and turned into a thick sauce. And it worked when it was time to duck out of El Salvador, where he had been a CIA-covered captain during that country's war with Honduras in 1969. It got him out of Indonesia, where he crashed an old T-28 trainer he was ferrying for resale and found out that, unknown to him, the plane had been loaded with marijuana; in the dead of night, he spread the pasture containing the wreckage with the contraband. ("Bet there were some happy cows the next morning.") And it worked best of all in the late '70s, when he'd been "involved with certain agencies of the U.S. government" in a situation that had "proved less than satisfactory."

By "less than satisfactory," Pappas meant that he had been caught in something so profoundly unsatisfactory that he'd had to leave North America in a big hurry with whatever he could scrounge. He ended up with $20,000 and a suitcase. The episode had become a central focus of his life, the barroom story that not only defined him to others, but, in a more complete rendition, to himself as well.

The standard-issue version goes something like this: By the end of the '60s, Pappas was one of the best-known nonmilitary pilots in Canada and America, the subject of countless hangar lies and the hero of some truly thrilling flying feats. After years of hooting along the skyways, he decided to settle down in, say, Tucson, Arizona, and spend his days fixing beat-up airplanes. But by then it was the early '70s, and nothing was easy, especially not for a distracted dad. The boys settled in well enough, but he watched in alarm as his daughter, Tammy, began experimenting with drugs. He tried to pre-empt the kid's interest in personal chemistry by teaching her to fly and letting her in on the repair side, too. She was brilliant at both. "Tammy had the best hands I ever saw," a family friend told me. "She was even a better pilot than her dad. And she could fix anything by just looking at it." Soon, the girl was a regular feature of the Southwestern sky, looping loops, touching and going. She was a good young pilot, but she liked drugs too much, and things started to unravel. After a while, the family friend said, "she was almost never straight."

So, at least according to the familiar version, Pappas decided to wreak revenge for his daughter's corruption, and when he was approached by one of the wealthier, more influential men in the Southwest, a stalwart of the old Democratic party machine, to fly a drug-run from South America to a desert strip just north of the Baja border, Pappas said sure, then went to a friend, a local border-patrol agent who flew for fun, and said he'd like to work with the Drug Enforcement Administration to get this bad-ass drug smuggler. No problem. "I asked him if he was sure about what he wanted to do and he said he was, so I put him in touch with the DEA," the agent told me. "Dumbest thing I ever did."

The DEA assigned two agents to work with Pappas and in a meeting (also attended by the border patrolman, who told me he has a tape recording of the meeting) made arrangements for Pappas to fly not only the wealthy Democrat's planeload of dope, but also another shipment about which the DEA had received a tip. It was another marijuana haul, the proceeds of this one apparently going to benefit some new-left coalition that threatened the state's old Democratic power elite.

Pappas flew in the first shipment—the one for the rich Democrat—as planned. Trouble was, the DEA was nowhere to be found when he landed. "They just didn't show up," Pappas told me. "Can you imagine that?"

Pappas called the agents, who unreeled some long tale of bureaucratic heartbreak. "Something about one office thinking the other office was handling it," is how Pappas got it. "Basically," he said, "they fucked it up."

Never mind, the DEA said. Let's go after the other one. So, as planned, Pappas went south of the border again and returned to the rough desert airstrip. This time, the DEA was there. They made their bust. And they also arrested Pappas. The hot, dry Mojave air grew wet and heavy. "I was gone," he said.

Somebody told him about a DC-3 for sale in Portugal. Out on bail, he skipped the country with his twenty grand and put it into the airplane. "I had to make money," he said, then added something that I had heard paraphrased by dozens of other freight flyers. "The easiest way to make lots of money is to find a place that's at war, unstable or in some kind of trouble. The more danger there is, the more money you make."

Given his circumstances, then, one might have assumed that Pappas could turn a fortune in his own backyard. But you don't need a degree in economics to spot the point of diminishing returns in some situations, so Pappas headed for Zaïre, a country that experienced economic catastrophes with an encouraging frequency. By the end of 1978, he had been joined by his daughter (and his daughter's girlfriend), and his escapade became the source of rich anxiety; every passport renewal was fraught with peril, he felt. More, with each retelling, the story would become a little more baroque, a little less clear, until finally the whole episode assumed a greater importance to him than it could ever have for the DEA. Ultimately, he took comfort in the fact that he had become a millionaire, and, it seemed, had made a home for himself in Kinshasa, truly the last place on earth.

One day Pappas decided to take me on a mechanic's tour of Kinshasa. He had been eager to illustrate his oft-repeated thesis that more hardware was scattered in bits and pieces around the capital than existed in most industrialized nations.

Pappas's tour passed acres of abandoned buses, parked neatly in rows on hillsides, like crops. The broken-down buses, gifts from the Belgians, had been replaced by stake trucks with names like SUPER SONIQUE CONCORDE and DC-10 painted on their rear bumpers. The stake trucks littered the roadsides, withered green branches—Zaïrian for "Out of Order"—protruding from their tailgates (this universal symbol for machines no longer in operation appeared again and again, as I noticed green branches sticking out of telephone kiosks, Coke machines, and once, so help me, a wheelchair). We passed miles of disconnected water pipes spread in disarray like pickup sticks. Here, an abandoned generator; there, a tractor graveyard or a telex machine that would work only if the post office was in receipt of a $15-a-day bribe. According to Pappas, Africa was called the Dark Continent because the electricity is usually cut off.

"The Belgians really screwed over these people," he told me. "They used them as menial laborers, sold them as slaves, gave them damned little education. The average Zaïrois doesn't know how things work, because things usually don't work at all. If they have tools, they don't know how to use them; if something breaks, forget it, they don't know how to fix it. My theory is that it's impossible to grow up in a Western country without picking up some basic mechanical skills; just dealing with our poorly made consumer items makes the average American learn how to use a pair of pliers or something. But here, that tradition is missing; they've never had any *reason* to master mechanical skills on any level.

"Listen, a guy I know—a Belgian—was building a new house in Binza [a fashionable Kinshasa suburb, at the time the home of President Mobutu Sese Seko, as well as George Pappas, the Czech embassy, several expensive restaurants and the government's execution center, which was located down the street and around the corner from Pappas's in a large, pleasant-looking, California ranch-style house]. The construction was falling way behind schedule and the costs were rising, so he tried to figure a way to make the work go faster.

"He noticed that the workers were moving stones and dirt from around the foundations by piling the waste material on metal sheets which were lifted and placed on another guy's head. Then he'd take it to the bottom of the hill and dump it. So this Belgian imported three wheelbarrows from Europe and took them up to the building site. The next day, he went back to see how they were getting along, and there were two guys lifting a wheelbarrow and putting it on another guy's head." The story had made Pappas laugh.

"They've got their own logic, but if you ever figure out what it is, then you know you've been here too long."

The house Pappas had rented in Binza was nothing native. Stucco and low, it was straight out of the standard U.S. tract-home catalog, but decorated by the landlord in remnant baroque. Patterns—in the drapes, the floor tiles, the wallpaper—exploded in a punk synthesis of bad taste. A long drive—patrolled by one of the ubiquitous *sentinelles,* sort of barefoot Pinkertons, armed with bows and semicircular arrows, and pulling down a dollar a day for their twelve-hour shift—stretched up to the house from a heavy steel gate. If you could have found a place among the propellers, crates of gauges, spare parts and old airplane tires that decorated Pappas's terrace, you could have seen all the way across the Congo River, across Stanley Pool, to Brazzaville. You could have seen the relentless siege of the capital, surrounded by a very ambitious jungle. You could have seen trees growing through the broad boulevards and vines prying away the old Belgian colonial façades; you could have seen the hive-like marketplace and the endless sprawl of the crate-and-mud-hut *cité,* where more than a million Zaïrians had sought the refuge and cold cash of the capital, their tin-roofed homes stacked randomly in neighborhoods where hundreds of record shops broadcast distorted selections from their inventories through bullhorn speakers, and where specious Mercedes garages shared quarters with hairdressing salons. Kinshasa is the largest city in black Africa, the unrivaled commercial center of millions of square miles nearly bereft of commerce, and you could have seen it all, spreading out below you like Miami after World War III, from Pappas's terrace, if you could have found a place on Pappas's terrace to stand, which would have been impossible. Huge engines, a wing flap, drums of av gas and cartons of hardware competed for space in Pappas's front yard and on Pappas's fabulous terrace with a couple of gray parrots, mean as hell, two loud but docile dogs, redheaded lizards and strolling king-size cockroaches.

Once, during a morning walk, I drew a disapproving look from the people next door, who at least tried to keep up appearances, and ventured down toward the execution center, where, I had been told, the quiet neighborhood was often awakened by the morning rattle of a machine gun. A young boy, a pioneer of small-business go-getting, stood alongside the road with a half-dozen parrots perched on his shoulders and a small stack of hubcaps in front of him. (A friend of Pappas's had earlier complained to me that once a week he had to go find the hubcap salesman and buy his own hubcaps back; if he was late by a day or two for some reason, they were held for him. "One of the benefits of being a regular customer," he had said.) So I struck up a conversation with the kid. After a few minutes, the first in a series of military trucks rounded the corner, headed in the direction of the execution center. The kid said he liked watching the trucks come and go; they came in full, he said, every one of them. But not all of them left that way. He'd figured out a ratio: Three trucks full of live bodies equaled one truck full of dead ones.

We sat one night inside Pappas's house, where the magical splendor of Freon somehow compensated for the kaleidoscopic decor, drinking and talking about women. "My personal life is a little complicated," Pappas told me with apparent understatement. While he had no trouble finding girlfriends, he thought he was finally getting along better with his wife.

"But she's in Montana, isn't she?"

"That's right," he said. I laughed, but he didn't, so we sat drinking quietly for a while.

"Not that I could go back there. I go back and I get arrested. Besides," he added, "all I do there is get in trouble and go broke." Pappas went on slowly but rancorously about the evils of government, taxes and women, all of whom, in his eyes, competed with equal skill for his cash. "I can do without them," he said. "I came here two years ago with an old DC-3; now I've got a million-dollar business, and both the government and women want to take it from me." Besides, he said, he was concerned about his advancing years, and thought maybe he should retire to some nice place.

Obviously, it wasn't yet time. Pappas was full of entrepreneurial zeal. We would spend all night working out a proposal to sell the American embassy monthly charter flights to look for gorillas near the Rwanda border; the next night would be devoted to working out a way to retrieve an old, jungle-abandoned DC-3 that Pappas had bought after he learned it had once belonged to Eisenhower. He figured a round-the-world flight could be made to the Ike Museum, where he would donate the plane to posterity and pocket a hefty profit from Eisenhower fans who would want to go along for portions of the ride.

Or, during that near coup in 1979, where you got all the suppressed pandemonium of the real thing with none of the blood-and-guts weirdness, you could see how the only people with their feet on the ground were those who were most frequently high in the sky anyway—Pappas and his colleagues. They knew the trouble was coming, and they'd planned ahead. In a demonstration of the crucial albeit casual role played by freight flyers, I went along one night with a carload of Kinshasa's leading businessmen. They were panic-stricken at the unraveling economic mess in Kinshasa, and worse, they were stuck with a serious oversupply of old currency. They made their way up the boulevard du 30 juin, skirted the swollen Congo River and drove up and into the hills as I guided them to Pappas's house. They were convinced he was a man who might be able to help them in their dilemma.

Pappas was asleep when they arrived, but, rubbing his eyes and yawning loudly, he listened to their tale and solved their problem—a quick referral, a note and directions—pocketing a substantial profit in the process. Considerably relieved, the businessmen returned to the capital.

"We should have gone to him first," the driver—a hotel manager—told me flatly.

"We couldn't have afforded him at first," said one of his passengers. "Here," he added for my benefit, "pilots make money even when they don't fly." He paused. "And what's worse, now we owe him a favor."

"I can put that in the bank," Pappas said later when I told him about the conversation. Several years later, he put a quarter-million-dollar touch on the guy.

Flying antique cargo planes around Zaïre had offered a man like Pappas room to improvise. Flying expensive jets around South America and Europe cramped his style. Once, he had spent much of his time dealing with the jungle-addled; now he was putting on suits to see lawyers. He chafed at the restrictions with which he had burdened himself.

"I stayed a little too long in Zaïre," he told me. Shortly after I'd left, his wife had come over to "take care of the business end." That didn't work: "Hell, she refused to learn French, and she just didn't like blacks. And if you don't like blacks, you're in the wrong place if you're in Africa." She left (and he hadn't seen her since) and new competitors flying more fuel-efficient jet aircraft had moved into his turf, and, worse, the mechanics at Air Zaïre had finally figured out how to fix broken airplanes. Finally, UTA, the French airline, took over the day-to-day operation of Air Zaïre, and the airline began flying a more predictable schedule, hauling cargo as well as passengers. "The bottom just dropped out."

He had made one last killing in Zaïre: The West Germans had built what they claimed was a research-oriented launching facility on an isolated plateau in eastern Zaïre. When neighboring governments, justifiably worried about allowing Mobutu access to rocket launchers (the European press had got wind of the project and described it as a cruise-missile testing base), pressured for its removal, Pappas was called in to do the job. The equipment was sent to another base, this one near Sabha in central Libya. "We did it very quietly—no flight plans, nothing. It was an interesting transfer of technology." He also removed the base's "cover," the junk that seemed somehow like the kind of stuff a satellite-launching facility should have. The "launch tower," Pappas said, "consisted of a bunch of aluminum pipes." Tinkertoys.

"I think they were just trying to get the technology, and especially the scientists, into Libya," he said. "See, they brought a group of scientists down to the base in Zaïre just before it all ended. A week or so later, they claimed that all the scientists had been killed on a river-rafting trip. Just them and a raft, it was impossible. A bunch of scientists arrive in Africa in the middle of nowhere and decide to go on a rafting trip? Anyway, they never found the bodies.

"But I sure saw a lot of German scientists and technicians in Libya, I can tell you. It must have been a resurrection."

Cash in hand and back in Kinshasa, Pappas started selling off his airplanes, took the money and set up shop in Brazil, having worked out a deal to cart goods from South America and Europe down to Luanda. And, because it was damned difficult getting anybody to fly cargo into the isolated government outposts, he picked up contracts to carry whatever the government had going from Luanda into the interior.

12.

Have a nice day.

—Comrade Lenin, Saurimo, Angola

PAPPAS MET ME at the hotel the morning after my arrival, told me there was a flight to Luanda that night and did I know what a loadmaster was? Nothing to it, he said, "you just balance the pallets of cargo so that the airplane flies straight. Make coffee for the crew." He took out a match-book and drew a diagram on the cover outlining the thirteen pallet positions inside a DC-8. "It's like this:

```
        7
   6        8
   5        9
   4        10
   3        11
   2        12
   1        13
```

"Try to get them to balance, sort of. Number seven is the middle position, so it doesn't matter what you put there. But try to get position five to balance with nine and so on. Nothing to it, really. That's it."

He gave me maybe two minutes' tuition on aircraft weight-and-balance, and made the job sound like a stewardess for boxes. "It's easy. But, ah, maybe you shouldn't show your passport around." And I was off to Luanda, so long. Not until it was actually time to load the airplane did I realize how silly Pappas's instructions had been. I showed the matchbook to a crewman.

"Right. That's Pappas for you," he said. Then he handed me a load sheet filled with graphs, mathematics and blank spaces.

Pappas's flights should have had an exquisitely enervating quality, since, on paper, they were always the same. If it was a north-south trip, for example, you'd leave Europe in an overloaded airplane, plug in the coffee maker, fly south across the Mediterranean, toss a few eggs and some pork and beans in an old Sunbeam electric skillet and smoke cigarettes across the stark Sahara, which stretched on for hours, until the scrub grew thicker and thicker and turned to forest, then stop in Lagos for fuel, and, half a day later, land in Luanda and unload. If there were to be any internal Angolan flights, that cargo was then put aboard and taken to its destination the following day. Then back to Luanda for gas and straight home again. Three, four times a week. It should have been routine, like a regular drive on the New Jersey Turnpike with the world's worst Philly at the other end.

It wasn't, of course. For one thing, the instrument panel on the DC-8 was an analog freak in a digital universe, a gallery of dead needles lying flat and pointing at zeroes; it was like an old car, sort of jury-rigged to do its job in an informal manner. Maintenance was performed by a brilliant young Scandinavian mechanic and an Irish cohort, but they worked alone, often accompanied only by hangovers, and there was only so much they could do during the few hours the plane was on the ground in Brazil.

As a result, things were always going wrong. For example, the fire-warning system for engine number four was on the fritz, and on takeoff, the alarm indicating a fire in the number-four engine would always go off. Everybody knew it was a crossed wire or something, and when the red lights started flashing and the bells started ringing, somebody would reach up, punch the reset button, and the cockpit would become silent again. So, when you see the number-four warning erupt several dozen times, you think it's an inconvenience. When the number-*three* warning goes off, you think it's a fire, and you shut down the engine, dump $15,000 worth of fuel over the Mediterranean and look for a place to land in a hurry. In the day or so the airplane sat in Málaga waiting for money for gas (our creditworthiness somehow wasn't universally acknowledged, and an unscheduled stop meant money had to be sent from home), it was discovered that the faulty alarm system on the number-four engine had been switched to the number-three engine to see if it would behave better. It didn't.

Added to the problems of flying in a mechanically suspicious airplane were the complications of flying it in and out of Africa. When you're almost out of fuel and trying to make it to Lagos and discover that Lagos is closed because of weather, then you land someplace else, like Benin, and wait for gas money again.

It never went smoothly.

A bagful of maps and a view from only two miles up will tell you all the lies about Africa you need to know. To the high-flyer, for example, Angola looks like a successful 4-H project: enormous green pastures and rich, red earth. But that's not it: Fly a little lower, a little slower, and you see the big picture.

The bumper crop in Angola this year is land mines: Looking through holes in the cloud cover below us, we could see ugly craters that scarred the landscape. Bridges disappear under rivers, broken trucks litter the roadsides, the ruins of a national economy are clearly marked. Looks like everybody in Angola threw a *Road Warrior* party and forgot to clean up. Down there someplace, an Angolan general is escorting a *Washington Post* reporter through the countryside trying to find evidence of UNITA atrocities, secure in the knowledge that while civil wars don't produce agricultural breakthroughs, they do provide a surplus of outraged rectitude, a commodity that always finds a willing market in the West. Invited journalists receive interesting statistics: According to one especially intriguing report, the Angolan army claimed that 23,000 people are waiting in line, in a way, to get artificial arms and legs because of UNITA's efforts to disrupt harvests.

But even as African civil wars go, the Angolan one is sort of a bust. For one thing, all the players are superpower weirdos: The Russians and the 35,000 Cuban barking dogs of the Evil Empire are supporting the 100,000-man army of Comrade President José Eduardo dos Santos, while the CIA and the South Africans are backing Jonas Savimbi's 40,000 or so UNITA fighters. For another thing, the war's going nowhere. Sure it's moving into its second decade now, and sure plenty of people are getting killed, but nobody's going to win the thing. Someday, it's just going to stop. "The Russians can't keep propping up Angola forever," a British diplomat in Europe explained to me. "It's a bottomless pit." The country's broke: More than one-third of the $1 billion Angola will earn in foreign trade—almost all from U.S. oil companies—will go to import food to replace the harvests that haven't happened. Of the country's $3 billion–plus budget, at least half will go to fight the war.

For his part, Savimbi has mounted one of the most energetic and persistent job searches ever. "He doesn't expect to win," a pilot who

knows the rebel leader told me, echoing recent public statements by
Savimbi himself. "He just wants to force them [the Marxists] to invite him
to join the government." Indeed, quiet talks were held in 1986 in Great
Britain between Luanda officials and UNITA representatives. It seems
certain that someday soon, the government of backsliding Marxists will
give Savimbi, a backsliding Maoist after all, an expense account, a desk
at or near the top of the heap, a speech to read about the evils of American
imperialism, and that will be that.

It was becoming clear that we'd never find Saurimo, which meant we'd
have to take the goods—ingots of golden, bitter-smelling soap the size of
your arm, radio equipment, ugly yellow explosive canisters, rotting beans
and rice and a couple of pallets of fine, dry U.S. AID stuff—back to
Luanda. And, frankly, I'd had it with Luanda.

Luanda was pretty enough, built around a perfect lagoon, with pastel
buildings, narrow streets and delicate arcades. The Portuguese, I thought,
really know how to make an African capital. It was perfect, it looked like
a movie set, and at one time it was the most prosperous city in that part of
the continent, with waterfront cafés, first-rate restaurants and charming
hotels. But I'd been out cruising in an old Honda that was supposed to be
used for getting around the airport and I had driven up and down the local
version of Revolution Boulevard at eight o'clock at night on a Friday, and
the town was closed on account of war and Marxism. There was, for
example, one bar in town, and I thought, great, just one bar, good idea,
that must be where *everyone* goes. But to drink a beer, you had to make
reservations far in advance, plus you had to go with a woman or else you
didn't get in. Of the hotels in Luanda, the Panorama—situated out on the
spit of land that described the lagoon—was for Russians and visiting oil-
company execs, I guess. Another one, called simply "the complex," was
next to the airport, and was for aircrews and passengers caught in-transit
(there are no tourists in Angola); that's where I stayed, fighting for space
beneath the sheets with a neighborhood of cockroaches and some other
rather unusual insects. There was an inexpensive restaurant in Luanda,
but no menu; if you were inside between seven and nine, you got the
mystery meal of the day and a single can of Löwenbräu.

In the capital, a few citizens wandered about in silence, and the traffic
was so light that once I managed to travel the wrong way up a major
thoroughfare from one end to the other before I realized my mistake. (My
stupidity terrified me, since I had little interest in being caught as an
American without a visa—nobody checks the passports of aircrews—
carrying sometimes sensitive cargo in and out of a war zone controlled by
Cubans and Russians. In fact, on my first flight to Luanda, we had an

extremely taciturn Angolan airplane mechanic on board as a freeloader; the crew spoke to me only in French, since, as one of them told me, they all thought I worked for the CIA, and there was no reason the Angolans shouldn't think so, too, and they didn't know who this mechanic might *really* be. I admit, it's the sort of paranoia that makes a dull life exciting.)

In Luanda, the market was open, but almost empty, and the staple items that were on sale looked like they'd been priced by a ballpark concessionaire. Five bucks for a tomato. I figured a light meal for four would run about $200—or a couple of cans of beer, which, along with cigarettes, constitute the country's real pocket change. (The local unit of currency is called a kwanza, and it's about as useful as it sounds; barter is better.) Ten days in Luanda, I concluded, and you'd be in pretty good shape just from lugging six-packs of money around.

At the Fourth of February International Airport, once known more prosaically as Luanda International, nobody knew nothing. Missionaries wandered the tarmac looking for lost medical shipments; roving carloads of soldiers and minor airport officials appeared at our cabin door every ten minutes to demand Coca-Cola, and each time, in my anxiety, I thought they were looking for the likes of me. Huge throngs of passengers were shifted idly across the blacktop from one plane to another and another, each time carrying their corrugated baggage with them. Unloading and loading our plane was an organizational dilemma, although the cans of warm lager we brought with us served as currency to pay for the services of a high-loader, a tractor, a dolly and a team of handlers. Many of them wore powder-blue USA FOR AFRICA T shirts and had the remarkable ability to disappear for hours at a time in the middle of loading or unloading the plane, which, I must admit, was an unhealthy working environment (we were routinely parked at the far end of the airport; even upwind, you could smell the DC-8, which was alive with vermin, from a hundred paces). Though most of our cargo from Europe was clean enough—computers, food, hardware both military and civilian, and once a scary little box marked RADIOACTIVE—the stuff we put on board at Luanda for the flights into the interior was foul indeed.

For a major airport in the capital of a war-torn country, there was precious little security. Except for the day U.S. Assistant Secretary of State Chester A. Crocker was in town trying to make a deal to swap the removal of South African troops from Namibia for the removal of Cubans from Angola, I moved about with no hindrance, scooting around the airport in the Honda, either solo or with another crewman, flushing the cargo handlers out of hiding. All day long, Soviet military and civilian aircraft landed and took off; every now and again, a C-130 belonging to Southern

Air Transport, the alleged CIA airline so deeply involved in weapons shipments to Iran, would show up and disappear. Like us, they were flying for the Marxist government.* Huge Ilyushin 62Ms belonging to Interflug, the euphoniously named East German carrier, arrived and disgorged all-male tour groups, grim-faced guys in holiday clothes, with real short haircuts, all of whom had matching olive-drab canvas luggage. They were taken to a building next to the passenger terminal and marched through one door; minutes later, they reappeared through another door, wearing uniforms, and were put aboard the Soviet military transports. I didn't see why they bothered with the deception. Who cared? Maybe for them this *was* a vacation. I jealously noted, however, that the Interflug loadmasters all wore Kelly-green jogging shorts and black street shoes.

Aside from the lousy prospect of another night in Luanda, this load for Saurimo, the latest in a series of shipments, was especially bad. The rice and beans, imported from Cuba and Argentina, were in an advanced stage of decomposition caused by sitting in the sun and rain at Luanda for too long. The idea of carting it all back to the capital was repellent, since it would have to sit in the aircraft all night until we could go out again the next day. Besides, just getting away had been a chore this time; using my Franco-Español, it had fallen to me to inform an angry three-star general who arrived at the aircraft preceded by his stomach and bound for the front at Saurimo that we didn't allow military passengers, and those guys behind him could just put their pistols away, thanks. We split while he was away getting something signed that would override any objections I personally might make. Delays like that and having trouble finding the place were always bad; we had to get in and out of Saurimo during the midday "window" when the runway there was open, since after 4:30 in the afternoon, UNITA tried to poke holes in the tarmac with mortars, and not showing up at all would irritate the garrison. On a day like this one, knowing that we were supposed to show up, they had got up early,

---

* Their competitors, Santa Lucia Airways, which flies pretty sky-blue C-130s and 707s, were working the other side, flying weapons from the U.S. to Savimbi's forces, using bases in Zaïre. Santa Lucia was used to ferry weapons from Tel Aviv to Teheran, too, and frequently does U.S. military charters. One of their pilots described his three-week African tours as "tropical sweats." Despite Mobutu's denials, the *New York Times* breathlessly reports on weapons going to Savimbi through Zaïre from time to time, as though Mobutu, a very rich capitalist, would rather tolerate a Marxist neighbor than a South African patsy. The Angolan war is one of the most frequented venues in the world for cargo flyers. Arms are going to both sides from every side, and that's the news. By the way, when Santa Lucia isn't flying weapons to Savimbi, they're flying chickens to Libya.

marched out to the city limits and shot into the weeds, pushing the UNITA forces far enough away to make a safe zone for the aircraft's arrival.

Looking for Saurimo, the best and worst of all the government outposts, was what the Disney people would call a thrill ride. We would spin down through the clouds, everybody looking out the cockpit window for a familiar road, a certain twist in the river, something to follow on the tilted horizon; the deep green of the earth filled the windows for just a moment, just a peek, then up. By God, they might well hear us, but they'd never see us if we were clever boys. The pilot, nervous already—not only was it his first time into Saurimo, but I had dragged him out of a bar, roaring drunk, maybe five hours before we left—demanded over the protestations of the copilot to return to Luanda. To the copilot, who had flown for ten years through the eastern Zaïre jungle, where navigation had an intuitive quality and nothing else, looking for Saurimo was an amusement, a chance to do all the things in a big jet you always wanted to do but couldn't. "You never get to do this flying for Sabena," he shouted. He was damned straight on that one: If you were a passenger in an aircraft going through maneuvers like this, you'd be quite correct in assuming your life was nearly over. The pilot certainly assumed that, but since he'd taken the rap for the needless dumping of fuel a week or so earlier, he didn't want to mess this one up. So he sat grimly staring straight ahead, saying softly that this wasn't such a good idea. He was probably right. Just a few months before, UNITA had succeeded in attacking a Hercules as it landed. The loadmaster had been blown to smithereens, and the injured crew had been marched several hundred miles through the bush and out to civilization.

As usual, we had barely two hours before the window closed and some thirty tons of crap to get off the airplane once we were down. "It's getting close," the flight engineer announced. We made one more pass, twisted down, spotted the road, spotted the river and finally got lucky; there was a runway down there, and we assumed it must be Saurimo. In the surrounding forest, columns of smoke marked the perimeter where government troops were holding back the rebels. We skirted the perimeter in an arc I thought was somewhat luxurious, and put it down next to a little throng of locals who thought fun was seeing how close they could get to a landing DC-8. We dodged Angolans and potholes and finally turned off the strip and onto the taxiway where, at first, I thought for a moment I was at a winter-league training camp. Guys everywhere were hitting fungoes and playing catch, going through the windup, making the delivery, a Cuban farm team.

The idea was to get the cargo hatches and the cabin door open as soon as the plane stopped, since time was our nonrenewable resource. When I swung open the cabin door behind the cockpit, I found to my surprise that the ramp had already been pushed up to the plane, and standing at the top in a crisply pressed and starched uniform was the new local military honcho, a guy wearing Italian sunglasses and calling himself Comrade Lenin, who was armed with a handgun and a Sony Walkman. The gun was for security, I suppose, in case we'd brought in a load of South African GIs; the shades were to keep the sun out of his eyes as he lay on the bags of rice and dozed while his men swarmed aboard to throw down the cargo. From time to time in the distance you could hear the pop of the war.

I avoided Comrade Lenin like the plague, afraid to speak, worrying about my passport hidden behind the pilot's seat. Unidentified Americans drifting in and out of Cuban-Angolan front-line bases were fair game; these guys weren't just playing ball, they were fighting a nasty little war.

As had become routine, a truck was brought up, and all the U.S. AID groceries were gently handed down through the rear hatch, packed neatly into the truck by Angolan soldiers who were pushed and prodded into action by Cuban officers, covered with a tarpaulin and taken off to the Cuban barracks. (Nobody I met in Angola had ever seen a U.S. AID shipment go anywhere but to Cuban troops. I never bothered to find out how the stuff got to Angola in the first place, but you can figure there's a capitalist in the woodpile someplace.) Despite the huge throng of handlers—mostly Angolan soldiers in fatigue pants and old sport coats—it was more than an hour before we could get things organized. Comrade Lenin finally found motive power and barked a few orders. Then it was fury: The rest of the stuff was thrown out the main hatch onto the ground with abandon. The bags of rotten rice and beans split open on the asphalt beneath the aircraft, the soap was tossed on top of the pile of garbage. Cockroaches and rodents made for cover. One chap exhibited especially blind enthusiasm, bombarding his compatriots below with twenty-five-kilo bags, and in retaliation for the U.S. AID (I pay my taxes), I handed him a box of Russian radio equipment, which he lobbed out with zeal, wires and tubes flying everywhere.

Meanwhile, it started raining hard, and the soap began to foam all over the rice and beans. Several men on the ground started shoveling the sudsy mess into canvas bags and dragging it away from the aircraft. (I imagined the mess-hall dialogue: "What is it tonight, Cookie? More of that good, soapy rice 'n' roaches?") Time was running short, and sweating from the heat, humidity and fear, I mustered my best French-Spanish and asked Comrade Lenin if he could get his men to move the rest of the cargo from in front of the landing gear so we could taxi off. He obliged, saluted, and turning to leave, said, "Have a nice day" in perfect English. Gave me a bad chill, I don't mind telling you.

As I closed the main cargo door, I looked at the pallets that lined the freight floor. The bags of rice and beans had been stacked on the pallets, and it looked like a bag of rice had split open and had scattered all over the aircraft floor, until I realized it moved—maggots. The plane was filled with them, along with giant roaches and sundry vermin. I'd had it.

When we returned to Luanda, I drove over to the Panorama and thought about going inside to smell the air conditioning and see if I could spot a TAP stewardess. But standing around in front were a group of grownups wearing drip-dry khaki suits and pressed safari shirts; I looked like the cargo I'd been carrying and decided against it, opting instead for a Coke in the shade of a hangar at the airport, where imported Portuguese mechanics were fixing busted airplanes.

That's where I found my theory about civil wars in Africa. I call it the Theory of the Main Thing. Actually, it isn't my theory. I borrowed it from one of the mechanics, named, as best as I could make out, Manolo, who spoke English quite well but with a wicked accent and who had struck up a casual conversation with me about life in Luanda. He'd lived here for more than twenty years until independence sent him packing; it had given him his first chance to see Europe, and he didn't seem very happy to be back home in Angola.

"These places—Mozambique, Uganda. They get independence. Everybody in Europe feels good about it. That's okay. But who comes out ahead? Maybe ten guys on top. Everybody else in the country goes hungry, gets sick and dies."

I suggested that most Western visitors and observers saw these conflicts in terms of freedom fights and that long years of struggle had finally won people in Zaïre and Uganda the right to vote. He thought that was funny, too.

"Listen, I'll tell you one thing about this war. It's between two top men to see who will get the money from the country. Come here in five years, and you will see the main thing."

What, I asked was the "main thing"?

"The main thing is, it doesn't matter who wins."

I wondered if Pappas meant it when he said he was getting old. "What if I had a heart attack down there?" he asked one time. "Where would I go?

I've gotta start thinking about things like that." Besides, he said, he was swamped in paperwork and was having a deuce of a time getting the Angolans to pay up.

Whereas Pappas's workdays in Zaïre had stretched to sixteen and eighteen hours—tinkering with the planes, then flying them—these days he was working a nine-to-fiver, and whenever we sat around chatting, it was always about business. He seemed constantly on edge, and I thought maybe he was right, maybe he was getting old.

I think one of Pappas's principal virtues to me—aside from his penchant for risk taking—and the thing that made his invitation somehow irresistible, was that he was able to support himself quite nicely without taking what he did as seriously as, say, an adult insurance agent might. He flew cranky airplanes in and out of crazy places, he had fun doing it, and it made him a lot of money. "All I ever wanted to do was fly," he used to tell me, echoing bad scripts from long-ago matinees. Maybe he'd lost that, chasing invoices around a small room in an airport on the edge of South America.

Pappas was still haunted by his self-perceived failure to take care of his daughter's recurring drug problem. Tammy, who had been in Zaïre almost a decade, had spent her youth living on coke, smoke and native chow. After Pappas had left, she had tried to hang on by importing clapped-out motorcycles one week and fixing clapped-out trucks the next. Her teeth were rotting out of her head, and she weighed almost nothing. Pappas was afraid she'd contracted AIDS; he was determined to get her to Europe for good and thought out loud that maybe he should move closer to civilization as well.

Pappas talked nonstop about growing old, and complained bitterly about the demands his wife, his ex-girlfriend—a Dutchwoman named Betty—and his current girlfriend made on him. Once I found an envelope addressed to Betty; the name on the envelope, though, read "Mrs. Betty Pappas," and I knew Pappas had never divorced anyone. Complications.

Pappas had lost a certain edge, that's all. In Zaïre, in the old days, after a few flights to a place like Saurimo, we'd have sat around drinking and laughing. But I'd given up most booze, and Pappas didn't laugh much anymore. It was all hard work, long hours of boredom illuminated by moments of profound fear. Finally, the UNITA forces got some Stingers from Uncle Sam and shot down a couple of cargo transports. So one day I went in to say good-bye.

He was in an expansive mood. The Angolans had come up with some cash, he was going to sign a new deal to move hardware from Warsaw to Teheran, he had a new plan to operate a floating chicken ranch off the coast of Libya, and he'd just got back from a week in the South Pacific, airplane hunting.

"Taking off, huh?" He sounded unconcerned.

"I guess so."

He walked around his desk to stand in front of a National Geographic map of the world. "Maybe I'll do the same," he said, tracing invisible flight paths with his fingers. "There's going to be a lot of trouble in Angola, and it could get good." Or maybe Central America. "There should be some *good* action there."

He finally looked up. "You ought to stick around," he said.

I tensed.

"Look," he said. "I told you this once in Zaïre. And I'll tell you again here, then I won't say another word. Stick around." He pointed out the window toward the runway. The cracked and patched surface vibrated in the heat. "This is where it all happens."

PART FIVE

VILLAINY

13.

Without the white man, there's no hope.

—*Former British Foreign Secretary Lord Carrington, quoted by former Rhodesian Prime Minister Ian D. Smith*

HERE'S IAN SMITH, the devil, old-style: white sleeves rolled up to his elbows, hands in the pockets of his bagged-out chinos, fresh off the farm just yesterday, today sitting in a house filled with knickknacks and good furniture, next door to the Cuban embassy, a nest of radio antennas with a tract home attached. "No problem with security," he says. He's the devil, you wonder what he means by that, that stuff about security, what's he really mean?

Well, he says, just that the Cubans are "rather popular here at the moment," and the last thing this government wants is trouble right next door to its friends.

You kidding? They got the *devil* next door. Forget trouble. The cab-driver who gave me directions told me, "He's the devil," but that wasn't exactly news to me. I spent fifteen years reading about the devil and his work in Rhodesia. You don't have to tell *me* about the devil. Plus, I studied theology once. As I drove out there I said to myself, "Now you've really done it. Now you're going to the Devil." And I did.

The streets of Harare (once Salisbury), capital of Zimbabwe (once Southern Rhodesia, and once Rhodesia), are, for Africa, broad, tree-lined civic eccentricities (I read someplace the first white settlers built them to be wide enough to accommodate a U-turn by an oxcart). On either side are carefully pruned shrubs, obsessive lawns, neat pavements. Somebody ought to write a doctoral term paper sometime about the resemblance between Pasadena, California, and Harare, Zimbabwe. Nadine Gordimer, the writer, who came here in 1980 to pillory the already departed white regime and sanctify the incoming black one, called it "the most beautiful colonial city in Africa."* Same wide streets as Pasadena's, same pleasant landscapes, same giant houses built by rich white folks—and at about the same time. Even the same generally temperate climate and the same faintly Midwestern downtown, with early-twentieth-century buildings losing the battle to small-scale, vintage 1965 postmodern architecture. So Harare looks like Pasadena—except that it has lots of military vehicles in the streets, especially when Comrade Prime Minister goes shopping. Robert Mugabe, the new owner of Zimbabwe, travels with the biggest security entourage of any African leader, it is said.†

Once a quarter of a million white people (and 3.7 million black ones) lived in Zimbabwe. But that was when it was Rhodesia. Now maybe half that number of whites remain.‡ Once pictures of the Right Hon. Ian D. Smith and Queen Elizabeth II hung on the shop walls of Harare; now there are photos of Comrade Prime Minister Robert Mugabe and Comrade President Reverend Canaan Banana everywhere. "It certainly isn't the same," an airline employee told me.

Right. For one thing, the devil's gone to hell. Ian Smith, the villain of the '70s, the P. W. Botha of his time, the penultimate racist, has been booted out of politics forever. (Mugabe finally chucked him out of parliament for saying that it was stupid for a country like Zimbabwe, which finds a market in South Africa for 85 percent of what it produces, to advocate imposing trade sanctions against its major trading partner.) So we can breathe a little easier about the struggle for human dignity in Rhodesia, or Zimbabwe. And for another thing, the devil apparently took commerce with him, so the world's most self-contained economy, created by necessity after years of sanctions, has run out of steam. Mugabe, under enormous political pressure, has rapidly expanded public spending even

* Her front-line reporting was for *The New York Review of Books.* Among her observations: "One of the most stupid things whites ever did in Africa was to make the bar the first place where they would mix with blacks socially, and drinking the first pleasure to be openly shared by black and white. Almost without exception, the scattered incidents of violence that are occurring in the new state . . . happen in the vicinity of bars."

† And that's going some. Harare was the scene of a recent conference of non-aligned countries, which meant there were maybe a hundred Third World cranks running around town, each with a military parade preceding and following them. It was like Los Angeles. And there was at least one major disaster, when some prime minister's limo escorts plowed into some president's flotilla of motorcycles. It happened at a four-way intersection, but, according to residents, nobody's driver wanted to stop, since to do so might represent a life-threatening breach of protocol.

‡ Although, as the government has been boasting, more are returning, mostly because they cannot get their assets out of Zimbabwe, nor can they receive dividends, nor can they be paid rents or commissions.

as the foreign exchange evaporates, inflation demolishes the Zimbabwean dollar, the national debt skyrockets, jobs disappear, the roads slowly give way to potholes, and the phones get cranky.

Shortly after my friend P. J. O'Rourke returned from South Africa, I asked him what he thought about apartheid. "I think it's rude," he said.

A brutal incivility, the daily insult of a fearful government. Rude.

One day soon after my arrival in Zimbabwe, I asked a supporter of the Smith regime what he thought about apartheid. "Whose?"

I was stumped. Whose what?

"There's apartheid in South Africa," he said, "because they call it apartheid. We never have had apartheid here. We had a white government, as you might say, and that's different."

Rude. If there's one product for domestic consumption the white regime in Salisbury perfected, it was justification for bad behavior, for being rude. While it's true that the Smith government and the others that preceded his hadn't been violently oppressive (since the suppression of the native tribes in the late 1890s), they did manage to systematically justify denying black Africans access to governmental power—and, as Lord Blake, the historian, points out, whereas black governments in Africa may be bad governments, people have a right to bad government if they want it. In Rhodesia, whites could claim that this withholding of power wasn't apartheid; that claim wouldn't wash anywhere else, though, and ultimately, rude people were made to do the polite thing.

But it might be possible that, following a pattern established throughout Africa, the whites did the polite thing with another rude person, this one black. While everyone in Harare maintains a very polite attitude toward Robert Mugabe, the press maintains the same insulting propagandistic tenor established during the final years of white rule,* and the same oppressive emergency decrees imposed by the whites are still in place. Surliness has become government policy in much of Africa, and Zimbabwe's no exception.

If you ask people rude questions about Mugabe and his regime, you'll get impolite answers (variations on "I can't speak about that" or "Why do

* When the news isn't political jargon, it's trivial: The front page of a recent issue of the *Financial Gazette*, the white folks' weekly paper, carried a story headlined NEW NAME FOR LT. GEN. NHONGO. The General, it turns out, changed his name from Rex Nhongo to Tapfumaneyi Ruzambu Solomon Mujuru. An acquaintance told me the general's friends still call him Rex, though. And a Harare businessman said the story was put on a front page "because they have a dry sense of humor" at the *Gazette*.

you care?" lead the responses) about two-thirds of the time. One out of three, though, will give you an unexpected answer of some sort: "Mugabe is good, maybe better than Smith. But I cannot say I like him," a yuppie-looking black kid at a car-rental office said to me. If you are Matabele,* as was the young man, you cannot say you like him, "because he is against us. Just like Smith."

Another man, honored and decorated by the colonial government, Smith's U.D.I. (Unilateral Declaration of Independence) regime and Mugabe's administration, a white man, is a well-known leader in the business community in Harare, and, for the first five minutes of our chat, we're on the record. He's a fellow secure in his country's future, a booster of foreign investment and a fine spokesman for Zimbabwean economics. At the top of our hour, he's "pleased with the success between blacks and whites" in Zimbabwe. In fact, he says, "there's never been a better feeling in the country between blacks and whites." There is, he says, a "real future" in Zimbabwe, an "excellent chance that we will lead the continent in working out differences between whites and blacks and provide a tremendous economic opportunity for ourselves and for others."

This glad talk goes on for another three or four minutes—no more, I swear—until his voice begins to drop a little. Ten minutes later, we were off the record. In the time I spent with him—and another influential white businessman who joined us later—I asked just one question: "Do you really mean to encourage people to invest in this country?" I asked it several different ways, over and over.

It was clearly in his interest to simply say, "Sure." But he never answered the question. Instead, he digressed:

"The poor people here are earning less than Z$150 per month [about U.S.$90], and it's much harder for them to make ends meet than it was before the Mugabe government. After all, you have to look at the way the country's money is being spent. Twenty-one percent of the budget goes to the defense force [which has 12,000 troops supporting the crippled government of Marxist Mozambique] and a third of our foreign exchange goes to repay the national debt. Our currency has declined to 62 percent of what it was seven years ago, and we've gone from being one of the least indebted countries in 1980 to one of the most burdened today. There are 100,000 new employables [graduates from vocational schools, colleges

* Matabeles live in Matabeleland, mostly in the southwestern half of the country. Shonas are members of the Mashona tribe and live in Mashonaland, in the northeastern half.

and universities] coming onto the market each year, and that's where we can see Mugabe's dilemma.

"There's a crisis of expectation in the country. He [Mugabe] promised everything to everyone—that's how he gained such enormous support. How were they to know he couldn't possibly make good? We'd lied to them, too, after all, and they must have felt they couldn't trust anyone in sympathy with the white government. But Mugabe's promises have created a big problem for him. He must make good on what he said—and the country simply cannot afford to pay for that. Of the 100,000 young people trained for skilled work and looking for jobs, 7,000 of them will get jobs. That leaves 93,000 people who won't find any work at all."

In another part of town, at a small café near a library, one of the 7,000 lucky job winners is sporting me to a cup of coffee. He is a townie—but from a different town; he was born and raised in Bulawayo—and a university graduate who studied politics and economics. He had to come to Mashonaland to get a job, he said, even though he's from Matabeleland; he's working now for a tour company—not the job he wanted and was trained for, and he's a little disappointed. After a half hour of small talk about tourism and such, we began talking politics. I volunteered that despite the problems the government's having, Zimbabwe might be on the path already taken by Kenya. He seemed to be annoyed at that, and I wasn't up for a quarrel, so I looked for a way to backpedal. "Not," I added, "that the two are the same."

It was the wrong thing. He was pissed off, that's all, and launched into the angriest lecture I heard from anyone in Africa, including those from not a few pissed-off government ministers.

"You travel in this country, and you say it is different. But you don't see it. It's like all the others [African countries] here. *You* won't see that, of course. You don't know if a man is [Shona] . . . or from Matabeleland. You say you spent time in Kenya. Do you know a Kikuyu man from a man from another tribe? No."

Tribalism, he said, is the one constant political fact of life in Africa, an unchanging preoccupation that has done more to inform the continent's current crises than any problem left behind by the colonial powers. Tribalism *is* politics everywhere in Africa. "In every country—including this one—the struggle against the whites was to see which [African] tribe would have power over the others, and which man in that tribe would rule the country. You live in America, and there a black man is a black man and you think all this [black nationalism] is a good theory. [But] you do not see the reality. In my country, for example, you said, 'Smith is evil, he must go.' Good. So he went. But Mugabe is no different from Smith, *unless* you are part of his inner circle."

Mugabe is a Shona, he explained. "For me, what shall I say is the difference between this man [Mugabe] and that man [Smith]? There is no difference at all. Or maybe it is worse, because the white government did not slaughter as many villages in Matabeleland."

So, he demanded rhetorically, how did the cause of black liberation move forward in Zimbabwe when the power of government was given to a man who harbored tribal animosity toward half the country he wished to govern? "It did not move forward. It moved backward."

According to him, the way Zimbabwe "became independent gave us no freedom, only a new tyrant, a black one. And *we* know *you* cannot tell a black freedom fighter from a black tyrant. You can only tell a white man from a black man. So you are racists of the worst kind since your racism results in tyranny."

What, he wondered, would we do in South Africa to make sure we don't enfranchise one group at the expense of all the others; in essence, perpetuating another form of governmental discrimination? "You will do nothing because you cannot see the difference and because it will make you feel good to do it, even if it makes us feel bad. Which dictator will you establish in South Africa? It is ignorance . . . and it betrays us."

What was needed, he said, was a kind of glossary for well-meaning whites. "We have independence," but not, he said, freedom. "And what you call black nationalism is not the same thing as black liberation. We have no freedom, and we are not liberated. But we live in independent nations."

Like the young man at the car-rental office, he was a Matabele (or an Ndebele). His anger had been aroused by reports of renewed atrocities in Matabeleland caused by rampaging rebels or by army units, theoretically out chasing subversive tribesmen. There had been conflict in the region since independence, and a recent report by Zimbabwe's Roman Catholic Conference of Bishops called the army actions a campaign of terror and said that brutality was widespread. "People are beaten up . . . when they say they do not know anything about dissidents," the conference report said. The army, according to the report, was using a "policy of starvation" and telling Matabele villagers that they would "first have to eat their chickens, then their goats, then their cattle, then their children." Refugees were streaming out of the area; Matebele arriving in Botswana brought with them stories of rape and torture, according to a report in *Time* magazine. Most Matabele thought the army had been dispatched by Mugabe to squash resistance from Joshua Nkomo to Mugabe's one-party strategy. Once allied with Mugabe in the fight against Smith, Nkomo has had to flee from Zimbabwe—he claimed for his life—more than once, and the two are now apparently irreconcilable.*

The lecture I received from the young graduate was similar—though much more impassioned—to one I had once received a few months earlier from a black Mozambique National Resistance† fighter at ease in East Africa, where he had improbably slipped onto the UN payroll. On that occasion, the topic had been the Organization of African Unity (OAU) and how the colonial boundaries of Africa had been established at the 1969 OAU conference in Addis Ababa by those who were most vociferous in their rage at colonialism. "They knew that these boundaries are arbitrary," he said. "But they had each convinced the white governments to give power to them personally . . . almost all the elections in the stage leading to independence were scandalous. So the ones who had tricked the whites into giving them power had to hold it against other tribes and other powerful leaders. In all the history of black independence in Africa," he asked, "who do you think gained? Only a few politicians. The people lost. For them, it is as bad now. Why do you think they all want to leave their families and villages and go to South Africa? Because it is better there than anywhere else. They can earn a living there."

This was all delivered without Stepin Fetchit eye-rolling, mind you. The man was talking politics, and he was angry at politicians. If he hadn't been so universal in his annoyances, I'm sure I would have felt embarrassed, maybe offered a lame excuse or something. But he railed on against Americans—which relieved me—as well as against the Cubans, Mugabe, Samora Machel, the way U.S. arms always failed in the field (his "girlfriend's" nickname was "Kally," he said, "short for Kalashnikov," a more reliable Soviet weapon), and the OAU—especially the OAU. Imagine Idi Amin, he said, as president of the OAU, lecturing the world "on the evils in South Africa. . . . And next year it will be the turn of the Ethiopians, and Mariam Haile Mengistu, who has a government that has killed more people than all the white wars in African history, will preach to the

---

* In covering Nkomo's reluctance to work with Mugabe, the *New York Times* correspondent likened Mugabe's ambitions to something from Alexandre Dumas—a sort of jolly "one for all" esprit de corps. The reporter seemed to have confused one-party government with national unity. As this goes to press, Nkomo seems to have finally bowed to pressure from inside and outside Zimbabwe.

† The M.N.R. is alleged to be a South African–inspired group.

world." The civilized world will not say a word, he claimed, because
Mengistu is black.*

The first angry young man, the Zimbabwean, was right. I don't know
one tribe from another. Fifty percent of the time, maybe, a visitor can tell
whether somebody's Hamitic or part of some other general grouping. But
individual tribes? No way, no more than I can tell a Belgian from a
Dutchman or an Irish Protestant from an Irish Catholic. But small tribes
are the big picture in Africa, where tribal migration and usurpation are the
norm. White people, members of a tribe that usurped more than most, are
in Africa to stay, and, relieved of any of the ideological and political
considerations of colonialism, the new political realities of Africa make it
possible for sophisticated men from industrialized countries to plunder
and exploit to whatever extent a local government can be persuaded to
allow them to do so. And that, at least in the context of its history, is the
Rhodesian way.

* It happened just as he said.

14.

LORD METHUEN:
Gentlemen, have you got maps?

THE OFFICERS:
Yes, sir.

LORD METHUEN:
And pencils?

THE OFFICERS:
Yes, sir.

LORD METHUEN:

Well, gentlemen, your destiny is Mount Hampden. You go to a place called Siboutsi. I do not know whether Siboutsi is a man or a mountain. Mr. Selous, I understand, is of the opinion that it is a man. But we will pass that by. Then you get to Mount Hampden. Mr. Selous is of the opinion that Mount Hampden is placed ten miles too far to the west. You had better correct that; but on second thoughts, better not. Because you might be placing it ten miles too far to the east. Now, good-morning, gentlemen.

—*Major General (later Lord) Methuen, addressing the officers of the Pioneer Corps column of Volunteer Settlers on their departure to Rhodesia, June 24, 1890**

IF YOU'LL EXCUSE ME, a lot of history can be written around the need for a little fast money. In southern Africa, for example, in the last quarter of the last century there was a sizable constituency of men who had come from all over the world to share in what was shaping up to be one of the greatest land grabs in history. In 1869, the Star of Africa diamond had

* For background in this chapter, I have relied on Robinson, Gallagher and Denny and on David Caute's *Under the Skin: The Death of White Rhodesia;* Ian Colvin's two-volume biography of Dr. Leander Starr Jameson; L. H. Gann's *A History of Rhodesia, Early Days to 1933; The Birth of a Dilemma,* by Philip Mason; the autobiography of Sir Harry Johnston and his brother Alex's *The Life and Letters of Sir Harry Johnston;* Roland Oliver's *Sir Harry Johnston and the Scramble for Africa; The Life of F. C. Selous,* by J. G. M. Millais; and the biography of Cecil Rhodes, by William Plomer. I have been

been found in Kimberley, and overnight the area called Griqualand West, just south of the River Vaal, was overrun by prospectors. And when a major gold field was discovered in the Transvaal in 1886, the population of the rough Boer frontier republics north of England's Cape Colony grew dramatically.

In a gold rush, of course, not everyone strikes it rich, and by the middle of 1890, when Cecil Rhodes, the ultimate imperialist, and his agents began recruiting the 180 men who would later come to be seen as the Mayflower generation of Rhodesia, they had a fairly easy time of it. Rhodes canvassed various parts of southern Africa and came up with a likely bunch, told them stories about rich land and big nuggets and sent them a thousand miles or so north from Kimberley in the Orange Free State, across the Molopo River, through Lobengula's Matabele kingdom, past the ruins at Great Zimbabwe* to a grassy plain in the middle of Mashonaland, where they built the town of Salisbury—mostly because they lacked the means to get back to Kimberley again—and dreamed dreams of fast money. In fact, by sending them off, Rhodes himself was taking a huge step toward realizing his own obsessive dream—a Cape-to-Cairo British colonial empire.

Rhodes is often portrayed by writers—and by his contemporaries—as a zealous and compulsive empire builder, a man of great wit, charm and intelligence who would nevertheless swindle friend and enemy alike in order to achieve his desired ends. Those who see Rhodes this way are right, of course. And so are the historians who have painted him a reckless mercantile adventurer who had little use for native rights or governmental niceties.

Cecil John Rhodes was the youngest son of a Hertfordshire vicar, born on July 5, 1853, and educated at the local grammar school. At sixteen, as he was about to enter Oxford (either to study law or take holy orders, he wasn't sure which), he was stricken with the symptoms of a congenital heart malady. His family packed him off to visit his eldest brother, Herbert, who was in Natal, in the eastern part of southern Africa, growing

---

guided especially by Robert Blake's *The History of Rhodesia*. Lord Blake's survey not only corrects many inaccuracies in previous histories, but also provides a sensitive and concerned perspective. It's also very witty in places. The eighth volume of *The Cambridge History of the British Empire* is charming, if severely dated. Lord Methuen's memorable send-off is quoted in both Colvin and Blake.

* After decades of trying to convince each other that this once-great city must have been built by King Solomon or Arabs or Portuguese invaders, scholars now seem certain that Great Zimbabwe was built by indigenous Bantu inhabitants, probably in the fifteenth century.

cotton. His arrival, however, coincided with the Kimberley rush, and by 1871, the two brothers found themselves in the boomtown, surrounded by hustlers and whores, drunks and murderers. Kimberley was, according to historian Lord Blake, "one of the rowdiest places in the world." Within ten years, Rhodes had not only received his degree from Oxford,* but he had also become a very rich man and a member of the Cape Colony legislature. He had also become the target of slander—he was unmarried† and traveled with a coterie of young men—and ridicule, owing largely to his obsessive interest in imperialism and his voice, which must have sounded much like Mickey Mouse's, even though he was of some significant stature. He already had a large following of enemies, undoubtedly because of his ruthlessness in business. He was also beginning to fall victim to his heart ailment—doctors were always telling him how little time left he had. As it happened, he had until March 1902.

To accomplish his goal of spreading the empire north to Egypt, Rhodes established the last Royal Chartered Company—the British South Africa Company (BSAC)—and surrounded himself with a platoon of imperial misfits, perhaps the most impressive assortment of eccentrics in a continent jam-packed full of weirdos, including Dr. Leander Starr Jameson, who was to become Rhodes's best friend, and Harry Johnston, who was to become a bitter enemy.

Jameson, who has a pleasant hotel in Harare named after him, was a talented medical man who left England at twenty-five because of overwork, and ended up in Kimberley. He developed a reputation as a bad gambler but a good womanizer. Completely unpredictable—except that

---

* Historians are fond of pointing out the enormous influence Oxford had on Rhodes—the Rhodes scholarships and all that. Lord Blake, like others writing about Rhodes, takes special note of the effect the inaugural lecture delivered at Oxford in 1871 by John Ruskin had on Rhodes and other young men of the time. Blake has selected the most salient portion of that well-known address:

> We are still undegenerate in race; a race mingled with the best northern blood. . . . Will you youths of England make your country again a royal throne of Kings, a sceptered isle . . . ? This is what England must either do or perish; she must found colonies as fast and as far as she is able, formed of her most energetic and worthiest men; seizing every piece of fruitful waste ground she can set her foot on, and there teaching these her colonists that their chief virtue is to bear fidelity to their country, and that their first aim is to be to advance the power of England by land and sea; and that, though they live on a distant plot of land, they are no more to consider themselves therefore disfranchised from their native land than the sailors of her fleets do because they float on distant seas.

† Blake dismisses the notion of homosexuality as not necessarily likely, and not important, besides. "Some people . . . ," he writes with terrific clarity, "do not marry for the simple reason that they do not want the bother."

he was fearless and tireless—he managed to administer territories entrusted to him so badly that the price was still being paid as this book went to press. He also colluded in an important swindle of Lobengula, king of Matabeleland, and later provoked the native population under his control to rebel against the BSAC. During the last week of 1895, he led a small army of company troopers in a notorious and unauthorized raid on Johannesburg as part of a plot to overthrow Paul Kruger and the Boers in Transvaal.* After a term in prison, he dusted himself off, became prime minister of the Cape Colony and was eventually elevated to a baronetcy.

Sir Harry Johnston started as a friend and ally of Rhodes's, but ended as one of his many enemies. At the time of his knighthood (a K.C.B.) in 1896—for subduing the slavers operating around Lake Nyasa; shades of Frederick Lugard—he was, at age thirty-seven, the youngest member of any of the knighthood orders. He was an extremely eccentric soldier, scholar, scientist and diplomat, and, like Lugard, he's one of those characters in British colonial history in Africa that turn up everyplace—usually in a jam of some sort. A funny, imaginative, energetic, tiny man (again—Johnston was five-foot three; Africans must have thought Europeans were cute, miniature people), at the age of thirty, he looked like a twelve-year-old with a mustache. His enemies, including, later, Rhodes, called him the "prancing proconsul." But it was Johnston who first mooted the Cape-to-Cairo route—far in advance of Rhodes, who later claimed credit for the notion—in a *Times* piece published pseudonymously in August 1888. By the time he met Rhodes, he had traveled up the Congo (he subsequently reported to the Foreign Office on the brutal policies pursued by Henry Stanley and the Belgians) and, as a zoologist and artist, wandered widely through East Africa, where he attempted to secure Mount Kilimanjaro for England, and Zanzibar, where he won the admiration of Sir John Kirk, who wanted Johnston as his replacement when he finally left the sultanate. As a vice-consul posted to the Niger Delta, he helped to avert a native war and to bring the Oil Rivers district into the Lagos protectorate by subduing a brigand named Ja Ja.† Johnston also instituted a system of local councils

---

* Jameson's raid intimately involved Rhodes, who, at the time, was prime minister of the Cape Colony. As a result of the raid, he lost that position as well as his directorship of the BSAC.

† Ja Ja, a very energetic pirate leader, sent an embassy—consisting of his sons, Albert Ja Ja and Sunday Ja Ja, and two of his chiefs, wonderfully named Cookey Gam and Shoe Peterside—to London to put forth his case. No dice, said the Foreign Office. Nevertheless, Ja Ja, after his trial, received all the incomes from his property and a pension besides. He was sent to the Caribbean to cool his heels.

at several important outposts. Roland Oliver, in *Sir Harry Johnston and the Scramble for Africa,* quotes from what he calls "one of the most bizarre documents ever received at the Foreign Office"—a dispatch sent from Johnston after starting a treaty-making expedition up the Cross River. After gathering a few treaties, Johnston decided to wait until he heard from the government on whether or not they really wanted to rule the strange inhabitants in the upper Niger Delta area:

> They are inveterate cannibals, and are continually fighting among themselves. They accorded me a boisterous reception at first. In some cases they began by firing at my canoe . . . then they would wade out through the shallows armed with all kinds of weapons and compel me to stop. They would nearly sink the canoe in their excitement, but to do them justice, they never plundered me of the veriest trifle. In one instance, I was dragged out of the canoe by a score of cannibals, mounted on the shoulders of the biggest, and carried off at a run to the town, where I was put in a hut with the door open and had to submit to being stared at for an hour by hundreds of entranced savages. Almost over my head, hanging from the smoke-blackened rafters of the house, was a smoked human ham, and about a hundred skulls were ranged about the upper part of the clay walls in a ghastly frieze. Despite these sinister surroundings, however, as soon as my interpreters rejoined me, I entered into friendly conversation with my captors and we soon got on excellent terms. . . . Finally the same big black savage that had carried me out of the canoe carried me back, to the surprise and relief of my frightened Kru-boys. The town gave me a hundred yams and two sheep, and the old chief presented me with a necklace of human knucklebones from off his own neck.

These "enforced interviews" recurred every few hundred yards, as Johnston made his progress upriver. Finally, he felt enough was enough. He decided to "make a judicious retreat" and wait for London's instructions. He was later posted to Mozambique and quickly gained followers in the Foreign Office, both by colorful dispatches like this one as well as by his fanciful maps showing how Africa should be carved up.* After his brief encounter with Rhodes, he administered Nyasaland protectorate—a

---

* Sir Harry was also a poet of sorts:

  A Cannibal's Ode to His Aunt

  Search through the crowded market,
    Visit each cannibal feast,
      Where will you meet
      With a corpse so sweet
  As that of the dear deceased?

territory coveted by Rhodes, who suspected, falsely, that Johnston had done a deal with the Foreign Office behind his back—and ended his career as a special commissioner in Uganda. Sir Harry was a hypochondriac, a nonstop talker and a believer in Evolution as a god. He died in 1927.

The column of settlers sent to what would later become Salisbury followed a trail blazed by Jameson, who had been sent by Rhodes to strike an agreement for exploitation with Lobengula, and were seen as important pawns in Britain's maneuvering against Portugal—a colonial power trying to stretch a band of possessions across Africa, from Angola to Mozambique—and the Boers, who were agitating for independence for their semiautonomous republics in southern Africa.

The Matabele king Lobengula was the son of a warrior-chief who had broken away from the warlike Bantus—under the leadership of the formidable Shaka—in the early nineteenth century. After trying their hand at defeating early Boer settlers in the area that is now Transvaal,* the Matabele had been driven into Mashonaland, where they occupied half the territory, and sent the Shona packing to the district just south of the Zambezi River. When Jameson arrived to do business, he found the Matabele were pursuing a policy that involved periodic slave and cattle raids on the Shona—over whom Lobengula claimed sovereignty—with the conventional bloodthirstiness normally associated with African conflicts.

> Juicy she was and tender,
>   And little did we discern
>   The good we should reap
>   From the cost of her keep:
> She has made us a noble return.
>
>   Beauty we scarce remember,
>   Virtues we soon forget,
>   But the taste of our Aunt Eliza
> Clings, clings, to my palate yet.

Sir Harry also wrote a verse commemorating the introduction of female typists at the Foreign Office. Both are to be found in Oliver.

* Early trekkers noted that the veld had been almost completely depopulated as a result of the promiscuous raiding that had gone on there, with only dried bones and occasional burned-out villages as signs of human habitation. The Boer defeat of the Matabele took place in 1837.

After a good deal of negotiation and many threats, Jameson managed to deceive the Matabele leader, and the settlers began to arrive. Unlike any other British colony or protectorate in Africa—including South Africa, where the British, starting with the Cape Colony, had long exerted influence over native affairs—Rhodesia was settled American-style. That is, there was no governmental restraint on the abuse of the aboriginal population; settlers were encouraged to come, and the BSAC helped them by squeezing the native population, taking away their land and redistributing their cattle. Ultimately, of course, this sort of thing led to an uprising, first by the Matabele, who were defeated after they persisted in raiding Shona villages—and destroying the property of whites while they were at it—and then by the Shona, who resented the whites as much as they did the Matabele. By 1897, both tribes were subdued, and Salisbury boasted hotels, saloons, churches, schools, banks and, of course, a club.

The company ruled the territory until 1922, when the voters* were offered a choice in a referendum: union with South Africa or "responsible government," i.e., self-governing colonial status. The advocates of self-government used the same sort of jingoistic slogans that would once again become commonplace: "Rhodesia for Rhodesians, Rhodesia for the Empire," and the proposed union with South Africa was defeated. The vote was significant for a number of reasons: First, it showed that the politicians—almost all of whom anticipated union with South Africa—were out of touch with the sentiments of the settlers. Second, it showed that the settlers preferred to embrace membership in an empire that seemed prepared to protect their interests. As Lord Blake suggests, this same set of considerations later led to Ian Smith's Unilateral Declaration of Independence (U.D.I.) in 1965:

> It is fully in keeping and in no way inconsistent that very similar social and emotional forces should produce [U.D.I.]. . . . Then, too, there was a revolt against the people who had for so many years been ruling the country. Then, too, there was racialism—dislike of a different race, it is true, for the Afrikaners were in favor of U.D.I.—but the basic ingredient was similar, fear of an alien people whose advancement would in the end threaten the security and standards of the white artisans. The same forces which in 1922 propelled a majority of white Rhodesians to proclaim their loyalty to a Britain still believed to be on the side of the settlers, forty-three years later propelled them into breaking with a Britain which palpably was not.

* There were 20,000 white voters registered (out of a population of 35,000) and sixty blacks (out of some 900,000). The colony became self-governing in 1923.

The pattern of white Rhodesian politics was thus established: A somewhat parochial agrarian community would repeatedly unify to guard its interests in the face of outsiders who wished to alter—one way or another—the status quo. If any alterations were going to be done, it would be an inside job.

A series of "liberal" administrations—led first by Sir Godfrey Huggins (later Lord Malvern), who was in power in Southern Rhodesia from 1933 until his retirement as prime minister of the new Central African Federation of the Rhodesias and Nyasaland in 1956 (a stretch unequaled by any other British Crown prime minister)—slowly developed a set of policies that, among other things, rejected apartheid and moved gradually toward some more enlightened program of land reform. As early as 1941, Huggins had indicated that the so-called twin pyramid policy—in which the races should pursue parallel lines of development—would have to be scrapped and that segregation in jobs and on the land should not be enshrined as permanent national features.

By 1950 it seemed inevitable that the three colonies—Northern Rhodesia, Southern Rhodesia and Nyasaland—would be united in the Central African Federation. There were important differences in the three, however. While Southern Rhodesia—which had the largest white population by far—was a self-governing colony, the other two were protectorates with London-appointed governors at the head of the political structure. But whereas Nyasaland (whose white population was quite small) had always been somewhat outside the sphere created by Rhodes and Johnston, the white population of the two Rhodesias saw eye to eye on such issues as "partnership" between the races.* To Northern Rhodesia's Roy Welensky, a self-made politician and romantic advocate of empire, who was pressing for "responsible government" for the north, and to Huggins in Southern Rhodesia, the matter of partnership was a clumsy one, for both men believed that whites should be the senior partners for a long time to come. In the agreement that finally united the three territories, such areas as defense, currency, customs, highways, postal services and railways would be shared. What resulted was a white-dominated confedera-

---

* When Joseph Lelyveld was covering Rhodesia for the *New York Times* in 1965, he found himself being instructed in the notion of "partnership" by the wife of Douglas Lilford, a wealthy and influential early supporter of Ian Smith's. "Mr. Lilford's wife . . . complains that the rest of the world never quite grasped what white Rhodesians meant by the concept of racial 'partnership,' " Lelyveld wrote. "When my cook and I put on a dinner and it's a failure, both of us are at fault. When my cook and I put on a dinner and it's a success, both of us deserve credit. That, she explains, is partnership. But I never meant by partnership that my cook should say to me, 'Now you go into town and buy the cheese.' "

tion that had a compensatory soft edge on race relations; the federation carried with it the evolutionary views advocated by Huggins and a mandate from Britain to pursue the partnership issue. It was hoped in London that such an entity would be able to resist the still-compelling unionist movement that might eventually pull Southern Rhodesia into South Africa. Never mind that the federation was almost universally rejected by the African populations in the three states (although the Matabele nationalist leader Joshua Nkomo, who attended the federation deliberations in London, despite some reservations gave the plan his approval). In 1953, the federation was inaugurated. Huggins became its first prime minister.

The federation floundered along in a haphazard way until 1957, when Huggins's successor as Southern Rhodesian prime minister, Garfield Todd, a liberal committed to electoral reform, was confronted with a cabinet revolt. Although he was able to stave off his United party colleagues for a while, in 1958 the governor dissolved parliament and new elections were held. Todd's party lost every seat, and the opportunity for a multiracial Rhodesia—based on London's concept of partnership, not Welensky's or Huggins's—faded away forever.

Todd was succeeded by Sir Edgar Whitehead, an Oxford-educated, aloof figure, who, while he was even more liberal than Todd, was misunderstood not only by his own party, but, more important, by Nkomo and other black leaders. When elections were held in 1962, a new grass-roots right-wing party, the Rhodesian Front, under the leadership of a charismatic figure named Winston Field, was on the field. The electoral rules were changed, too. A new constitution was approved by referendum giving two separate registration rolls, both based on property and literacy; the A roll, granting fifty seats, was essentially for whites; the B roll, representing another fifteen seats, was for Africans.

Nkomo's decision to lead a black boycott of the constitutional negotiations, the referendum and, later, the election (there were some 5,500 Africans eligible for the A roll, but only 2,000 had registered to vote; of the 60,000 or more eligible for the B roll, less than 10,000 had registered) is now seen as a mistake, since he could have altered the constitutional deliberations significantly. Moreover, if 5,000 additional African B voters had cast ballots, Whitehead would have been returned to power with a mandate for increasing African representation. In the event, however, the Front won. Moved by events like the Mau Mau uprising in Kenya and the bloodbaths in the newly independent Congo, as well as by the advocacy of disruption and violence by African leaders inside the country, white voters decided to pull back from their awkward experiment with partnership.

By 1963 the federation was finished, disputes between the two African parties in Northern Rhodesia were resulting in what the *New York Times* called a "reign of terror" as Kenneth Kaunda maneuvered for power, and there was rioting in the streets of Lusaka as the territory, now without a credible government, moved toward independence. In Nyasaland, Dr. Hastings Kamuzu Banda moved quickly to consolidate his claim to power in an independent Malawi, as the country would be known.

By the following year, 1964, Kaunda had seized power in what would, in October, become Zambia, while in Malawi, one of the first acts of Banda was to reaffirm economic links with South Africa and Southern Rhodesia,* where Field had been ousted and replaced by Ian Smith, a dedicated right-wing hard-liner who was committed to independence for the colony.

Smith's overwhelming victory in subsequent elections—his supporters won every seat, save the fifteen reserved for Africans—reflected the growing insecurity of the settler population. He moved quickly to reassure his constituents, clamping down on black nationalist movements inside the country, while projecting a calm, confident image both at home and abroad. He told a reporter for the *New York Times* that reaction in Britain to Rhodesian independence wouldn't last more than a week. "For that reason," he said, "I think Friday afternoon would be a good time [to declare independence]. By Monday morning all the excitement would be over."

Smith was an enigma to many white Rhodesians. Until his final grab for power, he was rarely in the foreground of the political skirmishes that had been raging, usually playing secondary roles. Nevertheless, he had the cosmetics for success in politics—handsome, youthful looks with lean and serious features, slightly scarred from the plastic surgery that rebuilt half his face after he was shot down the second time while flying Spitfires for the RAF. (He spent five months behind the German lines fighting with Italian partisans, and rejoined the Allied armies only after disguising himself and crossing the Alps on foot.) Posters bearing his likeness and the slogan "An Honest Rhodesian. Trust Mr Smith" began appearing in Salisbury, and by May 1965, Smith was secure in his plans for declaring U.D.I. Finally, on November 11, 1965, Smith declared a state of emergency as well as his country's independence. Simultaneously, Rhodesia

---

* Among his other early measures was the sentencing of a white resident to six strokes with a cane for throwing things at a portrait of Banda.

became the subject of trade sanctions, UN condemnations and American and British threats, and the country was ousted from the Commonwealth. In the course of the next year, Smith would meet with the British prime minister—twice on ships in the Mediterranean—and with the Secretary of State and other American leaders, all for nought. Smith's war for independence was on, and it would continue, despite sanctions and threats and rhetoric, until the South Africans decided it should stop.

15.

I don't think anyone would have thought he
could ever be a prime minister—not even
his best friend. He was never a popular
speaker. There was something harsh and
grating about him—definitely not concilia-
tory.

*—A Rhodesian politician, quoted by Joseph
Lelyveld in the* New York Times,
August 22, 1965

I never voted for Smith. Not once. And I
never admitted it. Not once.

*—A white Zimbabwean
in Harare, 1987*

IAN SMITH'S LIVING ROOM contains few souvenirs of power—there
aren't any captured flags or plaques or pictures of Smith with his arm
around a Pope on the wall, or any of the other touches so much a part of
international political interior decor. Instead, there are the trophies of a
family man—kids with Mom, kids with Dad, the usual. Smith didn't
seem to realize that, at least in the high-contrast popular view, he was one
of the world's greatest living failures, a demon among men of goodwill,
the punctuation of a long sentence of colonial transience.

He solved that problem: According to Smith, the failure is not his, but
rather the rest of the world's. His regime, he told me, ultimately collapsed
"because it's the fashion to believe that a white man in Africa is exploit-
ing the black man. This is what the world has been led to believe, but
it's all part of a guilt complex on the part of the colonial countries
who were attacked—and this is something which came to a peak after the
last world war, when colonialism became a dirty word, everybody said,
'We must get out, we must give these poor people independence.' And

even . . . Roosevelt was in the forefront of saying [things like that], you see."

Who was behind this manipulation of reality? According to Smith, Moscow. "It's a communist ploy," he said. "I'm not one of these people who's just mad about communism and think that they're responsible for everything, but I have studied communism and analyzed it; I've spoken to a lot of people, and I think that communism is an evil [with] Russia as the main instigator. The most worrying thing is, though, that they find so many people in the free world who are prepared to aid and abet them—to be fellow travelers. . . .

"The theme [they advanced] generally was that colonialism was a bad thing; the white man used colonialism to exploit the Third World and Africa—just mine it, and get everything up they could. It isn't the case, you see. I mean, you look at this country and see what the white man has done here in less than a hundred years, less than ninety years. . . . When our forebears came here, these people couldn't read or write. The wheel hadn't even evolved; it was one of the few places in the world where they were so backward that the *wheel* hadn't evolved. Well, you look at them today. They're better off than the black people anywhere else on the continent of Africa.

"In the windup of the [Central African] Federation here—in those days I was Minister of Finance, and so I was chairman of the committee which dealt with the economic dismemberment of the federation—some very interesting facts were thrown up there by *British* civil servants, not our people, who said—and showed us the statistics—that the facts showed very clearly that we had done more than twice as much for our black people as Britain had done for their black people in Northern Rhodesia and Nyasaland in the fields of education and health and provision of special facilities and cultural facilities, that kind of thing.

"So when you look back on what we inherited here, one of the most primitive societies in the world, and when you look at these people today, see how well off they are and what they've inherited—this wonderful country, what wonderful educational facilities they have and so on—it makes it patently obvious to any fair-minded man that we spread lightness and Christianity and Western civilization here at an incredible pace. A handful of white people, and look what they've built. So, for some reason or another, it's a bit of a guilty conscience on the part of the people back in Britain and France and Belgium and all of those countries."

Smith was completely without emotion in telling me this, even the stuff about lightness and civilization. If I was expecting somebody to pull at my shirtsleeve and rant something about warning the world before it was too late or something, I was wrong. I got a chap who could sit down and say something like, "We spread lightness and Christianity and Western civilization here," and never miss a beat or crack a cynical smile. He believed it; you bet.

Finally, he said, the times caught up with what came to be seen as the anomaly of colonialism. "The world suddenly decided, after the last war," Smith went on, "that colonialism was bad and that white people from the West were mining Africa [and everywhere else—India and so on and so forth] and so the noble thing to do was to get out and give these people their freedom—that's what it was called, you see: They were being denied freedom."

Conventional wisdom demonstrates, and Smith knew, that it could be shown in almost every case where there's a healthy export economy that one did not have poverty or starvation or famine. So many people willingly made the decision that would ultimately cost so many people their lives, according to Smith, "because of a guilt complex.

"That's the only thing I can pin it on. I've given this great thought, having lived with it for so long. I remember, for example, at Lancaster House, [British Foreign Secretary Lord] Carrington and all of those people—and *dreadful* people they were—saying to us, 'It is now clear history has proven that whenever the white man pulls out of Africa, the country which they leave behind very quickly degenerates into bankruptcy and chaos and denial of liberty. So that's why we've now decided, from experience and hindsight, that we're going to introduce for the first time a constitution in your country which is going to enshrine the white man for quite a while in the hope that we can encourage him to stay and claim his spot—because if we can get him to do that, then there's hope. Without the white man, there's no hope.'"

"Carrington said that?" I had to ask. It just didn't seem likely.

"Oh, yes. Talked as blatantly and openly as that, but they didn't have the courage to really do it properly. Or the courage to do what they should have done—which they promised me they were going to do—and that was accept the previous government that had been brought in here, which already had a black majority and a big white participation—the [moderate Bishop Abel] Muzorewa government. They said, 'That's the sort of thing we want. If you get on and bring that about, we'll recognize you.'

"But the OAU was too powerful. The OAU said, 'No, no. That's not good enough. We want one man, one vote, and we want Smith and all of his cronies pushed into the background. We don't want them participating.' And they [the British and the West] gave in."

For the first time, Smith seemed to warm to the subject. But when I told him that none of the businessmen I had spoken to were willing to go on record recommending foreign capital investment in this country, he cooled.

"I try to get people to come here, in spite of the fact that I'm critical of this government. I think one has to be critical—I don't think you can condone what is wrong and what is evil—but nevertheless, it *is* my country and I say to people, 'It's still a good country, and eventually we can save it. You must come in and help.' And I try to be positive. . . .

"They say, 'But, Mr. Smith, how can you say that to us when we see what's happening around us?' And I then know that in the end I've got to say, 'But of course, you're right.' I mean, they say, 'We can get a very good return on investment in our own backyard. We aren't taxed as heavily as we are here, and even if we do make a profit here—which is highly unlikely, with the cost of production here and the inflation and so on— then we are taxed another 20 percent on any [goods] we won't send up, and we know that we're going to wake up tomorrow morning and find our industry nationalized by a government which is clearly Marxist-Leninist. And you ask us to come and invest here?' So I say, 'No, okay.' I give up. . . .

"Just at the moment, we're going through a sort of twilight zone, waiting for them to be in a position where they can make these [political] changes [that would enable the Mugabe government to eliminate white representation in the parliament in 1987] . . . [but] the more important [changes] have to go on for another four years, until 1990. That's when they will have the right, for example, to create a one-party state, if they want to, a one-party Marxist-Leninist state. One hopes that there is a lot of rhetoric associated with that at the moment, but we don't know. If they go with that kind of thing, then that will be the final nail in the coffin of confidence from the outside world. Nobody would invest; they're not investing today because there's so much talk about it. . . . [The level of Marxist rhetoric] is very high, because it's playing to the gallery, and Mugabe wants to be the savior of the OAU by imposing sanctions against South Africa, which, far from saving it [the Mugabe government] will be a suicidal act.* But this is the atmosphere, the euphoria we're living in, the

* A few weeks after this interview, Smith was expelled from the parliament—effectively ending his political career—for condemning the Mugabe government's plan to impose sanctions against the Republic of South Africa. During our chat, he had said, "I would have liked to get out of politics on quite a few occasions—after my first five years, I find it easier to get in than to get out, because once you get in people do come to you and say, 'You know we hope you won't abandon us, we hope you won't desert us.' Nobody wants to be associated with that sort of thing, so you can get caught." That's one less problem Smith has to consider.

emotions—and the free world, for a while, was going along with it. Fortunately, they're beginning to stand up to it now; you've got a few people like Thatcher and Reagan who are not prepared to condone this. So they're beginning to have second thoughts. But for a long while, they were being encouraged in this. It was a wonderful thing to do: The sooner they did it and got rid of [and] smothered all the terrible whites, the better.

"That was the complex, the guilt complex which for some reason or another the free world was suffering from. You know, you've got a different sort of thing in America, where the white man there believes he has to apologize to the black man for what his forebears did to the black man—this dreadful thing of bringing slaves to America. Of course, it wasn't the Americans who did that at all. It was the slave traders from Europe who did it in conjunction with *all* of the black chiefs on the African continent. This was an annual thing, which they still do today, where the chiefs determine how much food they've got and whether or not they've got to get rid of some of their menfolk or not. Because if they haven't got enough food, they tell them to push off and work in the gold mines in South Africa. In those days, they used to tell them to get on the boats and go to America. Nothing to do with white Americans. The white Americans were really saving these poor people, and I don't miss an opportunity to tell Americans when I'm over there how taken aback I am at this guilt complex of theirs, which is absolutely false and unnecessary. And I say if you want to prove it, just say to any of these black people— especially the ones who talk about wanting to help their black brethren back in the African continent—that you'll pay their passage back if they want to do the noble act—and in fact give them a bonus of a hundred thousand dollars to everybody who goes back—you know how many takers you'll have? You won't have any."

A bit much, I thought, and said so. He was on a roll, however. "If the government of this day were prepared to practice what they preach—in other words, bring about *true* reconciliation, and they were working together with the white people and the black people and accepted the free-enterprise system, the only viable system in the world, because every-where where communism or Marxist-Leninism has been practiced the countries are bankrupt—if they were prepared to do that, and there are some cabinet ministers who say to me that that's what they think should happen. This is one of the things that does give me a little bit of hope occasionally. . . . When I speak to these [black] chaps . . . in parliament who say, 'Please keep going, Mr. Smith, because we want to tell you we agree with you.' And they say, 'You'd be surprised how many cabinet ministers agree with us, but we are not in the majority. We hope one day to be in the majority.' If we got to that stage, then this could still be a wonderful country, because it is inherently a rich country, it has many advantages—the fact that it had the white man here so many years building what you have here—there is still quite a decent infrastructure here. It could be jacked up. You've got a lot of skills and potential and expertise—we are the most sophisticated country in this part of Africa today, so we could become the workshop of Africa. Our farmers are wonderful farmers, amongst some of the best in the world. We produce tremendous things, I mean, the quality of things like our tobacco is as good as the Americans', which is the best in the world, you see. So it is here. It isn't too late now. But if we go on as we're going on now for another five years, then it might be beyond redemption."

According to Smith, it is a "correct assumption" that Mugabe is assembling all the trappings of a president-for-life personality cult. Smith didn't foresee, for example, any impact a future election might have on Zimbabwe. "These people don't believe in elections, you know. We mustn't trust ourselves about that. One man, one vote, *once*. One man, one vote, one time. That's what they don't understand, the rest of the world. They don't understand Africa, yet they want to tell us how to run Africa. They're quite taken aback when I tell them—presidents and prime ministers—when I say to them, 'Do you know how many times govern-ments change through the ballot box in Africa?' Do you know how many?"

I think he actually expected me to guess, but I wasn't doing the talking.

"Never. They don't believe in it. They think you're stupid. Once— before we had that government that was set up with [Abel] Muzorewa [a moderate black leader]—a bloke said, Alec Home [Sir Alec Douglas-Home] said to me, 'Make a plan with your local blacks. You can do that with the reasonable ones. Forget about the chaps outside. The world will have to accept you.' So we did it, and they didn't. They let us down. . . . But I was talking to the [Rhodesian Front] cabinet at the prime minister's residence here, and at the end of the meeting I said, 'Well, gentlemen, as you know, I'm now going into a general election, so this is the last meeting until after the election. If I'm still the prime minister, we'll pick it up here. If not, you'll have to speak to the next person, you see.'

"I saw [the blacks] talking to one another and I said, 'Just excuse me a moment,' and I went out into the lobby to do something before coming back to usher them to the door. When I came back, they were still very seriously involved in the discussion. I said, 'What's the matter, gentle-men? Have you got a problem?'

"One chap said, 'Yes. You know,' he said, 'Prime Minister, we blacks,

we don't understand you white people. There you are, you're the government. You're the prime minister. You've got complete control of *everything*. And now you tell us you're going to go to the people, the man in the
street, and give him an opportunity to throw you out.'

"He said, 'You know, we blacks wouldn't be so stupid.'

"It isn't part of their culture, it isn't part of their tradition. They've never
practiced it; they don't believe in it today. . . . But the Western free world
believed that before leaving they had to insist on [it] whether they liked it
or not, good or bad. It doesn't work. They don't want to know it. When
they become the government, they all say to themselves, 'This is for the
next thousand years, thanks, and if you let anybody put you out, you're
just a damn fool.' And Mugabe's the same. Of course he is.

"A handful of black politicians are not going to suffer. When there's
starvation and bankruptcy and corruption, which is one of the root causes
of the problems, the famine in Ethiopia, the politicians . . . didn't suffer.
They all [had] these big, fat motorcars, and fed on caviar and scotch
whiskey."

Was that, I asked, why in his view U.D.I. had become so essential?

"What was worrying me more than anything else was the exodus of
white people at that time. For the first time in our history, we were losing
whites. And I don't speak of whites as a racialist, I'm sure you understand, but because they were the people with the skills and the capital and
the know-how and all of that. Without the whites, it wasn't going to work.
So white people had begun to say to me, 'We can see we're going the same
way the rest of Africa has gone—the British are going to sell us out. And
we're not going to accept it, because there's no freedom in those countries—they just go down the drain.' What a lot of people don't understand,
have been misled into believing—and again this is part of the guilt
complex, and I think also communist propaganda—is that the reason for
U.D.I. was a conflict between whites and blacks in this country. *It had
nothing to do with that at all.* It was an argument between our government
and the British government. The British government promised us at the
Victoria Falls Conference that if we assisted them in winding up the
federation—because without Rhodesia's assistance, it could not be done;
this was the financial and industrial capital of the whole federation—and
even all the federal ministers . . . all said, 'You know, without you they
can't do it. You're in a strong position.' So we extracted from the British
government an undertaking—which is really all we wanted—that in the
event of the federation breaking up we would get our independence.

"And at the Victoria Falls Conference we were given that undertaking
by that dreadful Briton called Butler, R. A. B. Butler, in his pompous

manner telling us—I can remember I wasn't prime minister then, I was
Minister of Finance; Field was prime minister then—that he was happy to
tell us that Her Majesty's government had come to the conclusion that after
our wonderful record of service to Britain we would get our independence,
if not before, not much later than the other two territories [Northern
Rhodesia and Nyasaland]. And, of course, I didn't like that attitude. So,
that was a problem. We had proved our ability, we had run our country
successfully for fifteen years, we were economically a wonderful example, and so on and so forth. . . . During the last world war we sent more
people to fight in terms of population than any other country in the
Commonwealth. We argued with them for a couple of years, and in the end
we came to the conclusion that they were just leading us up the garden
path and people were losing confidence in the country.

"From the moment we declared our independence . . . the whole scene
changed. People started coming back, conditions started returning to
normal, we developed what many bankers and economists and industrial-
ists told me was the most efficient economy on this earth. We had a rate of
growth in our economy greater than any other country in the world at the
time. That's what we did. That was the reason for the argument between
Britain and ourselves. . . . [It had] nothing to do with black-white con-
frontation, but if you listen today to the OAU and all of these people, the
only reason why I declared independence was because I wanted to suppress the black people, you know. We had a constitution which allowed
equal access to black and white."

Surely he must have realized at the time that he was volunteering to play
the role of the white racist bastard. "Yes, but I was part of a scene of
history which was taking place here, and by character I'm not the sort of
person that runs away from a problem. I always say, you never solve a
problem by running away from it, and the greater the problem, the more, I
believe, one has got to dedicate oneself to it. And I think that being part of
history and having lived in the country as I had, when it came to a crunch,
had I skipped away, that would have been a cowardly act and that's
certainly not part of my character. I may have many weaknesses and
failings, but I think I have quite a little bit of character and a little bit of
courage and a little bit of determination, and I could never, under any
circumstances, run away from that. . . . I was so incensed at what the
British government was doing to us, the deviousness and sheer dishon-
esty—I'd been brought up strictly by British parents to believe that a
Britisher's word was his bond, that if there was anybody in this world you
could trust, it was a Britisher and so on, so I wasn't prepared to pull out in
the middle. It was my intention to make sure that I was going to stay for

this one before pulling out, unless, of course, I was asked to step out, and that wouldn't have been my decision."

Throughout the guerrilla war that raged through much of his administration, Salisbury remained relatively calm, an important symbol of control cultivated by Smith. "I never used to have any protection. I used to walk out of my office at lunchtime, and people used to be standing outside on the veranda and they see me and speak to me as I went out. . . . I had one or two security guards. I didn't want it, but I was told, you know, 'It's good for you to have a chap because every now and again you want a messenger to go and get this and go and do this.' You know, that's what those blokes are going to do for you.

"But you see we had wonderful race relations in this country. One of the things I loved was visitors saying to me, 'The happiest black faces we've ever seen anywhere in this world, we see here in this country.' We had fantastic relations. We'd go around together, we were friends, we worked together—there were no problems until the politicians came and created the problems and told the blacks that we whites were bad and that they must hate us."

When, I asked, did he finally say to himself, "Well, okay, this is it."

"We always had enough sense to realize that in the end we must try to come to a negotiated settlement. I mean, within months of our declaration I was talking to the British government and I had meetings with Harold Wilson on battleships in the Mediterranean on more than one occasion. So I want to stress the fact that we were not inflexible and dogmatic and pigheaded about this; we were always very reasonable. I think, basically, we are a reasonable people. I didn't want to fight, but I was incensed that the British government had betrayed me and misled me—[it was] absolutely dishonest. And in the end, we just insisted that they should implement their promise. I've had constitutional lawyers from America and Britain and the Continent telling me that there was nothing illegal about our declaration because all we were doing was insisting on the implementation by the British of the legal commitment to us. So, this was nothing new. . . .

"And I'd been to America and talked to Cyrus Vance when he was Secretary of State, people like that, you see. We were always talking to try to see if we couldn't bring back a bit of sanity . . . [but] we didn't want to compromise on our thinking. In the end, we were not beaten by our enemies, it wasn't a war or economic situation that brought us to here. In the end we were betrayed by our friends. And in the end there was only one country that could really force us [to do anything]. . . . I could tell the British and the Americans what to do, as we'd done for fifteen years, [but] you couldn't do that with South Africa because my lifeline leads through that country. That was the pressure in the end which forced us.

"It was strange. [South African Premier John] Vorster thought he was going to be the savior of the white man in southern Africa." Vorster, Smith said, was convinced that if he sacrificed Rhodesia, the rest of the world would get off *his* back. "I said, 'You don't believe it, do you?'

" 'Ah, my friend,' he said, 'you've been so out of touch with the world around you for so long that you don't know what's going on. It's unbelievable.' "

In hindsight, Smith said, Rhodesia's biggest mistake was to decline independence and union with South Africa when it was offered to them in 1922. "At the time it probably was the right decision . . . because we were subsequently betrayed by the country that we then stood by. Huggins— when he was prime minister—told us after the last war [World War II] that he had been offered independence for Rhodesia because of this fantastic record that we had, and [because of] our reputation [for economic responsibility], and so on. We could have had it then [in 1946]. We virtually could have had it in '22 . . . because by going in with South Africa we would have had it. But [after the Second World War] Huggins decided that perhaps we would have been slow to have independence and that it would be better to try this thing called federation. . . .

"But when you go back to the '22 decision, it's a different ball game and problem altogether, and it opens up a much more complex vista, because the whole history of southern Africa would have changed. Had we gone in then with South Africa, [Jan] Smuts would have won the . . . election after the last war and not . . . lost it by one or two seats. God, we were almost . . ."

Smith broke off here and reflected for a moment. "If Smuts had won that election, the whole history of southern Africa would have changed, because at the end of the last war, Smuts hired three British [ships] to bring immigrants to South Africa. That was the sort of opportunity [that existed then], because people wanted to get out. We doubled our white population here in nine years. We brought in immigrants even faster than Israel. Now, if you follow that to its logical conclusion—I know it isn't practically possible to do—but had we doubled that every nine years, why, today we would have had more whites than blacks in this country. Which just shows you what statistics can do. But if you translate that to South Africa, they would have had a white population today of about twenty million. You can imagine how the whole history, the whole of southern Africa, would have been different, because as soon as the Nationalist party won in that first election, they canceled that agreement; they didn't want to bring white

immigrants [to South Africa] because they thought all the white Englishmen coming to South Africa would vote for Smuts and not them, you see.

"It's a mad world, eh?"

Indeed. We abandoned the living room and walked outside and looked
at the garden, spoke a little about his children and took photos. Finally,
returning to politics, we chatted about the South African government's
veto of the Natal referendum, which would have created a multicameral
legislature for the state and have provided blacks with meaningful representation for the first time. I wondered aloud if South Africa had failed to
learn the lesson offered by Rhodesia. Smith would have very little of that.

"I think [South African State President P. W.] Botha is a man of great
character," he said. "He's made more changes in favor of liberalizing
South Africa in the last few years than were made in the previous thirty
years, forty years. I'm surprised at how much he's done. He's gone so far,
so fast, that he has antagonized many of his oldest and loyal supporters,
who are now calling him a traitor. I think people in all fairness have to give
him credit for what he has done.

"You know, politics is the art of the possible. One of the things a
politician always has to be very careful of is that he doesn't distance
himself too far from his electorate and find in the next election he's off the
field. Because if he does that, even the greatest player in the world can't
influence the game, and any politician who does that has bungled it. It's
the sort of problem that you have to accept, and that politicians live with. I
think Mr. Botha is getting a mandate in this coming election* now which
will strengthen his hand again. . . .

"I'm surprised that even reasonable whites say they are afraid he's
going too fast, and that if South Africa isn't careful they're going to land
up the same way as we did. That's a strong point which his opponents are
using: 'Look at Rhodesia, is that what you want to do to us?' And, of
course, there aren't any South Africans, even the liberals in South Africa,
[who would] say yes. I'm surprised how many liberal Rhodesians, people
who didn't support me—they thought I was too conservative—have left
now and are living in South Africa . . . [although] a few of them are
coming back because they can't get any dividends. They're economic
prisoners here."

Smith felt certain that South Africa would be able to avoid a bloodbath
and resolve the issues that had confounded his government, "You see,

---

* He did, but subsequent advances by right-wing Afrikaners have eroded his power
somewhat.

what gives me hope—and I think I'm right when I say this because I go to South Africa now and again and I meet people there and I meet black people—the majority of blacks in South Africa are very supportive of this government. They don't support [Oliver] Tambo [leader of the African National Congress (A.N.C.)] because they can see he's going wrong. . . .

"When I was in South Africa last year, I was introduced to a black woman [in Johannesburg], and she says to me that her daughter was one of the people killed in one of these random bomb blasts at a bus stop in Pretoria, and she said, 'If that's all the A.N.C. can offer us, then we're better off without them.'

"You know, these [random] murders that they do . . . are really bad, really barbaric. I've seen it on television, I don't know if you have. It's one of the most difficult things I've ever seen in my life. It's difficult to think that a human being can be associated with such a thing. But the blacks are beginning to say to themselves, 'Hold on.' You know how many immigrant workers there are in South Africa today, black immigrant workers? I think it's about one and one half million. I can't walk into a big shop or a store in Johannesburg without being surrounded by my own black Rhodesians or Zimbabweans who come and speak to me. . . .

"In one store there [where] I used to go . . . quite often, the manager used to say, 'Oh, yes, Mr. Smith. Where are you going to have your meeting today?' They used to all gather around me. And they have no excuse for coming back here. . . . When I say, 'When are you coming back home?' they say, 'You must be joking.'

"Why do all of those people go there? Because, they say, 'Well, we have a much better life here we're better off economically, and it's freer.' I would think that's one of the strong things which the whites have in their favor there, that the blacks are beginning to realize that this black majority [movement] may be not what it's made out to be.

"But as far as a solution goes, it's not a simple problem, and I don't think there's a quick easy answer to it. I always say to people who ask me this question, 'The best way to help South Africa solve their problem is to leave them alone.'

"I think the nonsense which is going on today seems to me to be absolute madness and this Eminent Persons group's [a three-man "nonpartisan" delegation representing the Commonwealth] views are . . . so farcical and absolutely hypocritical [that] in the end South Africans will solve it, and no one else. The rest of the world is trying to blackmail [them], and the South Africans won't have anything to do with that and I don't blame them. I'm not supporting the South African government—

you know some of the things they do which I've queried. I'm talking about what the rest of the world is doing—trying to blackmail [them]. . . . If you analyze it, the rest of the world is really trying to say to the white people in South Africa, 'We want you to commit suicide.'

"It's a pretty involved, complicated system with a dozen different black tribes who don't trust one another. You say to the Zulus, 'Will you accept another black chap as your leader?' and they'll laugh at you. So, what do you do? It's not an easy problem.

"We're so close to them; I think it is wrong [to suggest sanctions]. . . . I'm strongly critical of this government attacking South Africa on the one hand, when on the other hand, they get 90 percent of everything they require from South Africa. I think that's being dishonest, hypocritical, two-faced."

I must say, I admired the job Smith had done with his world view. It was complete and steady, even if it represented some other world. I just wanted to know one other thing—what's left for the white man in Africa? Does he have a role to play at all?

I asked Smith, and Smith didn't know either. "It's not an easy question to answer, because politics is a pretty emotional game and an illogical one, even in countries where people are mature, where politics has been part of the system for centuries. It's a new game. . . . They've always had the tribal chiefs who were there by inheritance . . . and politics has never been part of this. Now it's a new toy that they've got, and it's exciting and it gives them power and they drive around in big motorcars and enjoy all of the things which colonialists brought and which they once condemned. Some of the greatest colonialists I've ever seen in my life are amongst the ministers of this [Mugabe's] government. So how long it's going to take to get that out of their system, it's difficult to assess, although there are already signs of people beginning to get a bit fed up.

"But if you have a totalitarian system, then you don't have much opportunity of expressing your views—especially if you disapprove. It's been going on in some of these countries for about twenty-five years now, hasn't it? They're still there. The only way they change a government is when there's a coup and a chap gets a bullet in his head or something like that. Whether Africa's going to go for a long time being different, I don't know. It is a different part of the world. Different people, different continent altogether. And whether it's the sort of thing that can come right in a couple of decades or whether it's going to take a couple of centuries, this is difficult to say."

One thing Smith does see that causes him distress is the patronizing attitude toward Africans by much of the West. To him, colonialism was more honest and more altruistic. "I think with a colonial attitude, the people who came here were motivated by an ideal; they were dedicated, and they felt that what they were doing was right. . . .

"But with paternalism, there's a difference. There's no moral issue there, you see? You're not dedicated to a cause. Patronizing is a bad thing, as opposed to colonialism, which I thought was a great ideal and which brought Christian civilization to half the earth, where people were killing one another . . . and other things worse than that. So the colonialists had the idea of trying to spread justice, law-and-order, decency, playing the game, Christianity. That was what colonialism was based on, and all of those are great ideals.

"But a patronizing attitude is, I think, almost an abyss. I think one should treat it with contempt. There is a very big difference. I think what the rest of the world has got to do is to face up to the fact that by patronizing people, you are encouraging them to go on following a course which is wrong. I think the only way you can get it right is by saying to them, 'Look here, you mustn't do that.'

"After all, white people [who live in Africa] are still admired here for our honesty and straightforwardness and for our playing the game with people . . . and I think with the passage of time, this is going to come out more and more. I thank the members of this government today; I think I have more support amongst the black people than they have—if the black people were free and allowed to express themselves. I walk down the streets here and black people come up to me and shake my hand and say, 'Will you please keep going?'

"Not only white people, but blacks, are becoming more and more concerned that things are going wrong with the passage of every day. They're not getting what they [were] promised . . . [and] unfortunately the government is trying to pretend that they are. And they control the mass communications, the media, [and] of course they're in a strong position."

Smith closed his eyes for a moment. A lifetime of being cast as a villain, I thought, and all for nothing. I wondered if he was a bitter man. So I asked him.

"No, I think I can honestly say no to that question, having been asked it before. So I've thought about it. I've always believed, and I've always said, I think bitterness and hatred are sterile things. . . . I think one must try to forget the past—other than . . . the fact that experience is always useful to try to help correct the mistakes of the past. Don't use it for discrimination, or rather for recrimination, because I think we've all got to get on together and make the best of this world today. Such a small world. . . . You can't live in splendid isolation anymore. You used to be able to once upon a time.

"I encourage people to try to eliminate bitterness and hatred, and I think I've succeeded in doing it pretty well. Maybe not completely— perhaps that would be absolutely impossible. I sometimes think back on how we've been betrayed by our own friends, our own kith and kin, and for a few moments I think what I'd like to do to them. But then I push it aside and get on with it—think what is before me and what I can still do in this world, because we live in a mad world and I see it particularly around me here and what's happening in southern Africa, my own people here calling for sanctions against South Africa, which I know will bring white Africa to its knees in a month, and I can't understand that kind of madness. I say there's much to do so let's get on with it and do it, even if it's only a mite that we can contribute, let's contribute, let's try to bring back a little bit of sanity to the world."

That was that. We retreated into the house, where Smith made a call to help me gain an appointment to see an acquaintance. The phone lines were on the blink, but he simply shrugged it off and tried again until the call was complete.

He didn't seem to have much to say as he walked me to the door. But as I walked across the yard, he took several steps off the porch.

"You know, I think I could honestly say that I don't indulge in bitterness and hatred."

Honestly.

End Notes

DRIVING SOUTH FROM HARARE, I detoured off the main road and found myself in Wildlife Central. Great, huge buffalo and awkward ostriches, a small herd of zebra and a large rap session of arboreal monkeys. It was all very educational until, like a jerk, I spotted some exotic beast and got out of the jeep. Although I'm a hopelessly inept picture taker, I pressed my eye to my camera viewfinder, zooming in on a distant antelope, and slowly shuffled backward through tall grass until I almost stepped on a wild hen of some sort. It squawked, and so did I, and we both ran off through the weeds screaming.

That's the deal in Africa. A few bad moves, lots of noise and lots of wildlife. But I suppose that out of all the species in Africa, the wildlife most comprehensible to me is white people. They aren't terribly plentiful, but they do make a lot of noise.

Some white people are Africans—Ian Smith, for example, can't be sent to some European or American homeland, as some have suggested—and some white people are simply living in Africa; but to most whites in Africa, the continent is not an abstract place or a convenient venue for finding application for various theories about justice or history. And I guess it's this notion of specificity that makes them interesting to people like me, because in the end, neither history nor politics nor popular civics—those self-absorbing social hobbies—travels very well.

Neither do I, by the way. As I mentioned at the start, I'm no grim adventurer slashing my way through the bush, and anything I know about nature and the wilderness I picked up at the zoo or on TV. I'm an ex-English teacher, and my idea of a great destination is the Air Conditioner of Khartoum (one of the Seven Wonders of the Third World—along with the Electric Light of Nairobi and the Drinking Water of Bulawayo and the other four). And the whites I met in Africa are living their lives more or less the way I'd live mine if I were in their boat, just going to work and trying to get along with the neighbors.

Somehow, though, they are all connected—a century of missionaries and managers, deMistura and Gordon, Lugard and Smith and Emin and Pappas and Shaw—all drawn together by the extraordinary place in which they live. It's a common observation these days that the "old" Africa is vanishing, and maybe that's okay, since whatever is replacing it is plenty fascinating enough, and for those members of the white tribe who remain, there will always be plenty of good stories, and most of them will be true.

Index

'Abdallahi ibn Mohammed, Khalifa, 76
Abu Klea (Sudan), 74
Abyssinia, 45, 52, 87
Addis Ababa Agreement, 115
Africa: The People and Politics on an Emerging Continent (Ungar), x
Africa and the Victorians (Robinson et al.), 38*n*., 57*n*., 187*n*.
African Lakes Company, 52
African National Congress (A.N.C.), 209
Africans, The (Lamb), x
AIDS, 174
Air America, 149*n*.–50*n*.
Air America (Robbins), 150*n*.
Air Zaïre, 163
Albania, 82, 83*n*.
Alier, Abel, 100 *n*3, 114
al-Mahdi al-Muntazar, 65*n*.
al-Mahdi, Sadiq, 76, 126*n*., 140
Ambukkol (Sudan), 74
Amin, Idi, 185
Angola, 44, 192
  civil war in, 148, 167–75
  freight fliers and, 148, 156, 164–75
Anne, Princess, 16
Ansar tribe, 74, 75, 126*n*.
Anson, Willy, 62
Anya Nya, 115–16
Anya Nya II, 115*n*.
Apartheid, 181, 194
Appropriate technologies, 116
Arabi Pasha, 59, 78
Arabs:
  European imperialism and, 39–53
  as slavers, 90, 91, 98*n*.
  in Sudan, *see* Sudan

Aruwimi River, 87, 89
Asians, ix
Askaris, 53, 97–100
  as the Uganda Rifles, 100
Atkinson, Dr. A. E., 28

Baader-Meinhof gang, 17
Back to Africa movement, 202
Bagamoyo (Tanzania), 97–98
Baganda tribe, 45
Bahr al-Ghazal Province (Sudan), 60, 134
  Gordon and, 64, 79, 80
  people of, 119, 122–23
Bahr al-Jebal (Nile River), 119–20
Baker, Sir Samuel, 46*n*., 60, 61, 62, 67, 119
Baker, Valentine, 65
Balfour, Arthur James, 26*n*.
Banana (Zaïre), 88, 97
Banana, Canaan, 180
Banda, Hastings Kamuzu, 196
Bantu tribe, 188*n*., 192
Baring, Evelyn (Lord Cromer), 57*n*., 59, 65, 81
  Gordon and, 67, 68–69, 70
Barttelot, Major Edmund, 90, 91, 93, 94
Basutoland, 66–67
Bearcroft, Michael "Punch," 8*n*., 9
Beard, Peter, x, 28*n*.
Belgian imperialism, 44, 67, 87, 190
  aftermath of, 151, 160
Benin, 44*n*.
Bennett, James Gordon, 87
Beresford, Lord Charles, 74
Berlin Conference, 49, 87*n*.
Bey, Ali, 39

215

About the Author

DENIS BOYLES is a journalist and writer whose pieces have appeared in *The New York Times, Geo, Playboy*, and other publications. He has spent many years in Africa and is at present working on a book about African lions.